**classic Great Dishes of the World**

# classic Great Dishes of the World

## Robert Carrier

BOXTREE

This edition published 1999 by Boxtree
an imprint of Macmillan Publishers Ltd
25 Eccleston Place, London SW1W 9NF
Basingstoke and Oxford
Associated companies throughout the world
www.macmillan.co.uk

0 7522 2167 1

Text and photographs copyright © Robert Carrier 1963

The right of Robert Carrier to be identified as the
author of this work has been asserted by him in accordance
with the Copyright, Designs and Patents Act 1988.

9 8 7 6 5 4 3

A CIP catalogue record for this book is available
from the British Library.

Design by Roger Hammond
Index by Sarah Ereira
Typeset by The Florence Group, Stoodleigh, Devon
Printed by Mackays of Chatham plc, Chatham, Kent

# CONTENTS

# FOREWORD
## TO THE 1999 EDITION

When I began to work on my last book, *New Great Dishes of the World* (published by Boxtree for Christmas 1997), I found great difficulty in leaving behind so many of my favourite recipes from the original edition, first published by Thomas Nelson more than thirty years ago. *Great Dishes of the World* – in its original version – had enjoyed a fabulous career: published in 1963 at the unbelievable price of 4 guineas (approximately £60 at today's prices), it nevertheless sold over 20,000 copies during the first week, 70,000 in its first two months, and altogether between two and three million copies in fourteen languages. Quite a record for a British cookbook.

So here it is again – perhaps my favourite of all the cookbooks I have written – that old classic, much loved in kitchens around the world, brought out shyly, and yet a little proudly, with its broken-spined, ragged, tatty covers and butter-stained, flour-smudged pages, as I met its owners on my frequent press tours and judging trips through New Zealand, Australia, South Africa and even France and Italy. Now named *Classic Great Dishes of the World*, it has been twinned, in paperback, for the millennium with its glamorous daughter *New Great Dishes of the World*, ready for another thirty years of hard use by cooks around the world. I'm a happy man.

I wanted the book to be pretty much as it was when it was first published, with many of its faults and all of its virtues intact. Books were a little looser then, not quite so circumscribed. And they were generous, too. You see, we didn't specify exact measurements for our terrines and tart tins and soufflé dishes in those days: we knew the average cook probably had only one or two of each in the cupboard. If the recipe gave us a little filling left over, we didn't worry; we exulted, in fact, and happily spooned the excess mixture into two or three ramekins, delighting in having enough left over for another surprise meal.

Of course I have titillated the original text a bit, bringing some of the chapter introductions a little more up to date, letting a small number of recipes go. I have added metric measures, centigrade temperatures, and in a few cases, more readily available exotic ingredients. But on the whole, I respected the rhythms and content of the original.

While many of these recipes have now been made easier thanks to products available in supermarkets, others require the maintenance of that old-fashioned thing: a good relationship with your local butcher and fishmonger. How else will you find boiling fowl and fat salt pork, and fresh clams and live lobsters? If you are unfamiliar with green bacon (a term I use in this book): who better to ask than your butcher? But I'll save you the trouble – it is simply unsmoked bacon.

I've always measured butter by the tablespoon. If you prefer to weigh it, a tablespoon of butter is 15 grams, or half an ounce. Use a 15 ml (half a fluid ounce) tablespoon to measure with, and have the ingredient, be it butter or whatever, level. Use fresh herbs unless 'dried' is stated in the recipe (an exception is the bay leaf, almost always used dried, and so given simply as 'bay leaf' in the ingredients). Fresh herbs are much easier to get hold of now than they were then and I've adjusted the recipes accordingly.

Here's my favourite *bouquet garni*, in case a recipe does not specify and you are not sure which to use: two short, thin stalks of celery (for flavour and for packaging) containing 2 sprigs of thyme, 3 of flat-leaf parsley and 1 of rosemary, tied together with string. Happy cooking!

# FOREWORD
## TO THE 1963 EDITION

The history of every nation lies visible on its table. Its wars and victories, its occupation in defeat, the marriages of its kings, its religion, its overseas empires – all have left behind them a dish or two destined to be adopted into the national life.

The Medicis, by marrying the Louis, transformed the French table, which then claimed the credit and conquered the world with its cuisine. The Auld Alliance, forged by endless interlocking marriages between the two kingdoms, still leaves many mementos in the Frenchified names of Scotland's food. A revolution gave us restaurants, when the chefs of the aristocracy were reduced to serving the very people who had so rudely cut off the heads they used to feed.

Civilisation itself, in fact, is founded upon food, for it began with the domestication of animals and the cultivation of crops. As soon as people could stay still – were released at last from the travail of following the game on which they fed – they ceased to live from hand to mouth, began to build up stocks and to store their wealth. With this wealth they bought leisure, and leisure brought them culture.

Then the wanderlust returned, forced on mankind again by the demands of food. The drives out from the Near East in search of pasture spread civilisation to Europe.

Greece and Rome flourished and fell, but Europe in the Dark Ages still needed spices. The quest for these, hidden behind the oratory of Saint Bernard and Peter the Hermit, led to the wonder of the East being rediscovered in the Crusades. For it was food, and not religion, that drove our forefathers to set out for years on the Crusades, to open up again the spice routes to the East closed down by the explosion of Mohammedanism in the Arabian desert.

It was food, once more, that made men brave uncharted seas – filled, as they thought, with monsters and evil spirits – to find the spice islands in the West. For spices were the measure by which wealth was counted in the Middle Ages, so coveted were they. So coveted, indeed, that Columbus died disgraced for having found only gold in America, and not the spices that he had promised.

This book assembles some of the most famous dishes of the world, dishes evolved from civilisations long past, dishes that have been favoured by every people that has tried them. Some still have to achieve international popularity. But each one of them is a part of the story of mankind. So let us approach them reverently. They have all history behind them. The first taste of some may surprise you, but adventure your palate as your ancestors did. And remember, the history of the world is written in this food. Culture stems from the stomach as well as the brain.

# SUCCESS WITH RECIPES

'I dislike feeling at home when I'm abroad,' said Bernard Shaw, his eyes fixed disapprovingly on those English tourists who spend their holidays searching for a good cup of tea and some plain, decent cooking. But what the master of paradox failed to mention was the delight of feeling abroad when we are at home.

The easiest way to carry yourself back to some favourite haunt is to recreate at home the dishes you enjoyed there. Or you can transport yourself to countries you have never even visited by sampling their cuisine. There is a tremendous variation in the food styles of the different nations of the world. Add to this the diverse regional cuisines of France, Italy, Spain, the United States and China, to name just a few, and you will have some idea of the delights that await you in this book.

Over the past fifteen years I have been collecting recipes on my travels abroad, experimenting with them in my own kitchens in America, Italy, Germany, France and England.

This book is the outcome of those years of pleasure, for an undoubted pleasure it has been, resulting in a collection of some of the world's most exciting recipes – *Great Dishes of the World* – each guaranteed to bring you the delights of travel without any of its inconveniences. No visas, no endless waits at airports, no inoculations and no luggage are necessary for the enjoyment of these dishes. Only the excitement of preparing something new, of tasting a quite original flavour, of sampling the exotic.

Do not be alarmed by the foreign names of some of these dishes, or by the seeming multiplicity of the ingredients used: you will find that you already have most of the ingredients in your kitchen. Most cooking – even of elaborate dishes – is merely the result of combining a number of very simple operations, but like everything else – walking, talking, driving a car, painting a picture – you learn best by actually *doing*.

In our grandparents' time, there were elaborate bicycling schools where people spent months learning how to stay balanced on two wheels. It seems that in the beginning we have to learn everything the hard way; later, it becomes almost second nature.

The great thing in cooking, according to the experts, is to master the principles and then to allow the application of the rules to special cases to follow as a matter of course. Thus, when you have learned how to cook a steak to pink-centred, charcoaled perfection, you will not need special lessons for grilling a lamb chop; when you have learnt to make half a dozen sauces, you will be able to make half a hundred without extra effort.

Whenever you try a new method of cooking, do not be disappointed if you are unsuccessful at the first or even the second attempt, but try to find out the cause of failure and remedy it the next time. For recipes are not like doctors' prescriptions; they cannot be repeated too often. In every case you must use your own judgement with regard to the time required for each cooking process.

# Chapter 1

# Appetisers

## Hors-d'œuvre Variés

It's time to bring back the *hors d'œuvres* trolley. At one time most of the glamorous restaurants of the world served a galaxy of titbits, both hot and cold, under the banner of *hors-d'œuvres variés*. These appetite stimulants were usually wheeled up to your table on a two- or three-tiered trolley, each tier of which held up to twenty small dishes or *raviers* containing a colourful assortment of vegetables, marinated in olive oil and lemon juice and served *à la vinaigrette*, or prepared *à la grecque* with wine, olive oil, finely chopped onion, carrot and herbs. These trolleys came to us via France from Russia where the *hors-d'œuvre* idea originated in the Russian *zakouski* table, set up in a room adjoining the reception room and wheeled in to satisfy far-travelling guests before dinner. Thus it is not surprising to find Russian salad, hard-boiled eggs with a mayonnaise or sour cream dressing, and pickled and preserved fish of all kinds included in the usual *hors-d'œuvre* assortment today.

The formula for *hors-d'œuvres* and *entrées chaudes* varied according to the whim of the *maître de la maison*. At the Restaurant de la Boule d'Or in Paris, for example, the *hors-d'œuvres* selection was limited to cucumbers in cream, sliced *saucisson*, tomato salad, asparagus *vinaigrette*, a duck pâté and a delicious dish of artichoke hearts, button onions and mushrooms *à la grecque*. The three hot *entrées* of the house were *quiche Lorraine*, a savoury tart of eggs, cheese and bacon; *pissaladière*, a Provençal tomato and onion tart; and delicately browned little ham patties.

La Petite Auberge, three-star restaurant of Noves, in the South of France, was famous for its starred vegetable appetiser, consisting of the following cooked and raw vegetables: button (tiny white) onions cooked in white wine and lemon juice, flavoured with nutmeg, pepper and herbs; leeks with a herb-flavoured vinaigrette sauce; coarsely grated raw carrots dressed with mustard-flavoured mayonnaise; finely sliced green peppers with an onion dressing; raw mushroom salad; poached celery with a Provençal dressing in which pounded anchovies, olive oil and wine vinegar played their part; highly spiced saffron rice studded with raisins; tomato slices with a tarragon cream sauce; marinated artichoke hearts; and asparagus tips, topped with puréed tomatoes, lightly flavoured with mustard and mayonnaise. Any one of these would be delicious by itself as a light starter, or try a combination of two or more to provide colour, flavour and texture contrast.

The real purpose of the *hors-d'œuvre* course is to stimulate the appetite, not to drown it. A correctly chosen complement of dishes should not contain too much mayonnaise or other different dressings but it should contain both cooked and raw foods so that tastes and textures will vary as much as possible. Serve *hors-d'œuvres variés* to best advantage in individual dishes or bowls, or follow the chefs of the Pacific Rim and serve a chilled mini-selection on each plate.

## Lentils and Sausages
### Forum of the Twelve Caesars in New York
Serves 4

225 g/½ pound green lentils
ham bone or 100 g/¼ pound
  bacon
16 cocktail sausages or 8 small
  chipolata sausages

150 ml/¼ pint olive oil
6 tablespoons wine vinegar
salt and freshly ground pepper
lettuce and quartered tomatoes

Cook the lentils in the normal way with the ham bone or bacon, and cool. Discard the ham bone or bacon. Bake the sausages in the oven and cool. Mix the lentils with the oil, vinegar, salt and pepper, and arrange on a bed of lettuce. Place the sausages on top. Serve with the quartered tomatoes.

## Bean Salad Vinaigrette
Serves 4 to 6

*Dressing:*
6–8 tablespoons olive oil
2–3 tablespoons wine vinegar
finely chopped flat-leaf parsley
  and garlic, to taste

salt and freshly ground pepper

700 g/1½ pounds young green
  beans

Combine the ingredients for the dressing. Top and tail the young green beans and cook them in boiling salted water until barely tender. Drain and toss immediately while still warm in the dressing. Chill.

## Mediterranean Fish Salad
Serves 4 to 6

350 g/¾ pound turbot
350 g/¾ pound halibut
a little milk
100 g/¼ pound cooked shrimps
150 ml/¼ pint olive oil
juice of 2 lemons

salt and freshly ground pepper
2–4 tablespoons finely chopped
  flat-leaf parsley
2–4 tablespoons finely chopped
  shallots
1 clove garlic, finely chopped

Cut the turbot and halibut into cubes about 1 cm/½ inch thick and poach in boiling salted water to which you have added a little milk to make the fish white. Reduce the heat so that the water barely bubbles. When the fish can be flaked with a fork, drain. Remove the skin and bones while the fish is still warm. Combine with the cooked shrimps and dress immediately with olive oil, lemon juice, and salt and pepper, to taste.

When ready to serve, add the parsley and shallots to taste, and the garlic.

# Onions 'Monégasque'
Serves 8

2 carrots, coarsely chopped
4 tablespoons olive oil
1 kg/2 pounds button onions,
   peeled
425 ml/¾ pint water
150 ml/¼ pint dry white wine
4 tablespoons lemon juice
50 g/2 ounces sultanas

2 tablespoons tomato purée
2 bay leaves
½ teaspoon dried thyme
salt and freshly ground pepper
cayenne
extra olive oil, to serve
finely chopped flat-leaf parsley,
   to garnish

Sauté the carrots in the olive oil until soft and golden. Combine in a saucepan with the onions, water, wine, lemon juice, sultanas, tomato purée, bay leaves, thyme and salt, pepper and cayenne, to taste, and simmer for about 1 hour, or until the onions are cooked through and the sauce has reduced a little. Chill. Just before serving: correct seasoning; add a little olive oil and sprinkle with parsley.

# Oriental Rice
Serves 4 to 6

½ teaspoon powdered saffron
¼ teaspoon powdered cumin
6 tablespoons dry white wine
600 ml/1 pint hot chicken stock
350 g/¾ pound risotto rice
½ green pepper, seeded and
   diced
½ red pepper, seeded and diced
½ Spanish onion, coarsely
   chopped

salt and freshly ground
   pepper

*Dressing:*
6–8 tablespoons olive oil
2–3 tablespoons wine vinegar
2 tablespoons finely chopped
   flat-leaf parsley
salt and freshly ground pepper

Moisten the saffron and cumin in the white wine and chicken stock and combine in a large saucepan with the rice, diced peppers, onion, and salt and pepper, to taste. Cover the pan and simmer until all the liquid is absorbed and the rice is tender. Add some more liquid if necessary.

Drain well and toss with the olive oil, wine vinegar, parsley, and salt and pepper, to taste. Add more olive oil or vinegar if necessary. Serve hot or cold.

## Haricots Blancs en Salade

Serves 4 to 6

350 g/¾ pound dried white beans
  (*haricots blancs*)
1 Spanish onion, finely
  chopped
2 tablespoons olive oil
1 clove garlic
1 bay leaf
1 teaspoon salt
1 small green pepper
4–6 tablespoons olive oil
wine vinegar
salt and freshly ground pepper

*Dressing:*
½ Spanish onion, finely chopped
4 tablespoons finely chopped
  flat-leaf parsley
1 teaspoon prepared mustard
1 clove garlic, finely chopped
salt and freshly ground pepper
olive oil
juice of ½ lemon
finely chopped flat-leaf parsley,
  anchovy fillets, black olives, to
  garnish

Soak the beans overnight in water to cover. Drain. Sauté the onion in the olive oil until golden brown. Add the garlic, bay leaf, salt and 1.5 litres/2½ pints water, and simmer the beans in this stock for about 2 hours or until tender. Drain. Seed and dice the green pepper and add to the beans along with the olive oil, vinegar, salt and pepper, to taste.

To make the dressing combine the onion, parsley, mustard, garlic, salt and pepper in a bowl. Mix well, and then pour in olive oil, drop by drop as if you were making a mayonnaise, beating all the time until the sauce thickens. Flavour with lemon juice.

Arrange the salad in a salad bowl. Add the salad dressing and toss until well mixed. Garnish with parsley, anchovy fillets and black olives.

## Jewish Chopped Chicken Livers

Serves 4 to 6

350 g/¾ pound chicken livers
chicken fat
¼–½ Spanish onion, finely
  chopped
2 hard-boiled eggs

1 stalk celery, finely chopped
¼–½ small green pepper, seeded
  and finely chopped
salt and freshly ground pepper

Sauté the chicken livers in a little chicken fat until firm, pink on the inside but not cooked through. Sauté the onion in the chicken fat until transparent.

Chop the hard-boiled eggs coarsely and then put through the finest blade of a mincer (or briefly chop in a food processor) with the chicken livers and onions.

Combine in a large bowl with celery, green pepper, and enough additional chicken fat to make the mixture smooth. Season to taste with salt and pepper.

# Marinated Herring

Serves 6 to 12

12 herring fillets
600 ml/1 pint double cream
6 tablespoons wine vinegar
1 tablespoon olive oil
3 medium-sized onions, finely
sliced
6 black peppercorns

1 large sour apple, peeled and
cut in thin strips
1 small cooked beetroot, cut in
thin strips
½ lemon, thinly sliced
3–6 small bay leaves

Wash the herring fillets; pat dry and arrange in a bowl. Mix the cream, vinegar and olive oil; add the onion, peppercorns, apple, beetroot, lemon and bay leaves. Pour over the herrings, cover and place in a refrigerator. Marinate 24 hours before serving ice-cold as an appetiser.

# Turbot Salad
## White Tower in London

Serves 4 to 6

1 kg/2 pounds turbot
150 ml/¼ pint milk
150 ml/¼ pint olive oil
juice of 2 lemons
salt and freshly ground pepper

2–4 tablespoons finely chopped
flat-leaf parsley
2–4 tablespoons coarsely
chopped onion

Cut the turbot into slices about 1 cm/½ inch thick and place in 1.2 litres/2 pints boiling salted water to which you have added the milk to make the fish white. Reduce the heat so that the water barely bubbles. It is important to cook the turbot very slowly so that it does not lose its juices in the stock. When the fish can be flaked with a fork, drain. Remove the skin and bones while still warm. Dress the fish immediately with olive oil, lemon juice, and salt and pepper, to taste. Add the parsley and onion, and allow to cool. Just before serving, correct the seasoning and add more olive oil and lemon juice if necessary.

This dish is best served soon after it has been prepared; it tends to lose flavour if kept too long.

# Ceviche
## Mexican Seafood Cocktail
Serves 4

450 g/1 pound halibut, or any firm white non-fatty fish
2 lemons or limes
225 g/½ pound tomatoes, peeled and seeded
1 small green pepper, seeded and diced
4 tablespoons olive oil

4 tablespoons finely chopped flat-leaf parsley
1–2 tablespoons wine vinegar
dash Tabasco sauce
½ teaspoon dried oregano
salt and freshly ground pepper
1 avocado pear, to garnish
6 stuffed olives, to garnish

Fillet, skin and dice the raw fish. Place in a glass bowl; pour lemon or lime juice over it and marinate for 3 hours, turning the fish pieces with a wooden spoon from time to time, so that the juice turns the fish snowy-white and non-transparent. It will look and flake like cooked fish.

Dice the tomatoes and add to the fish. Add the diced green pepper to the fish mixture with the olive oil, parsley, vinegar, Tabasco, oregano, and salt and pepper, to taste. Serve chilled, garnished with diced avocado and sliced stuffed olives.

# Taramasalata
## Greek Cod's Roe Appetiser
Serves 4 to 6

1 jar smoked cod's roe
6 slices white bread
¼ Spanish onion, grated
1–2 cloves garlic, mashed
8 tablespoons olive oil

juice of 1 lemon
2–3 tablespoons finely chopped flat-leaf parsley
green olives, to garnish
hot toast, to serve

Place the cod's roe in a mortar. Trim the crusts from the bread; soak the bread in water; squeeze and add to the cod's roe. Pound the mixture to a smooth paste. Stir in the grated onion and garlic, then add the olive oil and lemon juice alternately in small amounts, stirring well, until the mixture acquires a smooth, uniform consistency. Strain through a fine sieve. (The above can be done in a food processer and in that case the mixture does not need to be sieved.)

Serve in a salad bowl; sprinkle with parsley and garnish with green olives. Serve with hot toast. I also like to stuff short lengths of crisp celery with this mixture as a light appetiser.

## Guacamole
### Mexican Avocado Appetiser
Serves 4

2 ripe avocado pears
juice of 1 lemon
1 clove garlic, mashed
4 tomatoes, peeled, seeded and
coarsely chopped
½ Spanish onion, finely
chopped

4 tablespoons finely chopped
celery or green pepper
1 tablespoon finely chopped
coriander leaves or flat-leaf
parsley
2–4 tablespoons olive oil
salt and freshly ground pepper

Peel, stone and mash the avocados lightly with a wooden spoon. Add the lemon juice, garlic, tomatoes, onion and celery or pepper. Stir in the coriander or parsley, olive oil, and salt and pepper, to taste. Serve straight away. Mexicans serve *guacamole* with *tostaditos* (deep-fried wedges of *tortilla*).

## Tomatoes Guacamole
### Mexican Tomato and Avocado Appetiser
Serves 4

8 large ripe tomatoes
2 ripe avocado pears
juice of 1 lemon
1 tablespoon onion juice
1 clove garlic, mashed
salt and freshly ground pepper

crushed dried chillies
4 tablespoons finely chopped
celery or green pepper
1 tablespoon finely chopped
coriander leaves or flat-leaf
parsley

Plunge the tomatoes into boiling water, one by one, and remove their skins. Slice the top off each and carefully scoop out all pulp and seeds. Cover loosely with aluminium foil and chill in the refrigerator until ready to use.

Peel, stone, and mash the avocados lightly with a wooden spoon. Add the lemon juice and seasonings. Fold in the celery or pepper, and chill. Just before serving, fill each tomato case with this *guacamole* mixture; sprinkle with coriander or parsley.

# Terrine de Canard à l'Orange

Every French restaurant boasts its *pâté maison*; every great chef cherishes his own special *terrine* recipe incorporating chicken, duck or game. My favourite – and one of the world's great dishes – is *terrine de canard à l'orange*, a *terrine* made with the fillets of breast of duck marinated in orange juice, cognac, Noilly Prat and Madeira and encased in a savoury *farce* made up of the finely ground meats of the duck, together with pork, pork fat and veal, flavoured with the marinade juices, herbs and spices.

Far from being difficult to prepare, a *terrine* such as this one fits particularly well into the scheme of the busy host- or hostess-cum-cook. It can be prepared in advance – several days in fact – and chilled, thus eliminating much last-minute cooking. And it is easy to serve.

*Terrines* are usually baked in heavy earthenware baking dishes, round or oval in shape with straight sides and with a small hole in the cover to allow the steam to escape. Always line the bottom and sides of the dish with thin slices of fat pork or fat bacon. I usually cut mine paper-thin on a rotary cutter. Failing this, a useful trick is to cut the slices at least 6 mm/¼ inch thick; place them between two pieces of greaseproof paper; and then pound them with a wooden mallet to about 3 mm/⅛ inch in thickness. You will find that they cover the sides of your pâté dish better this way.

Aspic plays a major part in most *terrine* recipes. When I make a *terrine*, I always place a board or flat plate on top of it to weigh it down as it cools. The *terrine* shrinks in cooling and this weight (use an iron, tinned foods or a brick) compresses it just enough to eliminate the tiny air holes that make it difficult to slice when chilled. The *terrine* should be firm and moist, and must not fall apart as you cut it. The aspic serves to hold it together, as well as to add to the general flavour and appearance of the finished dish.

Any well-flavoured *consommé* will serve as a base for your aspic. For *terrines* of game and poultry, the bones of the animal or bird should be used in making the stock. It is usually wise to make sure that the aspic will set by chilling it thoroughly and re-melting it just prior to use. If the aspic fails to set during this preliminary chilling, strengthen it by adding a little unflavoured gelatine to the mixture.

## Terrine de Canard à l'Orange

**1 duck (and liver)**
**4 tablespoons cognac**
**4 tablespoons Noilly Prat**
**4 tablespoons Madeira**
**4 tablespoons orange juice**
**½ Spanish onion, finely chopped**
**½ teaspoon powdered thyme**
**½ teaspoon powdered savory**
**1 teaspoon grated orange rind**
**1 teaspoon finely chopped flat-leaf parsley**
**2 bay leaves, crumbled**
**salt and freshly ground pepper**
**crushed dried chillies**

**100 g/¼ pound duck or chicken livers, diced**
**100 g/¼ pound veal, diced**
**100 g/¼ pound lean pork, diced**
**50 g/2 oz fresh pork fat, diced**
**1 egg, well beaten**
**thin strips pork fat**
**50 g/2 oz fresh pork fat, cut into strips 6 mm/¼ inch in diameter**
**3 paper-thin slices orange with peel**
**liquid aspic made with powder and flavoured with**
**2 tablespoons Madeira**

Skin and bone the duck; remove the breast fillets and meat of the breast and cut into long, thin strips about 6 mm/¼ inch in diameter. Marinate the strips overnight in cognac, Noilly Prat, Madeira and orange juice with the onion, thyme, savory, orange rind, parsley, bay leaves, and salt, pepper and crushed dried chillies, to taste. Reserve the carcass and the remaining duck meat.

The next day, process the remaining duck meat in short bursts with the duck or chicken livers, diced veal, pork and fresh pork fat. Stir in the liquid in which the fillets were marinated, and also the beaten egg. Bake a spoonful of the finely ground meat mixture in the oven or in a nonstick frying pan, until cooked through. Taste; this is your chance to correct the seasoning.

Then, once satisfied with the flavour of your *terrine* mix, garnish the bottom and sides of an ovenproof terrine dish with thin strips of pork fat. Press in a thick layer of the pâté mixture; arrange strips of duck fillets over the mixture with a few strips of pork fat. Cover with another layer of mixture. Top with the remaining thin strips of pork fat.

Cover the *terrine*, place in a pan of hot water and bake in a moderate oven (180°C/375°F/gas 4) for about 1 to 1¼ hours.

Remove the cover and place a weighted plate on the *terrine* to compress it gently as it cools. Take the *terrine* from its container, remove the outside fat and replace in a clean terrine dish. Decorate with 3 thin slices of orange and cover with liquid aspic. Allow to set in the refrigerator overnight.

## Pâté Maison

225 g/½ pound bacon, thinly
  sliced
6 tablespoons brandy
1 kg/2 pounds calf's liver,
  minced
225 g/½ pound pork liver, minced
2 eggs, beaten
4 tablespoons double cream
2 tablespoons lemon juice
1 clove garlic, crushed

salt and freshly ground pepper
crushed dried chillies
1 truffle, coarsely chopped
  (optional)
100 g/¼ pound chicken liver,
  coarsely chopped and sautéed
  for 1 minute in a nonstick
  frying pan until lightly
  coloured

Cut the rind from the bacon slices and line a pâté mould with most of the trimmed bacon; sprinkle with one third of the brandy. Mix the minced livers with the beaten eggs, cream, the remainder of the brandy, lemon juice, garlic, and salt, pepper and crushed dried chillies, to taste. Mix well with a fork and half-fill the pâté mould with the mixture. Place the coarsely chopped truffle and sautéed chicken liver in a row down the centre. Cover with the rest of the pâté; then cover the top with bacon. Stand the mould in pan of water and bake in a slow oven (160°C/325°F/gas 3) for about 2 hours, covered with foil. Remove and cool. Put a weight on the top to press down firmly, and chill overnight in the refrigerator. Turn out of its mould just before serving.

# Truffled Duck Pâté

1 medium-sized duck
2 shallots, chopped
pinch of dried thyme
4 bay leaves
salt and freshly ground pepper
crushed dried chillies
125 ml/4 fluid ounces dry white
   wine
450 g/1 pound calf's liver, diced
6 tablespoons butter

4 Cox's Orange Pippins
1 teaspoon sugar
juice of ½ lemon
1 egg, beaten
225 g/½ pound fat salt pork,
   thinly sliced
sliced truffles
liquid aspic made with powder
   and flavoured with 2
   tablespoons Madeira

Bone and skin the duck. Cut the breast in long thin strips. Combine the shallots, thyme, 2 of the bay leaves, crumbled, ½ teaspoon salt, a little pepper and crushed dried chillies, and dry white wine. Marinate the fillets in this mixture in the refrigerator overnight. The next day, sauté the calf's liver and the duck liver in 4 tablespoons of the butter until medium rare. Peel the apples; add the sugar and cook in lemon juice and the remaining butter until soft. Process the livers and apples together in short bursts in a food processor; add the beaten egg and season to taste with salt and pepper. Blend mixture until it is very smooth.

Line a pâté dish or earthenware casserole with some of the thin slices of fat salt pork. Add half the liver and apple mixture and cover with layers of marinated duck fillets. Stud with sliced truffles rolled in thin slices of fat salt pork; cover with the remaining liver and apple mixture and top with the remaining fat salt pork. Place 2 bay leaves on the pâté and cover the casserole. Place in a pan of hot water and bake for about 1½ hours in a slow oven (160°C/325°F/gas 3).

Remove the cover and place a weighted plate on the pâté to compress it gently as it cools. Take the pâté from the casserole; remove the outside fat and replace the pâté in a clean pâté dish. Decorate with slices of truffle and cover with liquid aspic.

# Mousse de Foie Gras en Brioche

4 tablespoons double cream
225 g/½ pound tinned *pâté de
   foie gras*
4 tablespoons cognac
2 tablespoons finely chopped
   flat-leaf parsley

50 g/2 ounces finely chopped
   mushrooms
100 g/4 ounces butter
salt and freshly ground pepper
brioche dough
1 egg yolk
a little milk

Whip the cream. Combine the pâté, cognac and chopped parsley, and blend thoroughly with the whipped cream (in a food processor, if you like). Sauté the mushrooms in the butter over a low heat for 5 minutes or until golden. Season to taste with salt and pepper. Stir the mushrooms and butter into the pâté mixture and let stand at room temperature for at least 1 hour.

Line a large well-buttered *brioche* mould with a sheet of *brioche* dough 4 cm/ 1½ inches thick and about 2.5 cm/1 inch wider in circumference than is required to line the mould. Set the pâté in a ball in the mould and cover it with the overhanging dough. Form a piece of the dough the size of a cup into a ball and set the ball on top of the *brioche*. Let the mould stand for 20 minutes in a warm place to allow the dough to rise. Brush the top with egg yolk diluted with a little milk and bake in a hot oven (230°C/450°F/gas 8) until the *brioche* is browned and a wire tester comes out clean. Cool the *brioche* and lift it out on to a serving dish. Serve warm or cold.

# Quiche Lorraine

This hot cheese open tart, a native of Alsace-Lorraine, makes frequent and delicious appearances on tables throughout France. Slender wedges are served as an appetiser before dinner; larger portions make a perfect light luncheon dish when accompanied by a tossed green salad; and individual *quiches* provide a delectable first course for a more substantial meal.

Essentially custard, well flavoured with cheese and baked in a pie shell, the *quiche* varies from country to country. Germany and Switzerland have their own versions of this popular dish, but the most famous of all is the French *quiche Lorraine*. In Alsace-Lorraine, the home of the *quiche*, each village has its own special recipe and each jealously proclaims that its *quiche* is the authentic one. In some recipes, only cheese and custard are used; in others, finely chopped onions sautéed in butter add their subtle flavour; and in traditional versions, *lardons* of fat salt pork or green bacon are added.

I find the *quiche* an easily and quickly made, light-hearted *entrée*. But be careful, for your *quiche* should be satin-smooth on the inside with a crisp, golden crust. So do not let the *quiche* wait for guests. Serve it immediately, for it is at its best when piping hot.

The traditional *quiche Lorraine* is made with *lardons* of *petit salé* or fat salt pork, but you might like to try these variations on the basic theme, substituting for the bacon one of the following:

*Quiche aux crabes:* Remove tendons and bits of shell from cooked fresh crab; flake and add the white crabmeat to the *quiche* mixture. Shrimps, sliced tiger prawns and diced lobster may also be added for a *quiche aux fruits de mer*.

*Quiche aux champignons:* Clean and slice mushrooms thinly; sauté in butter and lemon juice; drain well and add to the *quiche* mixture.

*Quiche au poisson:* Poach halibut or turbot fillets in a well-flavoured *court-bouillon* of water and white wine, flavoured with onion, carrot, bay leaf, salt and pepper; drain well; remove skin and bones and flake fish into the *quiche* mixture.

*Quiche aux courgettes:* Sauté thinly sliced courgettes in olive oil with a little finely chopped onion and garlic and peeled, seeded and coarsely chopped tomatoes; drain and stir into the *quiche* mixture.

# Fingertip Pastry

225 g/½ pound plain flour　　　1 medium-sized egg yolk
1 teaspoon icing sugar　　　　　1 teaspoon lemon juice
½ teaspoon salt　　　　　　　　2 tablespoons iced water
150 g/5 oz cold butter

This is my favourite rich shortcrust pastry.

Sift the flour, icing sugar and salt into a large mixing bowl. Cut the cold butter directly from the refrigerator into 6 mm/¼ inch dice. Add these to the bowl and toss lightly in the flour mixture.

Using a pastry blender (or two knives, held one in each hand and cutting across each other like scissor blades), cut the cold diced butter into the flour mixture until it resembles coarse breadcrumbs. Then scoop up some of the mixture in each hand, and, holding your hands above the bowl, lightly rub your thumbs and fingertips together, letting the crumbs shower back into the bowl as you go. Repeat 6 or 7 times, or until the mixture is further reduced to the consistency of fine breadcrumbs.

Beat the egg yolk in a small bowl with a fork. Add the lemon juice and iced water and mix again.

Sprinkle the egg mixture over the contents of the bowl and, using a fork or spoon, stir it into the flour mix. When about three-quarters of the pastry is holding together, use your hand to form the pastry lightly and quickly into one piece.

Shape the pastry into a ball, pressing the ball lightly against the bottom and sides of the bowl to gather up any remaining 'crumbs'. Wrap the pastry ball in a sheet of greaseproof paper, or aluminium foil, and chill for at least 1 hour to allow the pastry to 'mature' before using.

**To Roll Out the Pastry:**  Leave the pastry at room temperature for 15 to 20 minutes before rolling it out, otherwise it will be a little too firm to roll out successfully.

Lightly dust your working surface and rolling pin with flour (I use a small strainer). Flatten the ball of pastry with a few strokes of the rolling pin. Then start rolling it out to a circle about 30 cm/12 inches in diameter and as thin as you can get it: about 3 mm/⅛ inch is perfect, but see the recipe instructions. Turn the sheet of pastry over once or twice on the working surface while rolling (dusting the surface with a little more flour if necessary) and don't worry too much if the pastry cracks or separates while you are rolling it: just press it lightly back into place with your fingers (that is why I call it 'fingertip' pastry). When the pastry is rolled out, dust off any excess flour with a soft pastry brush. The pastry is now ready for use.

# Quiche Lorraine
Serves 6 to 8

fingertip pastry for 20-cm/8-inch
quiche (page 00)
4 egg yolks
300 ml/½ pint single cream
salt and freshly ground pepper
grated nutmeg

100 g/¼ pound green bacon, or
fat salt pork cut in one piece
2 tablespoons butter
100 g/¼ pound Gruyère cheese,
diced

Line a loose-bottomed 20-cm/8-in pie tin with shortcrust pastry. Prick the bottom
with a fork; brush with a little beaten egg and bake 'blind' in a hot oven
(220°C/425°F/gas 7) for 15 minutes.

Whisk the egg yolks in a bowl; add the cream and whisk until thick and lemon-
coloured. Flavour with salt, pepper and freshly grated nutmeg, to taste.

Cut the green bacon, or fat salt pork, crosswise into fat fingers. Remove the
rind, then sauté the strips in the butter until golden.

Arrange the diced cheese and bacon strips in the pastry case. Pour over the
cream and egg mixture and bake in a moderate oven (180°C/350°F/gas 4) for about
30 minutes. Serve hot.

# American Clam Tart
Serves 6 to 8

fingertip pastry for 20–25-cm/
8–10-inch tart (page 00)
1 can chopped clams
3 slices bacon
butter
3 tablespoons finely chopped
onion

3 tablespoons finely chopped
flat-leaf parsley
3 eggs
150 ml/¼ pint cream
salt and freshly ground
pepper

Line a loose-bottomed 20–25-cm/8–10-inch pie tin with pastry, fluting
the edges; chill. Prick the bottom with a fork and bake 'blind' in a hot oven
(220°C/425°F/gas 7) for about 15 minutes, just long enough to set the crust without
browning it. Allow to cool.

Drain the clams, reserving the liquor, and chop them. Sauté the bacon in butter
until crisp. Sauté the onion in the resulting fat until transparent, and drain. Crumble
the bacon and combine with the clams, onion and parsley. Spoon into the pastry
shell.

Lightly beat the eggs; add the cream, reserved clam liquor, and salt and pepper,
to taste. Pour the custard mixture into the pastry shell and bake in a moderate
oven (180°C/350°F/gas 4) for 30 minutes, or until the crust is brown and the
custard has set.

# Italian Green Gnocchi Tart

Serves 6 to 8

fingertip pastry for 20-cm/8-inch
  tart (page 12)
350 g/¾ pound frozen spinach
2 tablespoons butter
salt and freshly ground pepper
225 g/½ pound cottage cheese

3 eggs, lightly beaten
25–50 g/1–2 ounces freshly
  grated Parmesan
6 tablespoons double cream
grated nutmeg

Line a loose-bottomed 20-cm/8-in pie tin with pastry, fluting the edges; chill. Prick the bottom with a fork and bake 'blind' in a hot oven (220°C/425°F/gas 7) for 15 minutes, or just long enough to set the crust without browning it. Allow to cool.

Cook the spinach with the butter, and salt and pepper, to taste. Drain thoroughly and then add the cottage cheese with the eggs, grated Parmesan, cream and nutmeg, to taste. Spread the mixture in the pastry shell and bake in a moderate oven (180°C/350°F/gas 4) for 30 minutes, or until the crust is brown and the cheese custard mixture has set.

# Pissaladière

Serves 6 to 8

dough – bread, brioche or
  fingertip pastry (page 12) –
  for a 23-cm/9-inch pie case
butter or egg yolk for case
4 tablespoons olive oil
6 large ripe tomatoes, peeled,
  seeded and chopped

2 tablespoons tomato purée
3 Spanish onions, sliced
2 tablespoons butter
fresh rosemary or tarragon
2 tablespoons grated Parmesan
1 can anchovy fillets
black olives

Use bread dough, *brioche* dough or fingertip pastry for this savoury tomato and onion tart. If you use bread or *brioche* dough, roll it out 6 mm/¼ inch thick and line a 23-cm/9-inch pie tin. Brush with butter and put in a warm place to rise slightly while you prepare the filling. If you use pastry, roll it out 6 mm/¼ inch thick; line the pan, fluting the edges, and chill. Then brush with a little slightly beaten egg yolk and bake in a 220°C/425°F/gas 7 oven just long enough to set the crust without browning it. Allow to cool.

Heat the olive oil in a pan; add the ripe tomatoes and tomato purée. Cook over a low heat until excess moisture is cooked away, mashing occasionally with a wooden spoon to form a purée. Simmer the Spanish onions in the butter with a little freshly chopped rosemary or tarragon until soft and golden but not brown.

Sprinkle the bottom of the pastry or dough case with Parmesan; add the onions and then cover with the tomato mixture. Arrange the anchovies in a lattice on top and place a black olive in the centre of each square. Brush the olives and anchovies lightly with oil and bake in a moderate oven (180°C/350°F/gas 4) for about 30 minutes.

# Miniature Fish Crescents

Serves 6

**100 g/¼ pound butter**
**100 g/¼ pound cream cheese**
**100 g/¼ pound flour**
**2 cans sardines, drained**
**lemon juice and curry powder**

**salt and freshly ground pepper**
**2 hard-boiled eggs, finely**
**chopped**
**1 tablespoon finely chopped**
**flat-leaf parsley**

Combine the butter and cream cheese and stir until well blended. Add the flour and mix with a fork. Knead the dough and form it into a ball before chilling. Refrigerate for 1 hour.

To prepare the filling, mash the sardines. Add a little lemon juice, curry powder, and pepper and salt, to taste. Add the eggs and parsley and mix well. Roll the dough on a floured surface to about 6-mm/¼-inch thickness. Cut into 10-cm/ 4-inch squares. Cut the squares in half to form triangles. Place a teaspoon of sardine filling in the centre of each triangle. Roll from the wide edge towards the point, twisting the ends to seal. Turn the ends to form crescents. Place on a baking sheet and store, covered, in the refrigerator until ready to bake. Bake at 220°C/425°F/ gas 7 for about 10 minutes or until golden brown.

Chapter 2

# Soups

## French Onion Soup

French onion soup spelled Paris in its most romantic mood, an aromatic vision of Les Halles at four in the morning, when its busy crowded streets were filled with the clamorous cries of an awakening city, where home-returning revellers mingled with hard-working marketmen for their one communal meal of the day.

In the very heart of the market, I used to love a tiny, crowded, smoky little workman's café which stayed open all night. There, porters and fruiterers, *camioneurs* and butchers complete with blood-stained aprons used to eat and drink around the crowded *zinc* in the early hours of the morning, and consume countless portions of the house speciality: an appetising *soupe à l'oignon*, served with a piping-hot crust of bubbling cheese.

Today Les Halles has moved to the outskirts of the city but the café is still there – enlarged and bedizened – with a smart upstairs restaurant for chic Parisians and foreign visitors. But downstairs it is still the same noisy, crowded, smoky room where the marketmen used to gather to swap early-morning stories and the onion soup is as good and as famous as it ever was.

French onion soup is nothing if not adaptable. Take a few onions, a little water or a little stock, a slice or two of toasted bread and a sprinkling of grated cheese, and you have a deliciously warming and inexpensive soup. Add a little dry white wine, a glass of champagne, or a dash or two of brandy, and you have a soup fit for the gods.

Pile an ovenproof earthenware dish high with slices of oven-toasted French bread; cover each layer with freshly grated Gruyère cheese; fill the bowl with your favourite French onion soup – choose from the two versions which follow – place it in the oven until the bowl is smoking hot and golden with melted cheese and toasted bread, and you have *soupe à l'oignon gratinée* as it is still served in Les Halles.

### Soupe à l'Oignon
#### French Onion Soup
Serves 4 to 6

24 small white onions
4 tablespoons butter
sugar
1.4 litres/2½ pints beef stock
125 ml/4 fluid ounces cognac
salt and freshly ground pepper

4–6 rounds of lightly toasted
  French bread or ciabatta
softened butter
freshly grated Gruyère cheese
crushed dried chillies

Peel and slice the onions thinly. Heat the butter in a large saucepan with a little sugar; add the onion rings and cook them very, very gently over a low flame, stirring constantly with a wooden spoon until the rings are pale golden brown. Add the beef stock gradually, stirring constantly, until the soup begins to boil. Then lower the heat, cover the pan, and simmer gently for about 1 hour.

Just before serving, add the cognac, and salt and pepper, to taste, and serve in a heated soup tureen or in individual serving bowls, each one containing toasted buttered rounds of French bread heaped with grated Gruyère cheese. Add a pinch of crushed dried chillies to each cheese-topped bread round. Serve immediately.

## Onion Soufflé Soup
Serves 4 to 6

**425 ml/¾ pint thick béchamel sauce (page 34)**
**6 tablespoons freshly grated Gruyère cheese**
**2 egg whites, stiffly beaten**
**salt, freshly ground pepper and grated nutmeg**

**1.4 litres/2½ pints well-flavoured onion soup (see above)**
**4–6 rounds oven-toasted French bread**
**softened butter**

To make the soufflé, prepare a thick béchamel sauce, remove from the heat and stir in the freshly grated cheese. Allow to cool, then fold in the stiffly beaten egg whites. Season to taste with salt, pepper and grated nutmeg.

Pour the French onion soup into individual ovenproof dishes (or one large ovenproof dish); top with toasted and buttered rounds of French bread and spoon the cheese soufflé mixture over this. Bake in a preheated hot oven (230°C/450°F/gas 8) for 8 to 10 minutes, or until the soufflé has risen and is golden. Serve immediately.

## Cold Borscht
Serves 6 to 8

**700 g/1½ pounds lean beef**
**2.4 litres/4 pints salted water**
**3 sprigs flat-leaf parsley**
**2 leeks, coarsely chopped**
**2 carrots, coarsely chopped**
**1 bay leaf**
**1 clove garlic**
**6 peppercorns**

**450 g/1 pound cooked beetroot, diced**
**½ red cabbage, coarsely chopped**
**2 potatoes, diced**
**2 onions, chopped**
**225 g/½ pound mushrooms, coarsely chopped**
**300 ml/½ pint sour cream**

Dice the beef and put it into a saucepan with the water. Bring the water slowly to the boil; skim carefully, and add the parsley, leeks and carrots, bay leaf, garlic and peppercorns. Simmer, covered, for 1½ hours, skimming from time to time. Remove the meat from the soup; strain the soup into a saucepan and add the beetroot, red cabbage, potatoes, onions and mushrooms. Bring to the boil; skim; and simmer, uncovered, for 1½ hours. Strain through a sieve; chill, and stir in sour cream before serving.

## Italian Leek and Pumpkin Soup
Serves 4 to 6

**450 g/1 pound pumpkin**
**225 g/½ pound potatoes**
**1 Spanish onion**
**50 g/2 ounces butter**
**100 g/¼ pound fresh haricot or broad beans**
**600 ml/1 pint milk**
**150 ml/¼ pint water**
**salt and cayenne pepper**

**50 g/2 ounces leek, cut in strips**
**600 ml/1 pint hot chicken stock**
**150 ml/¼ pint double cream**
**100 g/¼ pound cooked rice**
**2 tablespoons chopped chervil leaves or flat-leaf parsley**

Peel and dice the pumpkin and potatoes. Chop the onion and simmer in a large saucepan in half the butter until golden; add the pumpkin and potatoes, beans, milk and water. Bring to the boil; skim; lower the heat and simmer gently for 45 minutes, stirring from time to time to prevent scorching, and adding a little more water if necessary. Strain through a fine sieve into a clean saucepan; add salt and cayenne pepper, to taste.

Cut the leeks into fine strips and 'melt' in the remaining butter. Add to the soup, along with the hot chicken stock, and bring slowly to the boil. Just before serving, stir in the cream, cooked rice and chopped chervil or parsley.

## 'Fonda del Sol'
### Argentinian Pumpkin Soup
Serves 6

**1.2 kg/2½ pounds peeled pumpkin**
**1 litre/1¾ pints chicken stock**
**1 medium onion, chopped**
**6 spring onions, diced**
**4–6 plum tomatoes, chopped**

**300 ml/½ pint single cream**
**salt and freshly ground pepper**
**crushed dried chillies**
**150 ml/¼ pint whipped cream**

Cut the peeled pumpkin in pieces and place in a large saucepan; add the stock, onion, spring onions and tomatoes, and simmer until tender. Cool. Blend – or purée; add the cream; season to taste with salt, pepper and crushed dried chillies. Pour into pre-chilled cups. Just before serving, place a dollop of whipped cream on each portion.

## Corn and Tuna Bisque
Serves 2

1 tablespoon butter
1 tablespoon flour
600 ml/1 pint milk
1 chicken stock cube
1 can sweetcorn kernels

1 can tuna, drained and shredded
salt and freshly ground pepper
crushed dried chillies
curry powder or dry sherry
(optional)

Melt the butter in the top of a double saucepan; add the flour and cook for a few minutes, stirring constantly until well blended. Add the milk and chicken stock cube and simmer, stirring from time to time, until the sauce has thickened.

Stir in the sweetcorn and bring to the boil; add the tuna and heat through. Season with salt, pepper and crushed dried chillies and serve immediately. A little curry powder or sherry may be added, if desired.

## Scandinavian Fruit Soup
Serves 4–5

450 g/1 pound each ripe
   peaches, plums, cherries and
   apricots
1 litre/1¾ pints water
3 tablespoons lemon juice
sugar
powdered cinnamon

1 tablespoon cornflour
150 ml/¼ pint sour cream or
   crème fraîche

*Decoration:*
6–8 tablespoons fresh raspberries
6 sprigs fresh mint

Pit the fruit, but do not peel. Slice larger fruits. Combine the fruit in a saucepan with the water, lemon juice and sugar and cinnamon, to taste. Cover and simmer until the fruit is soft. Purée and return to the pan. Dissolve the cornflour in a little cold water; add to the fruit, bring to the boil, then simmer gently until the soup thickens. Chill. Just before serving, swirl in the cream and decorate with fresh raspberries and sprigs of fresh mint.

# Pot-au-Feu

*Pot-au-feu* – the great knife-and-fork soup often called the national soup of France – is one of the most rewarding dishes in the world to make. Although it looks complicated at first glance, you will find that this soup of many parts is well worth the effort involved. It is, in fact, two dishes – a first course of beef broth or *bouillon*, and a main dish of boiled beef or, as the French term it, '*le bouilli*', ancestor via Scotland of British 'bully beef'.

Serve the soup first and follow with the *bouilli* accompanied by vegetables from the *bouillon*: carrots, leeks, onions, and sometimes – cooked separately rather than in the *bouillon* – cabbage and potatoes.

# Pot-au-Feu
To make a pot-au-feu for 8, you will need:

1.8 kg/4 pounds lean beef
1 kg/2 pounds shin of beef
   (meat and bone)
100 g/¼ pound calf's liver
2 chicken livers
4.5 litres/8 pints water or water
   and stock
coarse salt
4 carrots

4 leeks
2 turnips
2 stalks celery
1 fat clove garlic
1 Spanish onion
2 cloves
1 *bouquet garni* (bay leaf, few
   sprigs flat-leaf parsley, thyme)

The secret of making a good *pot-au-feu* is to begin by covering the ingredients with cold water, bringing it slowly to the boil, a mere ripple on the surface, and then allowing it to simmer gently for hours without interruption at a low, regular heat.

Have your butcher bone the meat – chosen from the silverside, shoulder, top rib, or top round, although the last-mentioned is inclined to be a little tough in comparison to the others, or a combination of two of these, plus some shin of beef (meat and bone), so useful in making a *bouillon* for its gelatinous qualities. If I have it at hand, I sometimes add a knuckle of veal or a good-sized marrow bone or ½ pig's foot to these basics for extra flavour. For optimum flavour, you could do the same, availability permitting.

Your butcher will also cut the meat into large pieces, tie it up securely and break the bones for you. All you have to do when you are ready to make your *pot-au-feu* is to lay the bones in the bottom of a large stockpot; place the meat, calf's liver and chicken livers on top and add the water, or water and stock, and put the stockpot on the lowest possible heat so that the water comes to the boil very slowly. As it does so, the gradual heating of the water will tenderize the fibre of the meat and dissolve the gelatinous substances which it contains.

When the liquid barely begins to simmer in the pot, add a little salt to help the scum rise to the surface of the *bouillon*.

The scum which forms is thick and brownish-grey in colour. For a clear *bouillon* this must be removed. Let it become sufficiently compact and then skim it off with a perforated spoon, being careful to scrape away any remaining at the sides of the pot. When the water just begins to tremble, add half a glass of cold water to stop the boiling and to bring a new rise of scum to the surface. Skim and repeat this process several times for a matter of 10 to 15 minutes, until the scum is just a white froth which will of its own accord be consumed in the cooking. Simmer the meat and stock over the lowest heat, uncovered, for 2 hours, adding a little more water from time to time if necessary.

Now it is time to add the vegetables and *bouquet garni* (see below). If the vegetables bring a little more scum to the surface, skim carefully and cover the stockpot with a lid, tilting it so that the steam can escape. Keep the heat as low as possible so that the stock just trembles gently at one point only.

**The Vegetables:** The flavour and appearance of the vegetables in your *pot-au-feu* will be better if they are not overcooked. For the best results, carrots and turnips, cut in quarters, can be added to the *bouillon* after the first two hours of simmering, along with leeks, split if they are big, with most of the green cut off and tied together with the celery, plus an onion, stuck with cloves, garlic and a *bouquet garni*.

In the North of France they add a small *bouquet* of fresh chervil to the stock when the *pot-au-feu* is three-quarters cooked, and some cooks like to improve the colour of the *bouillon* by adding a few pea pods dried in the oven. Cabbage, not usually a part of the classic *pot-au-feu*, can be cooked separately, in water at first and then in a little of the *bouillon*, and served with the meat and vegetables. Potatoes, too, are sometimes boiled or steamed separately and served with a *pot-au-feu*.

**The Bouillon:** Take 2 litres/3½ pints of the *bouillon* with a ladle to a separate saucepan and bring to a fast boil; dip the soup ladle into the *bouillon* at the point where the boiling is most active. The fat will be forced to the side of the pot and your resultant *bouillon* will be less greasy. Pass the *bouillon*, ladle by ladle, through a fine muslin laid in a sieve, into a clean saucepan. Allow it to cool for a few minutes; skim any remaining fat from the surface; pour the *bouillon* into a clean saucepan and reheat to serve.

**The Meat and Vegetables:** To serve the beef and vegetables, remove them carefully from the stockpot and drain. Cut the strings from the meat and remove any small bones separated in cooking. Cut the meat to facilitate serving and place in the centre of a large hot serving dish. Surround with cooked vegetables, grouping them by colour. If you have added cabbage, place it in a sort of *bouquet* at one side of the dish. Potatoes can be served with the other vegetables or apart.

You can serve the *boeuf bouilli* alone '*au gros sel*' or you can accompany it by one or two kinds of mustard and small bowls of pickled gherkins, cocktail onions and small carrots, pimentos and green tomatoes in vinegar. I personally like to serve it with a sauce of whipped cream and grated horseradish or a piquant rémoulade sauce (page 40).

**Uses for Remaining Bouilli:** Put the beef through the mincer; mash equal quantities of boiled potatoes. Mix all together and work them well to blend, then bind with an egg and add salt and pepper, to taste. Butter a mould; fill with meat mixture; cover with a buttered paper and cook in a moderate oven (180°C/350°F/gas 4) for half an hour. This is delicious when served with a tomato or sour cream sauce.

Quite good meat balls or croquettes can be made in the same manner: mince the beef; combine with mashed potatoes and grated Gruyère or Parmesan cheese; season with a little nutmeg, salt and freshly ground pepper and sauté in butter until golden.

# Poule-au-Pot

| | |
|---|---|
| 1 large boiling fowl (or 1½ large roasting chickens) | thyme |
| | bay leaf |
| 450 g/1 pound lean pickled pork | butter |
| 1 small cabbage, quartered | *Vegetable Garnish:* |
| 1 large turnip | 12 small white onions |
| 1 large onion | 12 small carrots |
| 4 cloves | 12 small potatoes |
| 4 large carrots | 450 g/1 pound green beans, tied |
| freshly ground pepper | in bundles |

For a real *poule-au-pot* you'll need a boiling fowl, rather than a roasting chicken, to give the dish its rich full flavour.

If your butcher has not already prepared the boiling fowl, clean, singe and truss it. Wash the pickled pork thoroughly and halve it. Clean and quarter the cabbage and turnip, and place the vegetables in the bottom of a large stockpot together with an onion stuck with cloves, and the carrots, cut in quarters.

Place the fowl and pickled pork on the vegetables and sprinkle with pepper and a little thyme. Add enough hot water, or water and stock, barely to cover; place a bay leaf on top of the fowl and cover with a piece of buttered paper. Place the lid tightly on the stockpot; bring the stock slowly to the boil and simmer gently for about 1½ hours.

Add the small onions, carrots, potatoes and green beans, and cook for 20 to 30 minutes longer, or until the fowl is tender and the vegetables are cooked through.

To serve: place the fowl in the centre of a very large hot platter, place a piece of pork on each side and surround the meat with the vegetables, grouped according to colour. Reserve the broth for soup.

# Basic Stocks

It has been said that a cook's reputation rises or falls by the quality of her soups. A soup must be substantial enough to satisfy and at the same time light enough not to slacken enthusiasm for what follows. What an easy way to gain a reputation, for with the best home-made stocks you can provide a whole series of delicious soups from the world-famous *soupe à l'oignon* of the French (onions melted in butter and moistened with rich beef stock, served with grated cheese and rounds of toasted bread: see page 16) to the pride of the Greek cuisine, *avgolemono* (a handful of cooked rice, eggs whisked with the juice of a lemon and some fine rich chicken stock), a gold-tinted soup that is deliciously creamy and fresh-tasting. But first you will need some well-flavoured stocks to serve as delicious bases for consommés, soups, sauces ... and to enrich the great dishes of world cookery.

## Basic Beef Stock

| | |
|---|---|
| **1 kg/2 pounds shin of beef (meat and bone)** | **2 stalks celery, sliced** |
| **1 kg/2 pounds shin of veal (meat and bone)** | **1 *bouquet garni* (flat-leaf parsley, 1 sprig thyme and 1 bay leaf)** |
| **100 g/¼ pound lean raw ham** | **1 fat clove garlic** |
| **6 small carrots, roughly chopped and browned in butter** | **4–6 peppercorns** |
| **1 Spanish onion, roughly chopped and browned in butter** | **3.4 litres/6 pints cold water** |

Bone the meat. Cut all the meat, ham included, into large pieces and tie together. Break up the bones as finely as possible; sprinkle them with a little fat and brown them in the oven, stirring round from time to time. When the bones are slightly browned, put them in a large saucepan with the carrots, onion, celery, *bouquet garni*, garlic and peppercorns, but no salt. Add the cold water and bring to the boil. Skim carefully; wipe the edge of the saucepan, put the lid half on and allow the stock to cook gently for 4 hours. Then remove the fat; pass the liquid through a sieve and allow it to cool.

Put the meat in a saucepan just large enough to hold it. Brown a little in some fat; then drain it entirely of fat. Add 300 ml/½ pint of the prepared stock; cover the saucepan and let the meat simmer over a low flame until the stock is almost reduced, turning the meat from time to time so that it is bathed on all sides in the stock. Pour the remainder of the stock into the saucepan; bring to the boil and then simmer very slowly and evenly with the lid off. As soon as the meat is well cooked, remove the fat from the stock; strain through a fine sieve; cool and store in the refrigerator. The meat may be served in a great variety of ways.

## Basic Beef Stock (Quick Method)

450 g/1 pound veal knuckle
450 g/1 pound beef knuckle
4 tablespoons beef, veal or pork
  dripping
900 g/2 pounds lean beef
2 chicken feet (optional)
2 leeks (white parts only)
1 large Spanish onion stuck with
  2 cloves

2 stalks celery, tops included
2 carrots, coarsely chopped
4 sprigs flat-leaf parsley
1 fat clove garlic
3.4 litres/6 pints cold water
salt and freshly ground
  pepper

Have the veal and beef knuckles coarsely chopped by your butcher, brush with meat dripping and brown them in the oven. Place in a large stockpot with the lean beef, chicken feet, if you have any, and leeks, onion, celery, carrots, parsley and garlic. Cover with the cold water and bring slowly to the boil, removing the scum as it accumulates on the surface. Simmer gently for 1 hour; add salt and pepper to taste, and continue to simmer for another hour, or until the meat is tender. Correct the seasoning and strain the stock through a fine sieve. Cool, remove the fat and re-heat, or store in the refrigerator for later use.

## Basic Chicken Stock

1 boiling fowl
1 veal knuckle
2 chicken feet
3.4 litres/6 pints cold water
sea salt
6 peppercorns
2 leeks
6 small carrots

1 Spanish onion stuck with 2
  cloves
2 stalks celery, tops included
1 *bouquet garni* (flat-leaf
  parsley, 1 sprig thyme and
  1 bay leaf)
1 clove garlic

Place the boiling fowl in a large stockpot (with the veal knuckle and chicken feet for their extra gelatine content) and cover with the water. Add the salt and peppercorns and bring slowly to the boil. Simmer, with the water barely bubbling, for at least 1 hour, skimming the scum from the surface frequently. Then add the leeks, carrots, onion, celery, *bouquet garni* and garlic, and continue to cook for 1½ to 2 hours longer, or until the chicken is tender. Remove the fat, correct the seasoning and strain through a fine sieve. Cool and store in the refrigerator. The chicken meat can be eaten.

# Basic Chicken Stock (Quick Method)

1 chicken (about 2kg/4 pounds)
450 g/1 pound veal knuckle
3.4 litres/ 6 pints cold water
2 leeks, white parts only
1 Spanish onion, stuck with
  2 cloves

2 carrots, coarsely chopped
2 stalks celery, tops included
1 fat clove garlic
4 sprigs flat-leaf parsley
salt and freshly ground pepper

Place the chicken and veal knuckle in a large stockpot with the water and bring to the boil, skimming until the scum no longer rises to the surface. Simmer for 1 hour. Add the leeks, onion, carrots, celery, garlic and parsley; add salt and pepper to taste, and continue to simmer for 1 hour. Correct the seasoning and strain the stock through a fine sieve. Cool, remove the fat and re-heat, or store in the refrigerator.

# Basic Aspic

225 g/½ pound beef bones
1 duck's carcass
1 calf's foot (or 4 cleaned
  chicken feet)
1 onion, sliced
1 leek, sliced
1 carrot, sliced
1 stalk celery, chopped

1.2 litres/2 pints cold water
salt and freshly ground pepper
1 *bouquet garni* (flat-leaf
  parsley, 1 sprig thyme and
  1 bay leaf)
1 egg white
100 g/¼ pound raw lean beef,
  chopped

Combine the first ten ingredients in a large stockpot; bring slowly to the boil and simmer gently for about 4 hours, skimming from time to time. Strain and cool before skimming off the fat.

To clarify the stock, beat the egg white lightly, combine with the beef and add to the stock; bring very slowly to the boil, stirring constantly. After the stock has boiled up a few times, it will be clarified. Reduce the heat and simmer the stock very gently for about 25 minutes. Strain while hot through a flannel cloth.

**For Sherry Aspic:** stir in 4 tablespoons dry sherry.

**For Madeira Aspic:** stir in 4 tablespoons Madeira.

**For Tarragon Aspic:** when clarifying the aspic jelly, add several sprigs of tarragon.

This recipe will make 1.2 litres/2 pints of jelly and will keep for several days in the refrigerator.

# Chicken Consommé

2.4–2.8 litres/4–5 pints chicken
  stock

whites, lightly beaten, and shells
  of 2 eggs

Strain the chicken stock into a large saucepan. Add the egg whites and shells and bring to the boil. Simmer for 1 hour; strain through a fine cloth and cool. Skim and keep in the refrigerator; it will keep for several days.

# Beef Consommé

2.4–2.8 litres/4–5 pints beef stock
450 g/1 pound minced lean beef
2 leeks, chopped
2 stalks celery, chopped
2 carrots, chopped

½ Spanish onion, chopped
freshly ground pepper
whites, lightly beaten, and shells
  of 2 eggs

Strain the beef stock and combine in a large saucepan with the beef, leeks, celery, carrots, onion, pepper and the whites and shells of 2 eggs. Simmer for 1 hour; strain through a fine cloth and cool. Skim the grease from the surface and pour the stock carefully into storage jars, being careful not to disturb any sediment which lies at the bottom of the stock.

# Stracciatella alla Romana
Serves 4 to 6

3 eggs
2 tablespoons chopped flat-leaf
  parsley
2 tablespoons grated Romano or
  Parmesan cheese

1.5 litres/2½ pints well-seasoned
  chicken stock

Beat the eggs. Stir the parsley and cheese into the egg mixture. Bring the chicken stock to a fast boil and add the egg mixture slowly, stirring constantly. Continue stirring while the soup simmers for 5 minutes more.

# Tortellini in Brodo
Serves 4 to 6

225 g/½ pound flour
2 eggs
50 g/2 ounces *prosciutto*,
  minced
100 g/¼ pound cooked chicken,
  minced
50 g/2 ounces cooked pork,
  minced

1 egg
1 tablespoon chopped fresh
  basil, tarragon or chervil
salt, freshly ground pepper and
  grated nutmeg
2 tablespoons freshly grated
  Parmesan cheese
1.5 litres/2½ pints chicken stock

Make a well of the flour on a large pastry board; break the eggs into the well and slowly mix the flour and eggs together. Work the dough with your hands for 15 minutes, adding more flour if necessary. Sprinkle the board with more flour and roll out the dough as thin as possible. Cut into circles about 5 cm/2 inches in diameter.

To make the stuffing, combine the meats, egg, herbs, seasoning and cheese, and place 1 teaspoon of this mixture in the centre of each circle. Fold the dough over, closing in the stuffing, and press the edges together with your fingers to give the shape of a little cap.

Bring the chicken stock to the boil; add the *tortellini* and cook for about 20 minutes, or until the pasta caps are tender.

## Cold Beet Soup
Serves 4

½ **Spanish onion, sliced**
2 **tablespoons butter**
225 **g/½ pound cooked beetroot, peeled and sliced**
1 **boiled potato, peeled**

**salt and freshly ground pepper**
**juice of 1 large lemon**
300 **ml/½ pint cream**
425 **ml/¾ pint chilled chicken stock**

Sauté the onion in the butter until soft.

Put the beetroot, sautéed onion and boiled potato into a blender or food processor (or press through a fine sieve); add salt, pepper, the lemon juice and cream, and blend until smooth. Chill. Just before serving, add the chilled chicken stock and blend for 1 minute, adding a little stock or cold water if the soup is too thick.

## Curried Apple Soup
Serves 4

2 **tablespoons butter**
1 **Spanish onion, coarsely chopped**
600 **ml/1 pint chicken stock**
1 **tablespoon curry powder**
1 **tablespoon cornflour**
2 **egg yolks**

150 **ml/¼ pint hot double cream**
2 **eating apples**
**salt and freshly ground pepper**
**juice of ½ lemon**
**watercress leaves, to garnish**

Melt the butter; add the onion and cook until soft but not brown. Stir in the chicken stock and curry powder, then add the cornflour mixed with a little water. Bring to the boil and then simmer for 8 minutes. Add the egg yolks to the hot cream and stir gradually into the hot soup.

Remove from the heat immediately and transfer the mixture to a blender or food processor with 1 apple, peeled, cored and sliced. Blend until smooth or pass through a fine sieve. Season to taste with salt and pepper. Chill. Peel, core and dice the remaining apple and marinate in lemon juice to keep its colour. Just before serving, stir in the diced apple and enough watercress leaves to garnish.

# Gazpacho
## Spanish Iced Soup
Serves 4 to 5

6 large ripe tomatoes
2 small cloves garlic
1 Spanish onion
½ large green pepper
½ cucumber
6 tablespoons olive oil
4 tablespoons lemon juice

salt and cayenne pepper
450 ml/¾ pint chilled tomato
juice
450 ml/¾ pint chilled vegetable
stock
2 tablespoons butter
2 slices bread, crusts removed,

Blend 4 tomatoes and 1 clove garlic in a blender or food processor; add ½ the onion and ¼ green pepper, cut in rough pieces, and ¼ cucumber, peeled and cut in cubes, and blend again. Strain the mixture into a large tureen or serving bowl and chill in the refrigerator. Just before serving, blend together the olive oil, lemon juice, salt, cayenne pepper, tomato juice and vegetable stock; stir into the above mixture and add a small block of ice.

*Gazpacho* is traditionally served accompanied by individual small bowls of raw vegetables and garlic *croûtons*. Guests help themselves to a little of each. To prepare: chop or dice the remaining vegetables – tomatoes, onion, cucumber and green pepper – and put each vegetable into a separate bowl. Heat the butter with the remaining clove of garlic, chopped; add the diced bread; fry until crisp and golden and put into a small serving bowl.

# Cream of Cauliflower Soup
Serves 4

1 cauliflower (about 1 kg/
   2 pounds), in florets
4 tablespoons butter
4 tablespoons flour
900 ml/1½ pints chicken stock
1 onion, coarsely chopped
1 stalk celery, coarsely chopped

2 sprigs flat-leaf parsley,
   chopped
2 egg yolks
150 ml/¼ pint double cream
salt, freshly ground pepper and
   grated nutmeg

Poach the cauliflower in boiling salted water for 5 minutes and drain. Melt the butter in a saucepan; add the flour and cook, stirring continuously until a smooth paste is formed. Add the chicken stock, onion, celery and parsley, and simmer for 20 minutes. Strain the stock; add the cauliflower and cook until the cauliflower is softened. Rub the soup through a sieve. Bring back to the boil; stir in the egg yolks and cream. Simmer, stirring, for about 3 minutes, taking care that the soup does not boil, or it will curdle. Correct the seasoning with salt, pepper and a little nutmeg, and serve.

# 'Four Seasons' Watercress Vichyssoise
Serves 6

5 potatoes, peeled and sliced
2 large leeks, sliced
1½ bunches watercress
1 ham bone (optional)
1.2 litres/2 pints chicken stock

salt and freshly ground pepper
600 ml/1 pint double cream,
  chilled
sprigs of watercress, to garnish

Cook the potatoes, leeks and watercress with the ham bone (if using) in the stock until done. Put through a blender or purée through a fine sieve. Season with salt and pepper, and chill. Just before serving, add the chilled cream. Serve with sprigs of watercress.

# Vichyssoise Verte
Serves 5 to 6

225 g/½ pound raw potatoes,
  diced
50 g/2 ounces raw leeks,
  chopped
225 g/½ pound raw green peas

900 ml/1½ pints chicken stock
salt, freshly ground pepper and
  celery salt
425 ml/¾ pint double cream
finely chopped chives

Simmer the potatoes, leeks and peas in the chicken stock until barely tender. Put through a blender or purée through a fine sieve. Season to taste with salt, pepper and celery salt. Cool the mixture slightly and stir in the double cream. Chill thoroughly and sprinkle with finely chopped chives.

# Leek and Potato Soup
Serves 4

6 large leeks
4 tablespoons butter
4 medium potatoes
900 ml/1½ pints chicken stock

salt, freshly ground pepper and
  grated nutmeg
300 ml/½ pint double cream
finely chopped chives, to garnish

Cut the green tops from the leeks and cut the white parts into 2.5-cm/1-inch lengths. Sauté the white parts gently in butter until soft. Do not allow to brown.

Peel and slice the potatoes and add to the leeks with the chicken stock, and salt, pepper and nutmeg, to taste, and simmer until the vegetables are cooked. Strain the vegetables and stock. Add the cream and serve sprinkled with the chives.

# Italian Minestrone

If, as has been claimed, one of the best things ever to come out of Italy is spaghetti in all its myriad variations, one of the finest uses for *pasta* is in the many wonderful soups and *brodi* of the Italian provinces. Delicate broths of chicken or beef – *cappelletti in brodo* (chicken stock studded with subtly flavoured 'little monks' caps' of meat and herbs) and *farfallini in brodo* (beef stock with small *pasta* bows) vie with the thick fish soups of the coastal regions – *zuppa di pesce alla romana* (fish soup Roman style), *burrido* and *cacciucco* (squid, lobster, scallops and sliced fish, simmered in stock with olive oil and dry white wine) – for first place in our affections. But the most famous of them all, and certainly one of the 'great dishes of the world', is Italian *minestrone*.

*Minestrone* is, by its very nature, a peasant soup, basically a mixture of beans, macaroni and fresh vegetables simmered in bean broth and rich beef stock or water with meats, herbs, olive oil, *pasta* and freshly grated cheese. But like most great peasant dishes, it is fit for the most sophisticated palate. Italian restaurants serve it as a first course, but in some Italian homes it often provides the whole meal. I like *minestrone* so thick, so full-bodied, so rich with meat and vegetables, that you can practically cut it with a knife.

The variations on the *minestrone* theme are legion. I sometimes add celery, spinach or sliced courgettes to the vegetables in the following recipe; diced Italian sausage, ham or a ham bone do no real harm; and a handful of finely chopped fresh basil elevates this country soup into the *gourmet* class.

Serve *minestrone* with additional cheese, freshly grated Parmesan or, if available, Roman *pecorino* and a slice or two of Italian bread, even though the Italians themselves frown on eating bread with a soup that contains *pasta*.

## Minestrone
Serves 6 to 8

225 g/½ pound dried kidney or
  haricot beans
100 g/¼ pound salt pork
2 cloves garlic
1 Spanish onion
2.4 litres/4 pints beef stock
4 carrots
4 stalks celery
½ small head cabbage
4 sprigs curly endive
4–6 tomatoes

225 g/½ pound green beans
100 g/¼ pound frozen peas
100–150 g/4–6 ounces macaroni,
  broken into 5-cm/2-inch
  lengths
salt and freshly ground pepper
2 tablespoons finely chopped
  flat-leaf parsley
2 tablespoons olive oil
4 tablespoons freshly grated
  Parmesan

Soak the dried kidney or haricot beans overnight. Drain. Simmer the beans in 1.2 litres/2 pints salted water for 2 hours.

Dice the salt pork and sauté in a thick-bottomed frying pan until brown. Finely chop the garlic; cut the onion into quarters or eighths; sauté with the pork until golden. Pour in the beef stock and simmer gently, adding the finely sliced carrots and celery. Slice the cabbage, endive, tomatoes and green beans in fairly large pieces and add them to the soup. Bring to the boil, cover, and reduce the heat until the soup barely simmers. Simmer for 1½ hours.

Twenty minutes before serving, add the peas and macaroni or other pasta, bring to the boil and then simmer until the pasta is tender. If the soup is too thick, add a little water. Add salt and pepper to taste, and just before serving, stir in the finely chopped parsley and olive oil. Serve hot, sprinkled with freshly grated Parmesan.

## Zuppa di Fagioli
### Italian Double-Bean Soup
Serves 4 to 6

**225 g/½ pound dried white beans**
**1.5 litres/2½ pints cold water**
**salt and freshly ground pepper**

**4 tablespoons olive oil**
**2 cloves garlic, chopped**
**2 tablespoons chopped flat-leaf parsley**

Soak the beans overnight. Drain and put them into a stockpot with the cold water. Bring to the boil and simmer the beans as slowly as possible for 2 to 3 hours, or until they are tender. Remove half the beans, purée them in a blender – or press them through a fine sieve – and return this purée to the soup. Season to taste with salt and pepper.

Heat the olive oil in a small saucepan and simmer the garlic in it until just golden. Add chopped parsley to this mixture and pour it into the soup. Serve very hot.

## Green Pea Soup
Serves 6

**2 Spanish onions, thinly sliced**
**350 g/¾ pound dried green peas**
**1.8 litres/3 pints cold water**
**6–8 peppercorns**
**1 tablespoon salt**
**4 cloves**

**1 teaspoon dried mustard**
**2 stalks celery, thinly sliced**
**100 g/¼ pound bacon, cut in thin strips**
**¼ teaspoon dried oregano**
**fried *croûtons***

Combine the first nine ingredients in a large saucepan and bring to the boil; skim and then cook very slowly, covered, for 2 to 3 hours, adding more water if the soup becomes too thick. Add the oregano after the soup has cooked for 2 hours. Serve with *croûtons*.

# Lentil Soup
Serves 4 to 6

175 g/6 ounces brown lentils
1.5 litres/2½ pints beef stock
ham knuckle or 100 g/¼ pound
  salt pork

2 baking potatoes, diced
1 tablespoon butter
1 tablespoon flour
freshly ground pepper

Wash the lentils and drain them. Cover with cold water and leave to soak for 2 hours. Drain. Cover with cold water again and bring to the boil. Boil for 10 minutes. Drain again; add the beef stock and ham knuckle and bring to the boil. Lower the heat; cover the pan and simmer gently for 2½ to 3 hours, or until the lentils are tender.

Twenty minutes before the lentils are done, add the potatoes. Just before serving, make a *beurre manié* by creaming together the butter and flour. Stir this into the soup, bit by bit, and continue to cook for a few minutes longer. Add pepper, to taste.

Chapter 3

# Sauces

## Great Sauces

'A sauce-maker,' according to the *Dictionary of Jovial Gastronomy*, 'must be adroit and sensitive to the most delicate nuance as sauce-making includes chemistry, harmony, flavour voluptuousness, vigilance and other virtues . . . all crossed by the lightning stroke of genius.' No wonder so many cooks hesitate to look into this awesome subject and discover for themselves that, given a few practical rules and a little experience, the whole magic realm of sauce-making is theirs for the asking. But don't get me wrong, I don't claim that your version of *quenelles de brochet* will ever equal the ethereal *pain de poisson* served with an unctuous *sauce Cardinale* created daily by Alexandre Dumaine in his restaurant at Saulieu.

Yet sauces, like soups and stocks, have their place in everyday good cooking as well as in the kitchens of international hotels. A home-made sauce can lend certain magic to the simplest ingredients and make a memorable meal out of humble beginnings.

The French have a way with sauces. Ever since the days of the famous Carême, sauce-making has been the key to French *haute cuisine*, ranking foremost among the many skills that any aspiring cook must learn, practise and finally master.

## White Sauces

*Béchamel* – named after the *maître d'hôtel* of Louis XIV – is the mother sauce of all white sauces and is exceedingly simple to prepare. A simple béchamel sauce can be made with just flour, butter, milk and a little minced onion, but I think you will find that the following classic recipe which includes a little chopped veal or a paper-thin slice of Serrano ham adds greatly to the savour of this delicious sauce. The secret of making a good white sauce – and most other sauces – is to cook it slowly.

# Béchamel Sauce

Makes about 600 ml/1 pint

4 tablespoons butter
½ onion, finely chopped
3 tablespoons flour
900 ml/1½ pints hot milk
50 g/2 ounces lean veal or ham,
  finely chopped

1 stalk celery, finely chopped
1 small sprig thyme
½ bay leaf
white peppercorns
freshly grated nutmeg
extra butter

In a thick-bottomed saucepan, or in the top of a double saucepan, melt 3 table-spoons of the butter and cook the onion over a low heat until it is transparent. Stir in the flour and, stirring constantly, cook for a few minutes or until the mixture cooks through but does not take on colour.

Add the hot milk and cook, stirring constantly, until the mixture is thick and smooth.

In another saucepan, simmer the veal (or ham) and the celery in the remaining butter over a very low heat. Season with the thyme, bay leaf, white peppercorns and nutmeg. Cook for 5 minutes, stirring to keep the veal from browning. Add the veal to the sauce and cook over hot water for 45 minutes to 1 hour, stirring occasionally. When reduced to the proper consistency (two-thirds of original quantity), strain the sauce through a fine sieve into a bowl, pressing the meat and onion well to extract all the liquid. Cover the surface of the sauce with tiny pieces of butter to keep a film from forming.

# Béchamel Sauce (Short Method)

Makes about 600 ml/1 pint

2 tablespoons butter
½ onion, finely chopped
1 stalk celery, finely chopped
2 tablespoons flour
600 ml/1 pint hot milk

1 small sprig thyme
½ bay leaf
white peppercorns
freshly grated nutmeg

Melt the butter for the *roux* in a thick-bottomed saucepan or in the top of a double saucepan. Cook the onion and celery in it over a low heat until the onion is soft but not browned. Remove the pan from the heat, stir in the flour, return to the heat and cook gently for 3 to 5 minutes, stirring constantly, until the flour is cooked through. Add a quarter of the milk, heated to boiling point, and cook over water, stirring vigorously. As the sauce begins to thicken, add the remainder of the milk, stirring constantly with a wooden spoon until the sauce bubbles. Add the thyme, bay leaf, white peppercorns and nutmeg, to taste, and simmer the sauce gently for 15 minutes. Strain through a fine sieve and dot the surface with butter.

Using either version of the béchamel sauce above, you can make a variety of sauces to accompany meat, fish, eggs and vegetables.

**Cream Sauce:**  For fish, poultry, eggs and vegetables. Add 4 tablespoons double cream to 600 ml/1 pint hot béchamel sauce and bring to boiling point. Add a few drops lemon juice.

**Mornay Sauce:**  For fish, vegetables, poultry, poached eggs, noodle and macaroni mixtures. Mix 2 slightly beaten egg yolks with a little cream and combine with 600 ml/1 pint hot béchamel sauce. Cook, stirring constantly, until it just reaches boiling point. Add 2 tablespoons butter and 2 to 4 tablespoons grated cheese (Parmesan or Swiss cheese is best).

**Aurore Sauce:**  Excellent with eggs, chicken or shellfish. Add 2 to 3 tablespoons tomato purée to 600 ml/1 pint hot béchamel sauce.

**Onion Sauce:**  For fish, lamb or veal. Chop 1 Spanish onion, cover with hot water and parboil for 3 to 5 minutes. Drain and cook the onion in a saucepan with a little butter until soft. Add 600 ml/1 pint hot béchamel sauce and cook for approximately 15 minutes longer. Strain through a fine sieve, pressing the vegetables well to extract all juice; return to the heat and gradually add 4 tablespoons double cream. Correct the seasoning with salt and white pepper, and serve.

## Velouté Sauce
Makes about 400 ml/⅔ pint

2 tablespoons butter
2 tablespoons flour
600 ml/1 pint hot white stock
  (chicken or veal)

salt
white peppercorns
4 button mushrooms, chopped

Melt the butter in a saucepan; add the flour and cook for a few minutes to form a *roux blond*. Add the hot stock, salt and peppercorns and cook, stirring vigorously with a whisk. Add the mushrooms and cook slowly, stirring occasionally, skimming from time to time, until the sauce is reduced to two-thirds of its original quantity and is very thick but light and creamy. Strain through a fine sieve.

## Rich Cheese Sauce
Makes about 600 ml/1 pint

3 tablespoons butter
3 tablespoons flour
425 ml/¾ pint hot chicken stock
300 ml/½ pint double cream

2 tablespoons each freshly
  grated Gruyère and Parmesan
salt, freshly ground pepper and
  grated nutmeg

Melt the butter in the top of a double saucepan; stir in the flour and cook over water for 3 minutes, stirring continuously until smooth. Blend in the hot stock and then the cream, using a wire whisk to avoid lumps.

Stir in the grated Gruyère and Parmesan and season to taste with salt, pepper and a little nutmeg. Continue to cook over water on the lowest of heats for about 20 minutes, stirring from time to time to keep a skin from forming. Good for poultry, fish, vegetables and eggs.

## Rich Prawn Sauce

Makes about 600 ml/1 pint

3 tablespoons butter
3 tablespoons flour
425 ml/¾ pint fish *fumet* or rich
    fish stock, strained
300 ml/½ pint double
    cream

350 g/¾ pound frozen prawns,
    coarsely chopped
2 tablespoons butter
salt, freshly ground pepper and
    cayenne
2 tablespoons cognac

Melt the butter in the top of a double saucepan; stir in the flour and cook over simmering water for 3 minutes, stirring continuously until smooth. Add the fish *fumet* slowly, stirring continuously until the sauce is rich and creamy. Simmer gently for 20 minutes; then add the cream and continue cooking, uncovered, stirring from time to time to keep a skin from forming, until the sauce is reduced to the desired consistency.

Sauté the chopped prawns in the butter until heated through; season to taste with salt, pepper and cayenne pepper. Flame with cognac and add to the sauce. Good for poached fish and fish and shellfish soufflés.

# Brown Sauces

There is only one basic brown sauce – *sauce espagnole* – used as the base for many famous French sauces. As this sauce keeps very well, make it by the quart and store it in the refrigerator in a covered jar for future use. *Sauce espagnole*, or basic brown sauce, will keep indefinitely in the refrigerator if it is boiled up again once a week, and returned to the refrigerator in a clean jar.

Use *sauce espagnole* as a base for many exciting sauces, and as it is to lend interest to braised onions, carrots and celery, or to add to the butter that steaks and chops have been cooked in.

## Sauce Espagnole

Makes 1.2 litres/2 pints

3 tablespoons beef dripping
75 g/3 ounces fat salt pork or
    green bacon, diced
3 carrots, coarsely chopped
1 Spanish onion, coarsely
    chopped

2 stalks celery, coarsely
    chopped
3 tablespoons flour
1.8 litres/3 pints hot home-made
    beef stock

1 *bouquet garni* (3 sprigs flat-
leaf parsley, 1 sprig thyme,
1 bay leaf)

1 clove garlic
150 ml/¼ pint rich tomato sauce
or 3 tablespoons tomato purée

Melt the fat in a large, heavy saucepan; add the salt pork (or green bacon), carrots, onion and celery, and cook until golden. Sprinkle with the flour and cook gently on a very low flame, stirring frequently, until well browned. Add a third of the boiling stock together with the *bouquet garni* and garlic, and cook, stirring frequently, until the sauce thickens.

Add half the remaining stock and cook very slowly over a very low heat, uncovered, stirring occasionally, for about 1½ to 2 hours. Skim off the scum and fat rising to the surface as it cooks. Add the tomato sauce (or purée) and cook for a few minutes longer. Then strain through a fine sieve into a bowl, pressing the vegetables against the sieve to extract all their juice.

Clean the saucepan; return the mixture to it; add the remaining stock and continue cooking slowly until the sauce is reduced to about 1.2 litres/2 pints, skimming the surface from time to time.

Strain again. Cool, stirring occasionally. Store *sauce espagnole* in a covered jar in the refrigerator until ready for use.

**Madeira Sauce:** Reduce 600 ml/1 pint *sauce espagnole* until it is half the original quantity. Add 6 tablespoons Madeira. Heat the sauce well, but do not let it boil, or the flavour of the wine will be lost.

**Sauce Bordelaise:** Cook 2 finely chopped shallots in 150 ml/¼ pint red wine until the liquid is reduced to a third of its original quantity. Add 300 ml/½ pint *sauce espagnole* and simmer gently for 10 minutes.

Remove the marrow from a split beef bone; cut it into small dice and poach it in boiling salted water for 1 or 2 minutes. Drain, and just before serving the sauce add 2 tablespoons of the diced beef marrow and a little finely chopped flat-leaf parsley.

**Sauce Lyonnaise:** Sauté ½ Spanish onion, finely chopped, in 2 tablespoons butter until golden. Add 8 tablespoons dry white wine and simmer until reduced to half the original quantity. Add 600 ml/1 pint *sauce espagnole*; cook gently for 15 minutes; add 1 tablespoon chopped flat-leaf parsley and 'finish' the sauce by swirling in 1–2 tablespoons butter.

## Sauce Perigueux

600 ml/1 pint sauce espagnole
3 tablespoons Madeira
2 tablespoons truffles, finely
  diced

1 tablespoon truffle liquor
1 tablespoon butter

Reduce the *sauce espagnole* in a thick-bottomed saucepan to half the original quantity. Add the Madeira and bring slowly to the boil, stirring occasionally. Take off the heat and stir in the truffles and truffle liquor. Add the butter to the sauce, melting it in by moving the saucepan in a circular motion until the butter is completely absorbed.

Serve with baked eggs, eggs *en cocotte*, beef, chicken and veal.

## Tomato Sauce

1 Spanish onion, finely
  chopped
2 cloves garlic, finely chopped
2 tablespoons butter
4 tablespoons olive oil
6 tablespoons Italian tomato
  purée
1 large can Italian peeled
  tomatoes
2 bay leaves

2 tablespoons finely chopped
  flat-leaf parsley
¼–½ teaspoon dried oregano
1 small strip lemon peel
6 tablespoons dry white wine
6 tablespoons water
salt and freshly ground
  pepper
1 tablespoon Worcestershire
  sauce

Sauté the onion and garlic in the butter and olive oil in a large, thick-bottomed frying pan until transparent and soft, but not coloured. Stir in the tomato purée and continue to cook for a minute or two, stirring constantly. Pour in the peeled tomatoes; add the bay leaves, parsley, oregano and lemon peel. Add the dry white wine and water, and salt and pepper, to taste, and simmer gently, stirring from time to time, for 1 to 2 hours. Just before serving, stir in the Worcestershire sauce. Good for *pasta*, meat, poultry and veal.

## Sauce Béarnaise

2 sprigs tarragon
3 sprigs chervil
1 tablespoon chopped shallots
2 crushed peppercorns
2 tablespoons tarragon vinegar

150 ml/¼ pint dry white wine
3 egg yolks
1 tablespoon water
225 g/½ pound soft butter
salt and cayenne pepper

Chop the leaves and stems of the tarragon and chervil coarsely and combine with the shallots, peppercorns, vinegar and white wine in a saucepan. Cook over a high heat until the liquid is reduced to two-thirds of its original quantity.

Place the egg yolks, herb and wine mixture, and water in the top of a double saucepan over hot, but not boiling, water and stir briskly with a wire whisk until light and fluffy. Never let the water in the bottom of the saucepan begin to boil, or the sauce will not 'take'. Add the butter gradually to the egg mixture, stirring briskly all the time, as the sauce begins to thicken. Continue adding butter and stirring until the sauce is thick. Season to taste with salt and a little cayenne pepper, strain through a fine sieve and serve.

## Sauce Hollandaise

| | |
|---|---|
| **1 teaspoon lemon juice** | **225 g/½ pound soft butter** |
| **1 tablespoon cold water** | **4 egg yolks** |
| **salt and white pepper** | **lemon juice** |

Combine the lemon juice, water, salt and white pepper in the top of a double saucepan or *bain-marie*. Divide the butter into 4 equal pieces. Add the egg yolks and a quarter of the butter to the liquid in the saucepan and stir the mixture rapidly and constantly with a wire whisk over hot, but not boiling, water until the butter is melted and the mixture begins to thicken. Add the second piece of butter and continue whisking. As the mixture thickens and the second piece of butter melts, add the third piece of butter, stirring from the bottom of the pan until it is melted. Be careful not to allow the water over which the sauce is cooking to boil at any time. Add the rest of butter, beating until it melts and is incorporated into the sauce.

Now remove the top part of the saucepan from the heat and continue to beat the sauce for 2 to 3 minutes longer. Replace the saucepan over hot, but not boiling, water for 2 minutes more, beating constantly. By this time the emulsion should have formed and your sauce will be rich and creamy. 'Finish' the sauce with a few drops of lemon juice, strain and serve.

If at any time in the operation the mixture should curdle, beat in 1 or 2 table-spoons of cold water to rebind the emulsion.

## Mayonnaise
Makes 300 ml/½ pint

| | |
|---|---|
| **2 egg yolks** | **lemon juice** |
| **salt and freshly ground pepper** | **300 ml/½ pint olive oil** |
| **¼ teaspoon mustard** | |

Place the egg yolks (make sure the gelatinous thread of the egg is removed), salt, pepper and mustard in a bowl. Use a wire whisk, fork or wooden spoon, and beat the yolks to a smooth paste. Add a little lemon juice (the acid helps the emulsion) and, drop by drop, beat in about a quarter of the oil. Add a little more lemon juice to the mixture and next, a little more quickly now, add more oil, beating all the while. Continue adding oil and beating until the sauce is of a good thick consistency. Correct the seasoning (more salt, pepper and lemon juice) as desired. If you are going to make the mayonnaise a day before using, stir in 1 tablespoon boiling water when it is of the desired consistency. This will keep it from turning or separating.

*Note:* If the mayonnaise should curdle, break another egg yolk into a clean bowl and gradually beat the curdled mayonnaise into it. Your mayonnaise will begin to 'take' immediately.

## Sauce Louis

300 ml/½ pint well-flavoured
  mayonnaise (page 39)
2 tablespoons chilli sauce
3 tablespoons olive oil
1 tablespoon wine
  vinegar
2 tablespoons finely grated
  onion

2 tablespoons finely chopped
  flat-leaf parsley
6 tablespoons double cream,
  whipped
salt, freshly ground pepper and
  cayenne
1–2 tablespoons chopped stuffed
  or black olives

Blend together the mayonnaise, chilli sauce, olive oil, wine vinegar, onion, parsley and whipped cream. Season to taste with salt, pepper and a dash of cayenne. Stir in chopped stuffed or black olives and chill for 1 or 2 hours before serving. Delicious for seafood cocktails and a 'must' for crab Louis.

## Sauce Verte

300 ml/½ pint well-flavoured
  mayonnaise (page 39)
4 tablespoons finely chopped
  watercress leaves
4 tablespoons finely chopped
  chervil

2 tablespoons finely chopped
  flat-leaf parsley
1–2 tablespoons finely chopped
  tarragon leaves
lemon juice
salt and freshly ground pepper

Whirl the mayonnaise, watercress and herbs in a blender or processor, or blend well with a whisk, and add lemon juice, salt and pepper to taste. Serve this sauce chilled with fish and shellfish, poached and grilled salmon, or fish mousse.

## Sauce Rémoulade

300 ml/½ pint well-flavoured
  mayonnaise (page 39)
2 tablespoons finely chopped
  tarragon, basil or chervil
2 tablespoons finely chopped
  flat-leaf parsley

1 clove garlic, finely chopped
1 teaspoon dry mustard
1 teaspoon capers
2 baby gherkins, finely
  chopped

Combine the ingredients; chill and serve with grilled fish, prawns and lobster. Excellent with cold pork chops.

# Greek Garlic Sauce (Skordalia)

2–4 cloves garlic, finely chopped
2 tablespoons finely chopped
 flat-leaf parsley
1 large boiled potato or an
 equal quantity of moist fresh
 breadcrumbs

50 g/2 ounces blanched and
 crushed almonds
olive oil
2–4 tablespoons wine vinegar
salt and freshly ground
 pepper

Pound the garlic, parsley, potato (or moist breadcrumbs) and almonds in a mortar. Add olive oil and the vinegar little by little, pounding the mixture until it is a smooth paste. Add salt and pepper, to taste, and continue adding olive oil, beating briskly, until the sauce is of the desired consistency.

# Sauce Gribiche

3 hard-boiled eggs
1 tablespoon Dijon mustard
2 tablespoons finely chopped
 parsley, chives and chervil
 (*fines herbes*)

150 ml/¼ pint olive oil
vinegar or lemon juice
salt and freshly ground
 pepper

Pound the egg yolks with the mustard and *fine herbes* in a mortar until smooth. Add the olive oil little by little, stirring all the time as for a mayonnaise. Season to taste with vinegar or lemon juice and salt and pepper. Chop the egg whites finely and add to the sauce. Stir just before serving.

# Rouille

2 fat cloves garlic
1 tablespoon paprika (or crushed
 red peppers)
1 slice white bread, trimmed of
 crusts

2 tablespoons olive oil
2–3 tablespoons mayonnaise

Pound the garlic and paprika (or crushed red peppers) in a mortar with the bread, which you have dipped in water and then squeezed dry. Add the olive oil and mayonnaise little by little and blend to a smooth paste.

## Provençal Tapénade

50 g/2 ounces stoned black
  olives
25 g/1 ounce anchovy fillets
25 g/1 ounce tuna fish
Dijon mustard

50 g/2 ounces capers
4–6 tablespoons extra virgin
  olive oil
cognac
freshly ground pepper

Pound the olives, anchovy fillets and tuna fish to a smooth paste in a mortar with Dijon mustard, to taste, and capers, adding the olive oil bit by bit as you would for a mayonnaise. Season to taste with cognac and pepper and force the mixture through a fine sieve. The *tapénade* mixture keeps well in a jar, and is excellent with hard-boiled eggs or as a highly flavoured *canapé* spread.

# Butters

## Beurre Noisette

100 g/¼ pound butter
juice of ½ lemon

salt and white pepper

Melt the butter and cook to a light hazelnut colour. Add lemon juice and salt and pepper, to taste. Serve with eggs.

## Garlic Butter

100 g/¼ pound butter
2–4 cloves garlic, crushed
1 tablespoon finely chopped
  flat-leaf parsley

1–2 tablespoons lemon juice
salt and freshly ground
  pepper

Cream the butter with garlic and parsley. Season to taste with lemon juice, salt and pepper. Chill. Serve with grilled steak.

## Prawn Butter

2 tablespoons butter
1 small onion, finely chopped
1 bay leaf

pinch dried thyme
crushed raw tiger prawn shells
100 g/¼ pound butter

Melt the butter and sauté the onion with the bay leaf, thyme and crushed raw prawn shells (which you have dried in the oven for a few minutes) for 20 to

30 minutes. Cool. Add the butter and pound in a mortar until creamy. Rub the mixture through a fine sieve and use as required in fish or shellfish soups, *bisques* and sauces.

### Lobster Butter

As above, but use shells and coral of lobster.

# Sweet Sauces

## Apricot Sauce

300 ml/½ pint apricot jam
150 ml/¼ pint water

2 tablespoons Kirsch, or
   mandarin liqueur

Combine the apricot jam and water in a saucepan and bring to the boil. Lower the heat and simmer gently, stirring from time to time, for 5 to 10 minutes. Strain through a fine sieve and stir in the Kirsch, or mandarin liqueur.

## Vanilla Custard Sauce

425 ml/¾ pint milk
½–1 teaspoon vanilla essence
4 tablespoons sugar

4 egg yolks
¼ teaspoon salt

Simmer the milk for five minutes; stir in the vanilla essence, and remove the pan from the heat. Combine the sugar, egg yolks and salt in a mixing bowl and whisk with a hand-held electric beater until fluffy and lemon-coloured. Pour a little of the hot milk into the egg and sugar mixture; blend well; then stir the egg mixture into the hot milk. Heat slowly in the top of a double saucepan over simmering water, stirring constantly, until the mixture coats the back of a spoon. Serve warm over cake, a sweet soufflé or ice cream.

## Zabaglione Sauce

3 egg yolks
25 g/1 ounce granulated
   sugar

3–4 tablespoons Marsala or
   sherry
1½ tablespoons brandy

Combine the egg yolks with the sugar and Marsala (or sherry) in the top of a double saucepan. Whisk the mixture over hot, but not boiling, water until the sauce coats the back of a spoon. Stir in the brandy, and serve immediately. For cakes, puddings, sweet soufflés and ice cream.

# Crème Pâtissière

**4 egg yolks**
**50 g/2 ounces sugar**
**2 teaspoons flour**

**300 ml/½ pint warm milk**
**¼–½ teaspoon vanilla essence**

Beat the yolks and sugar together until the mixture is fluffy and lemon-coloured. Mix in the flour; add the milk and vanilla and mix thoroughly. Place the mixture in the top of a double saucepan and cook over simmering water, stirring constantly, until it reaches boiling point. Boil for 2 minutes; remove from heat; put through a sieve and allow to cool.

# Rum Sauce

**2 egg yolks**
**2 tablespoons sugar**
**300 ml/½ pint double cream**

**4–6 tablespoons rum**
**½–1 teaspoon vanilla essence**
**sugar**

Beat the egg yolks with the sugar until fluffy and lemon-coloured. Whip the cream until stiff; add the rum and vanilla essence and whip until stiff again. Add more sugar to taste. Fold the beaten egg yolks into the whipped cream.

# Chapter 4

# Eggs

It was in France that I first learned to treat eggs with the respect that they deserve. Until then, I had always considered them as just another breakfast food or late-night snack. But in France, where an omelette can be a thing of fragile beauty and where the soufflé soars to gastronomic heights of distinction, the egg really comes into its own as *gourmet* fare for any occasion.

France also taught me to appreciate the egg in its hard-boiled state – eggs mayonnaise as the refreshing beginning to a meal on a sun-dappled terrace; eggs *en tonneaux*, whole hard-boiled eggs filled with anchovies and made to look like little caper-filled barrels; and stuffed and dressed eggs of every variety.

Eggs are good mixers. They go well with any meat, fish or sauce, are one of the most versatile of foods, and can be prepared in almost endless ways. To my mind, no single food is more essential to good cooking than the egg.

The most important thing to remember in cooking eggs is to use low heat. The making of an omelette is the outstanding exception, and here the higher heat is nullified by the short time the eggs are subjected to it.

Always store eggs in the refrigerator. Keep eggs broad end up and away from smells (the porous nature of the shell makes the contents particularly receptive to odours). Do not store them near highly flavoured cheeses or onions. For best cooking results, bring eggs to room temperature (about 45 minutes) before using them. Whites will beat up faster and to a larger volume and shells will not crack when you boil them. If they have just come from the refrigerator, run warm water over them for a minute or so to bring them to room temperature.

## Boiled Eggs

This is a misnomer. Eggs should never be boiled. Doing so produces an unpalatable tough white and a yolk which is dull yellow and rubbery. For the best results, eggs in the shell should be cooked in water which is barely simmering.

Fill a pan with enough water to cover the eggs thoroughly. Bring the water to a rolling boil and lower the eggs into it gently, using a spoon. Then lower the heat until the water is just barely bubbling; otherwise the eggs will bang against the side of the pan and the shells may crack. And eggs cooked more gently seem to taste better too.

The classic soft-boiled egg – the white coagulated but still on the soft side and the golden yolk runny – is cooked for 3 to 4½ minutes. A 6-minute egg (*œuf mollet*) has a firm white and runny yolk. A true hard-boiled egg is cooked in simmering water for about 10 minutes.

Remove the eggs from the water at once or they will go on cooking. Rinse them under cold water for a brief second to make handling easier.

## Poached Eggs

For the best results it is essential to use fresh eggs, preferably not more than three or four days old. I always find that the whites of older eggs tend to go stringy and the yolks are much more apt to break than those of fresh ones. A large wide pan is a necessity, too, if you intend to poach more than one egg at a time. And be sure it is deep enough to allow at least an inch (2.5 cm) of water over the eggs to prevent them sticking to the bottom of the pan.

Fill the pan with water; bring it to the boil and add 1 tablespoon of vinegar and a little salt to help the eggs keep their shape. Have your eggs ready, each broken into a separate cup. Holding a cup in each hand, tip the eggs into the gently simmering water. Remove the pan from the heat; as the whites begin to set, turn the eggs once with a perforated spoon to give them a proper shape; cover the pan and allow the eggs to cook gently, still off the heat, for about 3 minutes. Lift the eggs out with a perforated spoon, and, if you are not going to serve them immediately, slide them into a bowl of warm water. If you are, put them in cold water for a minute to stop cooking and to remove all taste of acidity; drain them dry on a clean towel and trim straggly bits of white with a pair of scissors.

## Œufs Mollets

Poached eggs are not easy, by any standards, to make successfully. I often prefer to use *œufs mollets* in recipes that call for poached eggs. An *œuf mollet* is the French culinary term for a shelled soft-boiled egg with the white delicately firm and the yolk deliciously runny. Cook *œufs mollets* as boiled eggs, but for 6 minutes only. Shell carefully under cold water.

Any French chef will tell you that certain egg dishes served with a special sauce or garniture require a poached egg, and that there are others which require an *œuf mollet*. As a matter of fact, these are practically interchangeable. So if, as I do, you find difficulty in preparing poached eggs, then by all means use shelled soft-boiled eggs instead.

## Baked Eggs

Butter individual baking dishes or soufflé dishes with a teaspoon of butter. Slide 1 or 2 eggs into each, being careful not to break the yolks. Sprinkle the top with pepper and salt to taste and add a small dab of butter. Place the baking dishes in a pan of hot water and bake in a preheated moderate oven (170–180°C/325–350°F/gas 3–4) for about 8 minutes, or a little longer if a firmer egg is desired. Be sure to remove the eggs from the oven before they are completely cooked. They will continue cooking from the heat of the baking dish.

## Baked Eggs with Cream
Serves 4

| | |
|---|---|
| 150 ml/¼ pint cream | 1–2 teaspoons prepared mustard |
| 2 tablespoons grated Gruyère | salt and freshly ground pepper |
| 2 tablespoons lemon juice | 8 eggs |
| 2 tablespoons dry white wine | buttered breadcrumbs |

Mix together the cream, grated cheese, lemon juice and wine; add the mustard and salt and pepper, to taste. Break the eggs into individual buttered ramekins or tiny casseroles, 2 eggs in each. Cover the eggs with the sauce and sprinkle buttered breadcrumbs over the top. Place the ramekins in a pan of hot water and bake in a moderate oven (180°C/350°F/gas 4) for about 15 minutes.

## Baked Eggs en Soufflé
Makes 8

8 eggs
salt and white pepper
butter

8 tablespoons double cream
4 tablespoons freshly grated
Parmesan

Separate the eggs. Beat the whites until very stiff and season generously with salt and white pepper. Butter 8 large individual ramekins or tiny casseroles and spoon beaten egg whites into each. Use rather large ramekins as egg whites tend to rise like a soufflé. Make a depression with the back of your spoon for each egg yolk. Place the yolks in the hollows (1 to each of the 8 ramekins); cover each yolk with 1 tablespoon cream and sprinkle with a little grated cheese. Bake in a hot oven (230°C/450°F/gas 8) for 8 to 10 minutes.

## Eggs en Casserole
Serves 4

4 hard-boiled eggs
1 tablespoon Dijon mustard
2 tablespoons olive oil
2 tablespoons finely chopped
   flat-leaf parsley
salt and freshly ground pepper
4 tablespoons freshly grated
   Parmesan

2 slices bread, crusts removed
2 tablespoons butter
300 ml/½ pint well-flavoured
   tomato sauce (page 38)
1–2 teaspoon(s) grated onion
1–2 tablespoons chopped stuffed
   olives

Cut the eggs in half crosswise and remove the yolks carefully. Mash the yolks and mix with the mustard, olive oil and 1 tablespoon parsley. Season to taste with salt, pepper and half the cheese. Stuff the egg cavities with this mixture.

Dice the bread and sauté in the butter until crisp and golden. Place the diced toast at the bottom of individual ovenproof baking dishes and arrange the stuffed eggs on top. Cover with tomato sauce to which you have added the remaining parsley, the onion and stuffed olives. Sprinkle with the remaining cheese and heat through in a moderate oven (180°C/350°F/gas 4) for 15 minutes. Serve alone as a hot first course, or with rice as a luncheon dish.

# Deep-fried Stuffed Eggs

Makes 12 'eggs'

6 hard-boiled eggs
1 can sardines
1 teaspoon French mustard
juice of 1 lemon
Worcestershire sauce

salt and freshly ground pepper
mayonnaise
flour, egg and breadcrumbs for
coating
corn or olive oil for frying

Cut the eggs in half lengthwise and remove the yolks. Sieve the yolks into a bowl; mash the sardines, add to the sieved yolk and mix well together. Add the seasonings and enough mayonnaise to make a firm paste.

Mound each egg half with the filling and with your fingers, or a spatula, form into the shape of a whole egg. Dip each re-formed egg shape in flour and then coat each 'egg' with egg and breadcrumbs. Fry about 2 minutes or until a golden-brown colour in deep hot oil.

# Œufs Farcis aux Anchois

Serves 4

4 hard-boiled eggs
4–6 anchovy fillets
4–6 capers
2–3 tablespoons finely chopped
flat-leaf parsley

150 ml/¼ pint thick béchamel
sauce (page 34)
salt and freshly ground pepper
fresh breadcrumbs
butter

Cut the eggs in half lengthwise. Remove the yolks and mash to a smooth paste in a mortar with the anchovies, capers and parsley. Add the thick béchamel sauce to this mixture and season to taste with salt and pepper. Blend well together. Take each half egg and mound the mixture on it to re-form the egg into a whole.

Place the re-formed eggs in a well-buttered baking dish, stuffing side on top. Sprinkle with fresh breadcrumbs. Dot each with butter and heat through in a moderate oven (180°C/350°F/gas 4) for 10 minutes.

# Œufs à la Tapénade

Serves 4 to 6

50 g/2 ounces stoned black olives
25 g/1 ounce anchovy fillets
25 g/1 ounce tuna fish
1 teaspoon mustard
25 g/1 ounce capers

4–6 tablespoons olive oil
1 tablespoon cognac
freshly ground pepper
4–6 hard-boiled eggs
lettuce, to garnish

Pound the olives, anchovy fillets and tuna fish to a smooth paste in a mortar with the mustard and capers (called *tapéno* in Provençal, from which this dish gets its name). When the mixture has been blended to a smooth paste, put it through a fine sieve and whisk olive oil into it. Add the cognac and pepper to taste.

To make *œufs à la tapénade*: cut the hard-boiled eggs in half lengthwise and remove the yolks. Blend the yolks with the *tapénade* mixture, adding a little more olive oil if necessary; fill the egg cavities and serve on a bed of lettuce. The *tapénade* mixture keeps well in a covered jar, and is excellent as a *canapé* spread.

## Eggs and Mushrooms au Gratin
Serves 4

| | |
|---|---|
| **8 eggs** | **300 ml/½ pint well-flavoured** |
| **225 g/½ pound mushrooms, sliced** | **béchamel sauce (page 34)** |
| **2 tablespoons butter** | **4 tablespoons grated Parmesan** |

Boil the eggs gently for about 6 minutes so that the yolk is still soft and the white not yet cooked hard. Shell carefully and chop coarsely. Sauté the mushrooms in butter, then add to the well-flavoured béchamel. Stir in the egg pieces and spoon the mixture into individual ramekins or mini soufflé dishes. Sprinkle with grated cheese and brown under the grill. Serve immediately.

## Stuffed Eggs Mornay
Serves 4

| | |
|---|---|
| **8 hard-boiled eggs** | **salt and freshly ground pepper** |
| **100 g/¼ pound cooked fish** | **300 ml/½ pint hot mornay sauce** |
| **16 capers, finely chopped** | **(page 35)** |
| **1–2 tablespoons olive oil** | |

Cut the eggs in half lengthwise. Remove the yolks and combine in a bowl with the cooked fish and capers and enough olive oil to make a smooth paste. Season the mixture to taste with salt and pepper. Fill the egg whites with the mixture, cover with mornay sauce and brown under the grill.

## Baked Eggs Lorraine
Serves 4

| | |
|---|---|
| **4 slices bacon** | **4 eggs** |
| **butter** | **salt and white pepper** |
| **2 thin slices Swiss cheese, diced** | **8 tablespoons double cream** |

Poach the bacon in boiling water for 5 minutes. Drain and dry; dice and sauté in butter until golden. Place the diced bacon in the bottom of 4 individual baking dishes and cover with a layer of diced cheese. Break 1 egg into each dish; season to taste with salt and pepper and cover with cream. Bake in a moderately hot oven (200°C/400°F/gas 6) for 20 minutes, or until the whites are set. Serve immediately.

# Bouillabaisse d'Œufs
Serves 4 to 6

2 leeks, whites only, finely
chopped
1 Spanish onion, finely chopped
6 tablespoons olive oil
3 tomatoes, coarsely chopped
4 cloves garlic, mashed
a little chopped fennel bulb

1 *bouquet garni*
1 piece of orange peel
6 potatoes, thinly sliced
powdered saffron
salt and freshly ground pepper
1 or 2 eggs per person
1 piece of bread per person

Sauté the leeks and onion in olive oil in a large saucepan until transparent. Add the tomatoes, garlic, fennel, *bouquet garni*, orange peel, potatoes and saffron, to taste, and generous amounts of salt and pepper. Cover with water, or water and stock, and boil as for a *bouillabaisse*. When the potatoes are cooked, poach the eggs in a little of the *bouillon*. To serve, pour *bouillon* over pieces of bread in individual soup plates. Serve the potatoes and eggs on a hot serving platter.

# Œufs au Foie Gras Louis Oliver
Serves 4

4 thin slices of *pâté de foie gras*
salt and freshly ground pepper
cayenne pepper

butter
8 eggs
Madeira sauce (page 37)

Season the slices of *pâté de foie gras* lightly with pepper and a little cayenne, and sauté gently in butter. Place in 4 buttered egg dishes (individual porcelain gratin dishes). Break 2 eggs per person into separate cups. Season to taste with salt and pepper and tip the eggs gently into the egg dishes. Cook on a low heat or, more safely, on a heat diffuser until the eggs are set.

When the eggs are cooked, pour a little hot Madeira sauce over them and serve very hot.

# Œufs en Meurette
Serves 4

100 g/¼ pound diced green bacon
1 tablespoon olive oil
1 medium onion, finely
chopped
1 clove garlic, finely chopped
1 tablespoon flour
150 ml/¼ pint hot beef stock
150 ml/¼ pint red wine
salt and freshly ground pepper
1 pinch dried marjoram

1 pinch dried thyme
1 bay leaf
1 tablespoon lemon juice
2 tablespoons finely chopped
flat-leaf parsley
3 tablespoons butter
8 eggs
lemon juice or vinegar
8 triangles or rounds of white
bread

Sauté the green bacon in olive oil until golden. Remove the bacon bits and reserve. Sauté the onion and garlic in the resulting fat until transparent; sprinkle with flour and blend well. Add the hot beef stock and wine alternately, stirring all the time, and simmer until the sauce is thick and smooth. Add salt and pepper to taste, marjoram, thyme and the bay leaf, and simmer, uncovered, over a low flame for 20 minutes.

Strain the sauce through a fine sieve; stir in the bacon bits, lemon juice, parsley and 1 tablespoon butter and keep warm.

Poach the eggs in water to which you have added a little lemon juice or vinegar; drain. Sauté triangles or rounds of bread in the remaining butter until golden. Place 1 poached egg on each slice of bread (2 per serving); pour the sauce over and serve.

## Œufs Florentine
Serves 4

8 eggs
salt and lemon juice
450 g/1 pound cooked spinach,
    finely chopped and seasoned
    with butter

grated nutmeg
300 ml/½ pint mornay sauce
    (page 35)
freshly grated Parmesan cheese

Poach the eggs in salted water containing a little lemon juice for added flavour and to help hold the eggs together. Butter ramekins or individual baking dishes large enough to hold 2 eggs and spread a good layer of seasoned spinach in each. Sprinkle with nutmeg and a little lemon juice and place 2 poached eggs in each. Cover with mornay sauce; dust with grated Parmesan and place under the grill for a few moments until nicely browned. Serve hot.

## Stuffed Egg and Tomato Salad
Serves 4

1 can tuna fish
6 hard-boiled eggs
4–6 tablespoons mayonnaise
juice of ½ lemon
salt and freshly ground pepper

6 tomatoes, sliced
French dressing (page 222)
2 tablespoons finely chopped
    flat-leaf parsley

Pound the fish in a mortar until smooth. Shell the eggs and halve lengthwise. Remove the yolks, mash them and add to the fish mixture. Stir in the mayonnaise, lemon juice, salt and pepper, and mix well. Taste and correct the seasoning. Add more mayonnaise or lemon juice if the mixture is too thick. Stuff the eggs with this mixture and serve on a bed of sliced tomatoes dressed with French dressing. Garnish with finely chopped parsley.

## Œufs à la Tripe
Serves 4

6 eggs

4 onions

2 tablespoons butter

300 ml/½ pint hot béchamel
sauce

salt and freshly ground pepper

Hard-boil the eggs for 15 minutes in boiling water. Remove the shells and slice the eggs. Slice the onions and sauté them in the butter until soft and golden; do not let them brown. Add the onions and the butter to the hot béchamel sauce; stir well; fold in the egg slices and add salt and pepper, to taste. Heat through in an ovenproof casserole and serve hot.

# Scrambled Eggs

Use plenty of butter in the pan. It should be hot when the eggs are added, but not smoking or browned.

Allow 2 eggs per person and add an extra one for the pan. Mix the eggs thoroughly in a bowl, but do not beat them. Add 1 tablespoon water or cream for each egg. Water will make exceedingly fluffy eggs; cream gives a richer, smoother texture.

Butter a small saucepan generously; pour in the eggs and cook over hot, but not boiling, water.

For fluffy or creamy scrambled eggs, allow the eggs to set slightly after you put them in the pan and then stir constantly with a wooden spoon, being certain to run the edge of the spoon around the edges and into the centre of the pan. Good scrambled eggs need constant and careful attention.

You may add seasonings when mixing the eggs or while they are cooking, or you may prepare the seasonings first, pour the eggs over them and scramble with the pre-cooked seasonings. Serve immediately on hot plates.

**Scrambled eggs with herbs:** Use fresh herbs; prepared herb mixtures for eggs are usually dry and tasteless. The most agreeable herbs are flat-leaf parsley, chives, chervil and tarragon, chopped fine and added to the egg mixture either before or during cooking. I like to sprinkle extra herbs over the eggs just before serving for added flavour.

**Scrambled eggs with smoked salmon:** Cut thin slices of smoked salmon *en julienne* and heat for a moment in butter. Add the eggs (2 for each person, 1 for the pan), slightly beaten with a little water or cream. Scramble. Add freshly ground pepper and salt, to taste. Cook as above. Just before removing from the heat, add a few drops of lemon juice and a little chopped parsley.

**Rumbled eggs:** Stir the eggs until well mixed; melt the butter in a saucepan; add pepper and salt, to taste. When the butter is hot, pour in the eggs and stir over a gentle heat until soft and creamy. The moment the eggs cream, scoop out on to hot buttered toast spread with a little anchovy paste and serve immediately.

## Scrambled Eggs with Oysters
Serves 4

12 raw oysters
butter
1 teaspoon anchovy paste
6 eggs
dash of Tabasco

salt and freshly ground
  pepper
1–2 tablespoons finely chopped
  flat-leaf parsley
*croûtons* of fried bread

Drain the oyster juices through a fine sieve into a bowl. Chop the oysters; reserve. Melt a little butter with the anchovy paste. Whisk the eggs with a dash of Tabasco. Pour the eggs into the hot anchovy butter and scramble as usual. When the eggs are just beginning to set, toss in the strained oyster juices and the oysters and finish scrambling. Season to taste with salt and pepper. Sprinkle with parsley and serve with *croûtons* of bread fried in butter and olive oil.

## Scrambled Eggs with White Truffles
Serves 4

6–8 eggs
½ clove garlic
salt and white pepper

3 tablespoons butter
1 white truffle, thinly sliced
6 tablespoons fresh cream

Rub the bowl in which you are going to beat the eggs with half a clove of garlic. Beat the eggs lightly, just enough to mix the whites and the yolks; add salt and white pepper, to taste.

Melt the butter in a thick-bottomed saucepan, and as soon as it is hot, add the sliced truffle and sauté for 2 minutes. Add the beaten eggs and cook over a low heat so that the eggs do not set too quickly. When the eggs just begin to set and are still quite liquid, stir in the cream and continue stirring until the eggs are creamy. Serve immediately.

# The Omelette

So much has been said as well as written about the omelette's capricious nature that otherwise daring cooks often refuse to attempt it. In actual fact, most of omelette making is easier to do than to explain.

Omelettes can be infinitely varied in flavour, for no other dish so lends itself to the inventiveness of the cook. And once you learn to make a basic omelette, its countless variations – *paysanne, provençale, parisienne, Parmentier, caviare, fines herbes* – become child's play. An omelette is perfectly easy to make and yet so easy to spoil. One false move and the dish is ruined. You might as well throw it away.

It takes talent to make it right and you must be on the job every moment it is in preparation, for speed and efficiency count above all. Every omelette must be made to measure – let your guests wait for the omelette, never let the omelette wait for the guests.

## The Basic Omelette

Small omelettes are much easier to make than big ones. Four to five eggs make an easily handled omelette for two, or even three people. If you have more guests, it is best to make several omelettes, for they then come hotter to the table and have a much better consistency.

For each small omelette, break 4 eggs into a bowl and season to taste with salt and pepper. Add, if desired, 1 tablespoon of water, milk or cream.

Heat the omelette pan gradually on a medium heat until it is hot enough to make butter sizzle on contact. Beat the eggs with a fork or wire whisk just enough to mix the yolks and whites (about 30 seconds). Add 1 tablespoon of butter to the heated pan and shake so the butter coats the bottom evenly. When the butter is sizzling, but before it has turned colour, pour in the beaten eggs, all at once.

Quickly stir the eggs for a second or two in the pan to assure even cooking, just as you would for scrambled eggs. Then, as the eggs start to set, lift the edges with your fork so that the liquid can run under. Repeat until the liquid is all used up but the eggs are still moist and soft. You can keep eggs 'slipping-free' by shaking the pan during the above operation. Now, remove the eggs from the heat and with one movement press the handle of the pan downwards and slide the omelette towards the handle. When a third of the omelette has slid up the rounded edge of the pan, fold this quickly towards the centre with a spatula. Then raise the handle of the pan, and slide the opposite edge of the omelette one-third up the side farthest away from the handle. Hold a heated serving dish under it and, as the rim of the omelette touches the dish, raise the handle more and more until the pan is turned upside down and your oval-shaped, lightly-browned omelette rests on the dish. Rapidly 'finish' the omelette by piercing a piece of butter with the tip of a knife and skimming the surface lightly to leave a glistening trail. Garnish with fresh parsley and serve immediately.

## The Omelette Pan

Although some cooks claim that an omelette can be made in any pan, I keep an iron pan exclusively for eggs. It is a pan expressly designed for omelettes alone – one of good weight, with rounded sides so the eggs can slide easily on to the plate when cooked. And unless you want your omelette to stick, never wash the pan. Instead, just rub it clean with a paper towel and a few drops of oil.

If the pan is new, you must 'season' it before using by slowly heating oil in it; then leave the oil to soak into the pan for at least 12 hours.

Your pan must not be too small or too large for the number of eggs used in the omelette. A pan 18–20 cm/7 or 8 inches in diameter is just about right for a 4–5-egg omelette.

# Variations on the Theme

Practice makes perfect and once you have mastered the basic omelette to your satisfaction you are ready to try some of the many exciting variations on the omelette theme. Some of the most delicious are the easiest to prepare; but always remember to make the omelette filling before you make the actual omelette itself. In this way your omelettes can come to the table crisply cased with a wonderfully moist interior and filling.

**Cheese Omelette:**   Perhaps the easiest version of all. Make your omelette as above and, just as the eggs begin to set, add 2 tablespoons finely grated Parmesan cheese and, if you like, 2 tablespoons double cream, or crème fraîche.

**Watercress Omelette:**   Add 2 tablespoons finely chopped watercress to the egg mixture, cook as above, and serve the omelette surrounded with fresh watercress.

**Omelette Florentine:**   Warm 4 tablespoons freshly cooked, well-drained spinach in butter. Keep warm. Rub the omelette pan lightly with garlic and make the omelette as above. When the eggs are just set, spread the spinach in the centre, fold and serve. Another version of this recipe chops the spinach and adds it to the egg mixture before cooking. In either case, make sure the spinach is well drained before using.

**Omelette aux Fines Herbes:**   Finely chop equal quantities of fresh flat-leaf parsley, chervil, tarragon and chives, enough to fill 2 to 3 tablespoons. Add half of this mixture to your beaten eggs and proceed to make the omelette as above. Mix the remainder of the chopped herbs with 1 tablespoon melted butter and pour over the finished omelette before serving.

Originally, the term '*fines herbes*' included some finely chopped mushrooms and truffles, sautéed lightly in butter, the perfect refinement for a delicious dish.

**Mushroom Omelette:**   Marinate 100 g/¼ pound sliced mushrooms in 1 tablespoon brandy for 15 minutes. Add 1 tablespoon butter and stir over heat until the liquid evaporates. Add 2 to 4 tablespoons cream, salt and pepper to taste, and keep warm while you make the omelette as above. As the omelette sets, spread with this mixture, fold and serve. A winner.

**Omelette Parmentier:**   Brown 4 tablespoons diced boiled potatoes in butter. Add ½ teaspoon each of finely chopped flat-leaf parsley and chives to the egg mixture and, just before pouring into the pan, add the lightly browned potatoes. Prepare the omelette as above.

# French Country Omelette
Serves 2

2 tablespoons diced salt pork or
green bacon
2 tablespoons butter
4 tablespoons diced boiled
potatoes
4 eggs, lightly beaten

2 tablespoons finely chopped
flat-leaf parsley
1–2 tablespoons finely chopped
chives
salt and freshly ground pepper
crushed dried chillies

Parboil the salt pork or green bacon in water for a few minutes. Drain and sauté in the butter. When the meat is browned, remove from the pan and keep warm. Sauté the potatoes in the fat until golden. Combine the lightly beaten eggs with the meat, parsley and chives; add salt, pepper and crushed dried chillies, to taste, and pour over the potatoes in the pan.

Cook as for the basic omelette above, and when the first odour of browning is evident, turn the omelette and brown it slightly on the other side. Slide it on to a hot platter and serve.

# La Pipérade du Pays Basque
Serves 2

1 green pepper, sliced
pork fat or olive oil
4 ripe tomatoes, peeled, seeded
and finely chopped
1 onion
½ clove garlic, crushed

2–4 tablespoons diced *jambon de bayonne*
salt and freshly ground pepper
1 tablespoon butter
4 eggs

Sauté the green pepper very gently in pork fat or olive oil. Add the tomatoes, onion, garlic and ham, and season to taste with salt and pepper. Add the butter and simmer the mixture slowly for about 30 minutes or until the vegetables turn into a rather soft purée.

Beat the eggs slightly with salt and pepper, and stir gently into the hot vegetable mixture. Be sure not to let them overcook, for this Basque omelette should be soft and wet, with almost the consistency of scrambled eggs.

# Madame Prunet's Pancake-Omelette
Serves 4 to 6

3 tablespoons caster sugar
400 ml/⅔ pint milk
3 tablespoons flour
3 eggs

dark Jamaican rum
peanut oil
melted butter
sugar

Mix the sugar with ½ glass of the milk. Add the flour and eggs and blend well. Pour in the remaining milk and flavour with rum to taste. The mixture should be smooth and rather light.

Heat an omelette pan and oil it lightly. Pour a ladleful of the omelette mixture into the pan and cook as you would a pancake. When it is cooked, roll it tightly and transfer to a warmed platter. Oil the pan again and continue cooking as above until the mixture is used up.

When ready to serve, place the rolled omelettes in a buttered baking dish, brush with melted butter and cook in a hot oven (230°C/450°F/gas 8) for 10 minutes. The omelettes will swell and become crisp. Sprinkle with sugar; flame with rum and serve immediately.

## Italian Frittata
Serves 4

| | |
|---|---|
| ½ **Spanish onion, finely chopped** | **salt and freshly ground** |
| 2 **tablespoons olive oil** | **pepper** |
| 6–8 **eggs, beaten** | **crushed dried chillies** |
| 2 **tablespoons each finely** | **butter** |
| **chopped flat-leaf parsley, mint** | **olive oil** |
| **and basil** | |

Sauté the onion in the olive oil until soft and transparent. Combine in a bowl with the beaten eggs, parsley, mint and basil. Add salt, pepper and crushed dried chillies, to taste, and mix well.

Cook slowly on one side in butter and olive oil until brown; add a little more butter before turning to cook other side.

## Fifine's Pipérade
Serves 4 to 6

| | |
|---|---|
| 4 **tablespoons olive oil** | **salt and freshly ground** |
| ½ **Spanish onion, coarsely** | **pepper** |
| **sliced** | 8–10 **eggs** |
| 4 **peppers (green, yellow and** | 2 **tablespoons freshly grated** |
| **red), seeded and coarsely** | **Gruyère** |
| **sliced** | 2 **tablespoons freshly grated** |
| 4 **tomatoes, skinned, seeded and** | **Parmesan** |
| **coarsely chopped** | 2 **tablespoons butter** |

Heat the olive oil in a frying pan; add the onion and sauté, stirring from time to time, until transparent. Add the peppers and cook over a low heat, stirring from time to time, until soft but not mushy. Increase the heat and stir in the tomatoes. Season generously with salt and pepper.

Break the eggs into a bowl and beat with a whisk until foamy. Pour the eggs over the vegetables, allow to set for a moment, then stir with a wooden spoon or spatula as you would for scrambled eggs. Sprinkle with finely grated cheese (Gruyère and Parmesan mixed) to bind the mixture, and fold the omelette into shape. Slide the butter under the omelette to add flavour, turn out on to a hot serving dish and serve immediately.

# The Savoury Soufflé

The soufflé – to many people one of the most awe-inspiring creations of French *haute cuisine* – is, in reality, nothing more than a simple airy mixture of eggs, butter, flour and a purée of vegetables, meat, fish or fowl. And the last-mentioned – unexciting and unpretentious as the case may be – are very often left-overs.

Try the soufflé as a perfect beginning to a meal, whether it be a simple cheese affair (try a combination of Gruyère and Parmesan), a concoction of fish or shellfish, or one made with a well-seasoned base of puréed vegetables (endive, rocket, onion or mushroom) and cheese.

Savoury soufflés also make light-as-air entrées of distinction for luncheon or supper parties. And there you can always let your imagination run riot. What do you risk? The basic soufflé mixture stays just the same. Add a breakfast-cupful of diced, grilled kippers to your basic soufflé mixture for an after-theatre supper for four. Spike a béchamel sauce with Parmesan cheese and a little cream; stir in beaten egg yolks; fold in beaten egg whites. Spoon half the mixture into your soufflé dish; add 4 poached eggs and cover with the rest of the soufflé mixture and you have the famous *œufs mollets en soufflé* created by Marcel Boulestin. Or take the same basic mixture (béchamel sauce, grated Parmesan, a little cream, beaten egg yolks and whites), flavour with a hint of cognac, and instead of poached eggs, bury a surprise catch of diced lobster meat which you have first flamed in cognac, or in a more sophisticated moment, in Pernod. It's as easy as that!

You will find that soufflés are quite easy to make if a few basic rules are followed. First and foremost: a soufflé must be eaten when ready. A soufflé will not wait for your guests: your guests must wait for this delicate and sometimes temperamental dish. A rich, smooth sauce is the base of all soufflés. Many French soufflé recipes simply require a thick, well-flavoured *sauce béchamel*.

The egg yolks and egg whites must be beaten separately; the yolks until thick and lemon-coloured, the whites until stiff but not dry. Always cool the sauce before adding the yolks and whites. Use an unbuttered soufflé dish for your first attempts so that the soufflé can cling to the sides of the dish and rise to its full height. For added flavour, if you butter the dish, sprinkle the buttered surface with fresh breadcrumbs or a little finely grated Parmesan cheese.

A slow to medium oven (170–180°C/325–350°F/ gas 3–4) is essential. If your oven is too hot, the soufflé will be well cooked on top and undercooked inside. As long as it remains in a warm oven a soufflé is pretty sturdy. The best way to determine when a soufflé is done is to open the door after 20 to 25 minutes and to give the dish a slight shove. If the top crust moves only very slightly, the soufflé is done. However, if it really trembles, leave it in a few minutes more.

Always cook a soufflé in a preheated oven.

# Basic Savoury Soufflé
Serves 4

2 tablespoons butter
2 tablespoons flour
300 ml/½ pint hot milk
5 egg yolks

100–175 g/4–6 ounces freshly
    grated Gruyère and Parmesan
    cheese
salt and freshly ground pepper
6 egg whites

Melt the butter in the top of a double saucepan; add the flour gradually and mix to a smooth paste, stirring constantly. Add the hot milk and cook over simmering water, stirring constantly, until the sauce is smooth and thick. Remove from the heat and add the egg yolks, one by one, alternately with the cheese. Mix well and return to the heat. Cook until the cheese melts. Add generous amounts of salt and pepper, remove from the heat and allow to cool slightly.

Beat the egg whites till they are stiff and fold into the warm cheese mixture. Pile the mixture in a buttered soufflé dish or casserole. Bake in a preheated oven (180°C/350°F/gas 4) for 35 to 40 minutes, or until the soufflé is golden. Serve immediately.

# Cheese Soufflé with Garlic Croûtons
Serves 4

2 tablespoons butter
2 tablespoons flour
300 ml/½ pint hot milk
5 egg yolks
100–175 g/4–6 ounces freshly
    grated cheese, such as Gruyère
    and Parmesan

salt and freshly ground pepper
crushed dried chillies
2 tablespoons butter or olive
    oil
1 clove garlic, minced
1 slice bread, cubed
6 egg whites

Melt the butter in the top of a double saucepan; add the flour gradually and mix to a smooth paste, stirring constantly. Add the hot milk and cook over simmering water until smooth and thick. Remove from the heat and add the egg yolks, one by one, alternately with the grated cheese. Mix well and return to the heat. Cook until the cheese melts. Add generous amounts of salt and pepper and a pinch of crushed dried chillies. Allow to cool slightly.

Melt the butter or oil in another pan; add the garlic and bread cubes and sauté until golden. Remove from the heat and drain.

Beat the egg whites until stiff and then fold into the warm cheese mixture. Fold in the garlic *croûtons* and pile the mixture in a buttered soufflé dish or casserole. Bake in a preheated oven (180°C/350°F/gas 4) for 35 to 40 minutes, or until the soufflé is golden. Serve immediately.

# Mushroom Soufflé

Serves 4

4 dried *porcini* mushrooms
4 tablespoons hot white wine
2 tablespoons butter
2 tablespoons flour
300 ml/½ pint hot milk
2 tablespoons grated Parmesan
salt and cayenne pepper

grated nutmeg
1–2 shallots, finely chopped
2 tablespoons butter
175–225 g/6–8 ounces
  mushrooms, thinly sliced
4 egg yolks
5 egg whites

Chop the dried *porcini* and place in a small bowl with the hot white wine. Reserve.

To make the soufflé, melt the butter in the top of a double saucepan; add the flour and cook until the flour just starts to turn golden. Add the hot milk and cook, stirring constantly with a wire whisk, until the sauce is thick and smooth. Add Parmesan and salt, cayenne pepper and nutmeg, to taste.

Sauté the shallot in butter until transparent; add the sliced mushrooms and cook until all the moisture has evaporated. Add the mushrooms and chopped *porcini* and their liquids to the hot sauce. Beat the egg yolks until frothy. Fold into the sauce mixture. Beat the egg whites until they are stiff but not dry, and fold into the mixture. Fill a buttered soufflé dish about three-quarters full and bake in a preheated oven 180°C/350°F/gas 4) for about 40 minutes.

# Crab Soufflé

Serves 4 to 6

4 tablespoons butter
3 tablespoons flour
300 ml/½ pint hot milk
8 tablespoons freshly grated
  Parmesan cheese

175 g/6 ounces cooked
  fresh crabmeat, well boned,
  shredded (white meat only)
sea salt and cayenne
4 egg yolks
5 egg whites

Melt the butter in the top of a double saucepan; add the flour and stir until well blended. Add the milk and cook over simmering water, stirring continuously, until the sauce has thickened. Stir in the cheese and heat until it has melted into the mixture. Add the crabmeat and heat through. Season to taste with salt and cayenne pepper.

Beat the egg yolks slightly and add the hot sauce to them. Whisk the egg whites stiffly and gently fold the mixture into them, a little at a time. Pour into a buttered and floured casserole and set in a pan of hot water. Bake in a slow (180°C/350°F/gas 4) oven for 25 to 30 minutes. Serve at once.

# The Sweet Soufflé

## Basic Sweet Soufflé

Serves 4

| | |
|---|---|
| 2 tablespoons butter | 5 egg yolks |
| 2 tablespoons flour | 4 tablespoons sugar |
| 300 ml/½ pint hot milk | ½ teaspoon vanilla essence |
| pinch salt | 6 egg whites |

**Step 1.** Melt the butter in the top of a double saucepan; add the flour and cook, stirring, until well blended. Add the hot milk and salt. Cook the sauce over simmering water, stirring constantly, until smooth and thick and then continue cooking, still stirring constantly, for a few more minutes. Let the sauce cool slightly.

**Step 2.** Beat the egg yolks well with the sugar and vanilla essence and mix well with the batter. Beat the egg whites until they are stiff, but not dry, and fold gently into the batter mixture. Pour the batter into a buttered and lightly sugared soufflé dish and bake in a slow oven (170°C/325°F/gas 3) for 35 to 45 minutes, or until the soufflé is puffed and golden. Serve at once.

## Soufflé au Grand Marnier

Serves 4

| | |
|---|---|
| 2 tablespoons butter | ½ teaspoon vanilla essence |
| 2 tablespoons flour | 2 tablespoons Grand Marnier |
| 300 ml/½ pint hot milk | halved sponge fingers |
| pinch salt | 2 tablespoons cognac |
| 5 egg yolks | 6 egg whites |
| 4 tablespoons sugar | |

Step 1 as for *Basic Sweet Soufflé*.

Beat the egg yolks with the sugar and vanilla essence and mix well with the batter. Stir in the Grand Marnier.

Preheat the oven to 170°C/325°F/gas 3. Line a buttered soufflé dish with halved sponge fingers sprinkled with the cognac. Beat the egg whites until stiff but not dry, and fold into the cooled mixture. Pour into the prepared soufflé dish. Bake for 35 minutes or until puffed and golden. Serve with apricot or vanilla custard sauce (page 43).

# Lemon Soufflé
Serves 4

2 tablespoons butter
2 tablespoons flour
300 ml/½ pint hot milk
pinch salt
grated zest of 1–2 lemons

3–5 tablespoons lemon juice
5 egg yolks
3 tablespoons sugar
6 egg whites

Step 1 as for *Basic Sweet Soufflé*. Then stir in the lemon zest and juice to taste.

Beat the egg yolks well with the sugar and combine them with the batter. Beat the egg whites until they are stiff but not dry, and fold into the cooled mixture. Pour the batter into a buttered and lightly sugared soufflé dish and bake in a slow oven (170°C/325°F/gas 3) for 35 to 45 minutes, or until the soufflé is puffed and golden. Serve at once.

## Chapter 5

# Fish

Cooks in Britain seem to regard fish as mainly something to fry. They seem afraid of its other propensities – why, I wonder, when such a variety of ways exist for its preparation.

'*C'est la sauce qui fait manger le poisson*' is the adage in France, and French culinary history is full of delicious recipes for grilled, poached and baked fish of all kinds, served with delicately flavoured sauces. Grilled fillets of sole or flounder with a shrimp sauce or a Hollandaise; turbot simmered in a *court-bouillon* and served with green butter; sole, flounder and turbot, marinated in a white wine marinade and simmered *en casserole* in their own juices; turbot cooked in red wine – these are but a few of the delights that French fish cookery can offer us.

The art of cooking with wine is made easier for us these days by the wonderful array of imported vintages at our disposal. Keep a good stock of Burgundies, both white and red. Yes, fish can be cooked in red wine – *rosé*, too, for that matter. This legend of white for fish and red for meat is just so much old-fashioned nonsense! There are no rules for this sort of thing and, indeed, anything goes. So add dry sherry and vermouth to your cooking cellar. Experiment with port and Madeira.

Of course, even the most superb wine sauce cannot transform fish that is stale or overcooked. Always buy fish with firm skin and scales and bright eyes. And cook it carefully to the point when the moist, opaque flesh can be easily flaked with a fork. More crimes are committed in fish cookery by plain, simple over-cooking than by any other means. Fish should be firm and moist, not an overboiled mush of watery tastelessness.

## Grilled Fish

In Provence, I learned to like my fish grilled on an outdoor fire that had been fed with aromatic herbs. Many are the midnight beach picnics enjoyed on the vast expanses of Pampelonne, at which barbecued fish, freshly caught from the gulf of Pampelonne, played the starring role, preceded by a cool salad of Mediterranean vegetables and cold *ratatouille*, a Provençal vegetable stew of tomatoes, aubergines and courgettes, served cold with a *vinaigrette* dressing, the fish accompanied by melted tarragon butter and plain boiled potatoes, and washed down by liberal quantities of chilled *vin blanc du Var*.

Basil, tarragon, parsley and rosemary have natural affinities for fish. Their fragrant perfume and the odorous smoke from the wood fire make fish a dish fit for a king. Try this on your own barbecue as the weather gets warmer. But be sure you use a hinged grill so that you can turn your fish easily without danger of breaking its tender flesh. Flour and oil all fish lightly before grilling, and if you are using fish steaks or fish fillets, be sure to baste them frequently with olive oil during the cooking time. Whole fish, with skins intact, require less attention. I like to stuff the cavities of fish with herbs before grilling them – a selection of fennel, parsley and thyme – and then baste them with olive oil as they grill, often using a switch of bay leaves as a basting brush to give added flavour.

## Flamed Fish

Along the coast from Marseilles to St Tropez, in the little sea towns on the way, it has long been the custom to serve grilled fish in a jacket of flaming herbs. This is a delicious way of dealing with any fresh fish. First grill your fish as above and remove it to a heated serving dish which has been covered with sprigs of fresh rosemary, fennel and thyme. The fish is then topped with additional herbs; 2 or 3 tablespoons of hot cognac are poured over it and ignited. The burning herbs give the fish a subtle flavour which, once you have tasted it, is irresistible.

## Fish Court-Bouillons and Fumets

When fish is to be served cold with a fish sauce, *vinaigrette* sauce or mayonnaise, or, for a special occasion, in a cool coat of shimmering aspic, it is always best to cook it in a well-flavoured fish *court-bouillon* to give it the utmost in flavour. A fish *court-bouillon* does for fish what a good chicken stock does for poached chicken.

## Fish Court-Bouillon

2 small carrots, finely chopped
2 stalks celery, finely chopped
1 large Spanish onion, sliced
3 tablespoons butter
3 tablespoons olive oil
600 ml/1 pint water
600 ml/1 pint dry white wine
1 kg/2 pounds fish trimmings
  (haddock, halibut, cod)

1 *bouquet garni* (celery, thyme
  and flat-leaf parsley)
2 bay leaves
6 bruised peppercorns
pinch crushed dried chillies
2 cloves
1 teaspoon salt

Sauté the carrots, celery and onion in the butter and olive oil until the onion is transparent but not brown. Add the water, white wine and fish trimmings and bring to the boil. Skim the froth from the liquid; add the *bouquet garni*, bay leaves, peppercorns, crushed dried chillies and cloves, cover the saucepan and simmer for 30 minutes. Strain; add salt, to taste, and use as required. Fish *court-bouillon* will keep, covered, in a refrigerator for 2 to 3 days. Halve the recipe for smaller quantities.

# Light Fish Court-Bouillon

1.8 litres/3 pints water
1 bottle dry white wine
1 large Spanish onion, sliced
4 carrots, sliced
2 stalks celery, sliced

2 bay leaves
1 *bouquet garni* (celery, thyme
  and parsley)
8–10 whole peppercorns

Combine the ingredients in a kettle or saucepan large enough to hold the fish to be poached; bring to the boil; skim; lower the heat and simmer for 30 minutes. Strain and use as required.

# Fish Fumet

225 g/½ pound whiting, hake or
  fresh cod
1.2 litres/2 pints cold water
150 ml/¼ pint dry white wine
2 carrots, sliced
1 leek, sliced

1 Spanish onion, sliced
6 whole peppercorns
1 *bouquet garni* (flat-leaf
  parsley, bay leaf, thyme)
1 clove garlic
salt

Combine the ingredients in a saucepan; cover and cook gently for 30 minutes. Strain and use as required.

# Concentrated Fish Fumet

Makes 900 ml/1½ pints

4 tablespoons butter
450 g/1 pound bones and
  trimmings of sole
4 tablespoons chopped flat-leaf
  parsley
1 carrot, chopped

1 onion, chopped
450 ml/¾ pint water
300 ml/½ pint dry white wine
3 bruised peppercorns
salt

Melt the butter in a saucepan, add the fishbones and trimmings with the parsley, carrot and onion, and sauté for 10 minutes. Then add the water, white wine, peppercorns and salt to the flavoursome aromatics, and allow to simmer gently, covered, for 20 minutes. Strain the *fumet* and use as required.

# Fish Aspic

Add 100 g/¼ pound any white fish, finely chopped, with the white part of 1 leek, finely chopped, 1 egg white and 1 crushed egg shell, to 900 ml/1½ pints fish *fumet*. Bring to the boil, stirring constantly, then simmer, uncovered, for 20 minutes. Strain through a fine sieve. Soften 1 tablespoon gelatine in 4 tablespoons dry white wine and stir it into the hot stock.

For moulds or glazing, use as soon as it is cool, but before it starts to set.

# Salmon Poached in Court-Bouillon

| | |
|---|---|
| 1 whole salmon | *Court-Bouillon:* |
| lemon slices | 1.8 litres/3 pints water |
| cucumber slices | 1 bottle dry white wine |
| fresh watercress or flat-leaf | 1 large Spanish onion, |
|   parsley |   sliced |
| | 4 carrots, sliced |
| | 2 stalks celery, sliced |
| | 2 bay leaves |
| | 1 *bouquet garni* |

Combine the elements of the *court-bouillon* in a kettle large enough to hold the salmon; bring to the boil; skim; lower the heat and simmer for 30 minutes. Let the *court-bouillon* cool slightly; then lower the salmon, wrapped in muslin, into it. Add more liquid if necessary. Simmer gently for 45 to 60 minutes or until the fish flakes easily with a fork.

Remove the fish carefully from the *court-bouillon* with the help of the muslin and carefully remove the skin, cutting it at the tail and stripping it to the head. Arrange the salmon on a hot platter and garnish with lemon slices, cucumber slices, fresh watercress or parsley. Serve for example with a *sauce verte* (page 40).

# Salmon Kedgeree
Serves 4

| | |
|---|---|
| 75 g/3 ounces rice | salt and freshly ground |
| 450 g/1 pound poached or |   pepper |
|   pan-seared salmon | crushed dried chillies |
| 4 tablespoons butter | 300 ml/½ pint hot cream sauce |
| 1 teaspoon curry powder |   (page 35) |
| 2 hard-boiled eggs | 1–2 tablespoons chopped chives |

Cook the rice in boiling salted water until tender but not mushy. Drain and keep warm.

Dice or flake the salmon, removing any bones and skin. Melt the butter in a saucepan; blend in the curry powder; add the fish and sauté gently.

Combine the chopped whites of the hard-boiled eggs with the rice and fish. Season to taste with salt, pepper and a pinch of crushed dried chillies. Fold in the hot cream sauce. Serve on a platter, or in a gratin dish, with the yolks of the hard-boiled eggs, pressed through a sieve or finely chopped, scattered over the top. Just before serving, sprinkle with chopped chives.

## Grilled Salmon Steaks
Serves 4

4 salmon steaks
salt and freshly ground pepper
4 tablespoons melted butter

2 pinches crushed dried chillies
lemon and parsley butter
lemon wedges

Season both sides of the salmon steaks with salt and pepper, to taste, and leave at room temperature for 20 minutes.

Place the steaks on a buttered, preheated baking tin; brush with melted butter, sprinkle with crushed dried chillies and grill for 3 to 5 minutes about 8 cm/3 inches from the heat. Turn the steaks, brush with the remaining butter and grill until the fish flakes easily with a fork (3 to 5 minutes). Serve with lemon and parsley butter and lemon wedges.

**To make the lemon and parsley butter:** Pound 100 g/4 ounces slightly softened butter in a mortar with 2 tablespoons finely chopped flat-leaf parsley and lemon juice, salt and pepper, to taste.

## Barbecued Fish with Tarragon
Serves 4 to 6

2 sea bass or grey mullet,
  cleaned and scaled
herbs: rosemary, fennel, sage,
  bay leaf
4 tablespoons dry white wine
6 tablespoons melted butter
salt and freshly ground pepper

*Serving Sauce:*
juice of 1 lemon
100 g/¼ pound melted butter
6 fennel seeds
4 tablespoons finely chopped
  fresh tarragon

Stuff the fish with the herbs. Secure the fish to a spit with thin wire or wet cord. Combine the wine and butter and season to taste with generous amounts of salt and pepper. Grill the fish over rather hot coals for 20 to 25 minutes, brushing from time to time with the wine-butter sauce. When the fish is done, it flakes easily when tested with a fork.

Serve with plenty of lemon and melted butter flavoured with fennel seeds and finely chopped fresh tarragon.

# Matelote à la Bourguignonne

Fish and wine have always seemed to me to have natural affinities . . . ever since the memorable summer of '31 when I was eight, my favourite brother was fourteen, and we lived on the banks of the Hudson river just twenty-five miles from New York. It was Prohibition – a zany period in American political history, when to indulge in a quiet drink between friends was punishable by law – and my brother and I spent the summer 'fishing' along with other members of the local citizenry for cases of champagne and caviare hastily thrown overboard during the summer nights when boatloads of bootleggers, temporarily at grips with the law, threw their forbidden cargoes into the river to avoid arrest.

Introduced to the illicit pleasures of fish and wine at such a tender age, it is small wonder that today I prefer fish and shellfish served in generous quantities of my favourite potions.

And I am not alone. The art of cooking fish in wine is as old as the art of gastronomy. The Rhône valley was probably the first to have its forests cleared and planted with vines by the early Romans when they conquered Gaul. Vines still flourish practically all along the Rhône today, coming into greater prominence below Lyons in the wine-growing districts of Châteauneuf du Pape, Hermitage and Côte Rôtie. Some of the most exciting little restaurants in France are to be found in this region; small bistros and unknown cafés where the food-conscious traveller is sure to find some of the best wine-simmered dishes in the country; simple little places with sawdust-strewn floors, where the chef is known to make the finest *matelote* in the region. The *matelote*, like the *pochouse bourguignonne*, combines the delicate meats of carp, pike, eel and other local fish, flamed in brandy and then simmered in a rich, smooth sauce of red or white wine, according to the tastes of house or region.

One of the best *matelote* recipes I know is that of Pierre Lefrank, genial French *antiquaire* and *bon vivant* of the rue Bonaparte, who used to entertain us so lavishly in Paris just after the war. Henri Sauguet, Christian Berard, Victor Grandpierre, Dior's decorator, and Prince Sturza were among those who enjoyed this famous dish.

## Matelote à la Bourguignonne
Serves 6 to 8

450 g/1 pound eel
700 g-1 kg/1½–2 pounds carp
700 g-1 kg/1½–2 pounds pike
2 tablespoons olive oil
2 tablespoons butter
100 g/¼ pound diced salt pork
1 Spanish onion, chopped
4 carrots, chopped
7 shallots, chopped
4 cloves garlic, mashed
4 tablespoons warm cognac
½ bottle good red burgundy, such as Châteauneuf du Pape
salt and freshly ground pepper

1 *bouquet garni* (thyme, bay leaf, flat-leaf parsley, celery, rosemary)
1 strip lemon peel
¼ teaspoon dried marjoram
4 tablespoons butter
2 tablespoons flour

*To Finish the Dish:*
12 tiny white onions, simmered in *court-bouillon*
12 button mushrooms, cooked in butter and lemon juice
2 tablespoons butter
fried *croûtons* and chopped flat-leaf parsley

Clean and skin the eel and cut into thick serving pieces (your fishmonger, from whom you will have to order in advance, can do this for you); cut the carp and pike into serving pieces; sauté them in equal parts olive oil and butter with the salt pork, onion, carrots, shallots and garlic. When the fish pieces begin to turn gold in colour, flame them in cognac. Shake the pan gently until the flames die down and add the burgundy and enough water to cover. Add salt and pepper to taste, the *bouquet garni*, twist of lemon peel and dried marjoram. Cook the fish slowly in this mixture until tender.

Melt the butter in a porcelain or enamel saucepan and make a *roux* by adding the flour; cook the *roux* for a few minutes without allowing it to take colour. Strain the liquid from the fish into the pan and cook over low heat, stirring from time to time to make a slightly thickened sauce. Add the fish pieces and pork bits, and garnish with the tiny onions and the button mushrooms. Finally, stir in 2 tablespoons butter and serve very hot with fried *croûtons* and chopped fresh parsley.

## Turbot in White Wine with Green Butter
Serves 4 to 6

**1.3 kg/3 pounds turbot, cut in serving portions**
**1 Spanish onion, thinly sliced**
**2–4 carrots, thinly sliced**
**1 *bouquet garni* (thyme, bay leaf, flat-leaf parsley, celery, rosemary)**
**dry white wine**
**salt and freshly ground pepper**

***Green Butter:***
**225 g/½ pound softened butter**
**2 sieved hard-boiled eggs**

**2 tablespoons olive oil**
**1 clove garlic, mashed**
**6 spinach leaves, stems removed**
**6 lettuce leaves**
**6 sprigs watercress**
**6 sprigs flat-leaf parsley**
**2 shallots, chopped**
**2 tablespoons capers**
**½ teaspoon French mustard**
**lemon juice**
**salt and freshly ground pepper**

Wipe the turbot with a damp cloth and place in a shallow, well-buttered baking pan. Add the onion, carrot and *bouquet garni*. Cover the fish with dry white wine and water in equal quantities, and add salt and pepper, to taste. Poach gently for 30 minutes or until the flesh of the fish flakes easily with a fork. When done, drain well, place on a heated serving dish and garnish each portion with a slice of green butter.

**To make the green butter:** Place the soft butter, sieved hard-boiled eggs, olive oil and garlic in an electric blender and blend until creamy. Add more oil if the mixture is too dry.

Blanch the spinach leaves, lettuce leaves, watercress, parsley and shallots. Drain well, chop and add to the butter mixture with the capers and French mustard. When well blended, add lemon juice and salt and pepper, to taste, and chill until you are ready to serve. This is also delicious with grilled salmon.

# Turbot à la Marinière
Serves 4

4 carrots, sliced
1 Spanish onion, sliced
2 tablespoons finely chopped
 flat-leaf parsley
2 bay leaves
1 pinch cinnamon
1 pinch dried thyme
salt and freshly ground pepper

150 ml/¼ pint dry white wine
150 ml/¼ pint chicken stock
150 ml/¼ pint water
4 tablespoons olive oil
450 g/1 pound potatoes, sliced
4 turbot fillets (about 225 g/
 ½ pound each)
melted butter

Combine in a pan the carrots, onion, parsley, bay leaves, cinnamon, thyme, salt and pepper. Add the white wine, chicken stock, water, olive oil and sliced potatoes, and cook on a high flame for 25 minutes.

Place the turbot fillets carefully in this *court-bouillon* and cook over a high flame until the fish flakes easily with a fork (about 20 minutes). Serve the fish and potatoes with *court-bouillon* and a little melted butter.

# Baked Fish Albert
Serves 6 to 8

6 medium-sized onions, finely
 chopped
4 cloves garlic, finely chopped
4 tablespoons each finely
 chopped flat-leaf parsley,
 chervil and tarragon
150 ml/¼ pint dry white wine
150 ml/¼ pint water

2 tablespoons Pernod
2 large sea bass (or 2.5–3 kg/
 5–6 pounds turbot or halibut)
4 tablespoons olive oil
1 large lemon, sliced thinly
100 g/¼ pound butter, diced
salt and freshly ground
 pepper

Combine the onions, garlic, parsley, chervil, tarragon, dry white wine, water and Pernod.

Place the fish in a large baking dish and moisten with the olive oil. Pour over the wine and herb mixture; cover with slices of lemon; dot with the butter and season to taste with salt and pepper. Bake the fish in a hot oven (230°C/450°F/ gas 8) for 30 to 40 minutes, or until it flakes easily with a fork, basting from time to time. If the fish becomes too dry, add a little more water and wine.

# Suprême of Red Mullet Niçoise
Serves 4

4 fresh red mullet, filleted
salt and cayenne pepper
dry white wine
fish *fumet*

white of 1 leek, cut in thin
 strips and cooked in butter
300 ml/½ pint double
 cream

4 tomatoes, skinned, seeded and
chopped, reduced to a purée in
a little butter

2 tablespoons butter
saffron

Put the fillets in a well-buttered ovenproof dish; add salt and a pinch of cayenne; add equal parts dry white wine and fish *fumet* to cover, and bake in a slow oven (170°C/325°F/gas 3) for 10 to 15 minutes. When the fish is flaky but still moist, keep it warm in several spoonfuls of the stock.

Reduce the rest of the liquid to half its original quantity with a fine *julienne* of cooked white of leek. Add the cream and the tomatoes. When this mixture forms a smooth creamy emulsion just thick enough to coat the back of a spoon, stir in the butter, mixed with a pinch of saffron. Heat well; place the fillets on a serving dish and cover with the sauce.

# Fish Soups

## Bouillabaisse for Northern Seas
Serves 6 to 8

4 carrots, sliced
2 Spanish onions, sliced
4 cloves garlic, bruised
2 leeks, sliced
150 ml/¼ pint olive oil
4–6 tomatoes
1 *bouquet garni* (thyme, bay
leaf, flat-leaf parsley, celery,
rosemary)
450 g/1 pound eel, cut in 5-cm/
2-inch lengths

1 kg/2 pounds fish (cod,
haddock, sea bass, etc.), cut in
5-cm/
2-inch lengths
4–6 potatoes, cut in slices
600 ml/1 pint fish stock (made
from fish trimmings)
½ teaspoon powdered saffron
salt and freshly ground pepper
cayenne
24 mussels

Place the carrots, onions, garlic, leeks and oil in a large, thick-bottomed, flame-proof casserole and sauté until golden brown. Seed and chop the tomatoes coarsely; add to the vegetables with the *bouquet garni* and eel, fish and potatoes and cook about 6 minutes, stirring gently from time to time. Add the fish stock and just enough water to cover the fish; season to taste with saffron, salt, pepper and cayenne, and bring to the boil. Cook for 15 minutes. Add the mussels and lobsters and continue cooking until the mussels open.

Serve this wonderful dish in two courses: the amber-tinted soup first in a deep soup tureen, accompanied by garlic-flavoured *croûtons* and *rouille*, and the fish and potatoes immediately after the soup.

## Soupe Aigo-Sau
### Provençal Fish Soup with Rouille
Serves 4 to 6

| | |
|---|---|
| **1 kg/2 pounds any firm white fish** | **2 sprigs flat-leaf parsley** |
| **1 leek, chopped** | **1 sprig fennel** |
| **1 Spanish onion, chopped** | **1 bay leaf** |
| **4 tomatoes, chopped** | **1 piece of lemon peel** |
| **6 potatoes, cut in thick slices** | **boiling water, to cover** |
| **salt and freshly ground pepper** | **sliced French bread** |
| **2 cloves garlic, crushed** | **olive oil** |
| | *rouille* |

Cut white fish of assorted kinds into pieces of the same size. Place in a large saucepan with the leek, onion, tomatoes and potatoes. Season generously with salt and pepper; add the garlic, parsley, fennel, bay leaf and lemon peel. Cover with boiling water and cook over a high heat for 20 minutes.

To serve: place slices of French bread in a soup tureen; sprinkle with olive oil and pepper. Strain the fish *bouillon* over and serve separately. Fish pieces and potatoes should be served together with a *rouille*.

**To make the rouille:**  Pound 2 fat cloves of garlic and 1–2 hot chilli peppers in a mortar with ¼ slice white bread with crusts cut off, which you have dipped in water and then squeezed dry. Blend to a smooth paste with 2 tablespoons olive oil, and then thin this *pommade* to the consistency of heavy cream with about 150 ml/¼ pint of hot fish *bouillon*. This is often served with *bouillabaisse*. (You will find another recipe for *rouille* on page 41.)

## Cotriade
Serves 6 to 8

| | |
|---|---|
| **4 large potatoes, sliced** | **salt and freshly ground** |
| **2 Spanish onions, sliced** | **pepper** |
| **1 *bouquet garni* (thyme, bay leaf, flat-leaf parsley, celery, rosemary)** | **1.5 litres/2½ pints fish stock (made from fish trimmings)** |
| **½ teaspoon dried marjoram** | **1.3 kg/3 pounds firm fish** |

Cook the potatoes and onions with the *bouquet garni*, marjoram, and salt and pepper to taste, in fish stock for 20 minutes. Add the fish – cod, haddock, fresh sardines, grey mullet, mackerel, sea bass, etc., cut in 5-cm/2-inch lengths – and enough water, if necessary, just to cover the fish; cook over a high heat until the potatoes are tender and the fish flakes easily with a fork (10 to 15 minutes).

Serve the soup in one bowl with garlic-flavoured *croûtons*; the fish and vegetables in another. Serve olive oil and vinegar with the fish.

## Creole Crab Gumbo
Serves 4 to 6

2 tablespoons butter
2 tablespoons olive oil
1 Spanish onion, chopped
1 small green pepper, chopped
2 tablespoons flour
salt and freshly ground
  pepper
1 *bouquet garni* (celery, flat-leaf
  parsley, thyme)
1 clove garlic, finely chopped
1 small thin strip lemon peel
dash Tabasco sauce

12 large cooked prawns,
  sliced
1 can (225 g/8 ounces) okra
  with liquor
1 large can Italian peeled
  tomatoes
300 ml/½ pint milk
150 ml/¼ pint cream
150 ml/¼ pint vegetable stock
350 g/¾ pound fresh crabmeat,
  flaked

Combine the butter and olive oil in a saucepan and heat until butter has melted. Add the onion and green pepper and sauté until tender. Blend in the flour and cook, stirring continuously, for 3 minutes. Add salt and pepper, to taste, the *bouquet garni*, garlic, lemon peel and Tabasco sauce. Stir in the prawns, okra and tomatoes, and heat to boiling point. Cover the saucepan and simmer for 20 to 25 minutes. Gradually stir in the milk, cream and vegetable stock. Add the flaked crab and cook a few minutes more over medium heat, stirring occasionally, until the crab is cooked through. Correct the seasoning, remove the *bouquet garni* and serve immediately.

## Zuppa di Pesce
Serves 6 to 8

1 large onion, thinly sliced
6 tablespoons olive oil
2 tablespoons butter
1 kg/2 pounds tomatoes, peeled
  and diced
2 tablespoons tomato purée
  diluted in 150 ml/¼ pint
  water
1 clove garlic, chopped
4 tablespoons chopped flat-leaf
  parsley

1.3 kg/3 pounds mixed fish
  (sole, mullet, mackerel,
  whiting), cleaned
1 small eel, cut in pieces
2 small squid, cut in pieces
  (optional)
boiling water
150 ml/¼ pint dry white wine
1 tablespoon wine vinegar
salt and freshly ground
  pepper

Sauté the onion in the oil and butter until soft, then add the tomatoes, diluted tomato purée, garlic and parsley. Simmer uncovered for 15 to 20 minutes, then add the fish, eel and squid, and enough boiling water to cover, and let it come to the boil. Add the white wine and wine vinegar and cook over a low heat for 15 minutes. Season to taste.

# Hawaiian Fish Chowder
Serves 6 to 8

100 g/¼ pound salt pork, diced
2 tablespoons olive oil
1 Spanish onion, finely chopped
450 g/1 pound cod, diced
450 g/1 pound new potatoes,
 sliced

4 ripe tomatoes, sliced
425 ml/¾ pint boiling water
300 ml/½ pint milk
salt and freshly ground
 pepper

Sauté the salt pork in the olive oil until golden. Remove. Add the onion and sauté in the resulting fat until transparent. Add the fish, potatoes and tomatoes, and sauté for a minute or two more. Then add the water and simmer for ½ hour, or until the potatoes are tender. Add the milk and simmer 5 minutes more. Season to taste with salt and pepper.

# Seafood Bisque
Serves 4

6 tablespoons butter
6 tablespoons flour
900 ml/1½ pints hot milk
4 tablespoons finely chopped
 shallots
1 teaspoon curry powder
1 cooked lobster
1 can minced clams

100 g/¼ pound prawns
3 tablespoons olive oil
150 ml/¼ pint dry white wine
salt and freshly ground
 pepper
2 tablespoons finely chopped
 flat-leaf parsley

Melt the butter in the top of a double saucepan; add the flour and cook over simmering water until the *roux* is well blended. Gradually add the hot milk, stirring continuously. Then add the shallots and curry powder and simmer, stirring from time to time, until the sauce is thick and well blended.

Shell the lobster and dice the meat; drain the minced clams, reserving the liquid. Sauté the shellfish in the olive oil until golden. Pour the reserved clam juice over the shellfish; add to the milk mixture and cook over a low heat, stirring constantly, until well heated. Just before serving, add the white wine, and salt and pepper, to taste, and sprinkle with parsley.

# Provençal Aïoli

A strange soaring elation always grips me as I drive along the winding coastal road from St Raphael and first catch sight of the pink-shaded towers of St Tropez across the glittering bay. There are certain places in the world for each of us – magic places where we immediately feel at home at first meeting, as if somehow, sometime, we had been there before. St Tropez holds this magic for me.

Sheer good luck – unearned and unadorned – is as satisfying as it is exciting. Newton sitting under an apple tree, for instance; or the owner of the left-bank café, Les Deux Magots, awaking one morning to find his corner the most famous rendezvous in France.

St Tropez is a case in point. I have watched its legend grow since the war and have often pondered on the pure chance that made virtual millionaires out of the simple folk I had come to know so well during the years that I owned a house there, the café owners on the port, the fishermen-turned-restaurateurs, the shopkeepers and the hoteliers of the town on whom this providential manna had fallen.

Summer visitors have flocked to St Tropez like migratory birds since the time of the legendary Mistinguett. How many of them realise, I wonder, that until just recently one of the best cooks in Provence could be found practically within arm's reach of the port?

Chez Fifine was a tiny restaurant on rue Suffren, where I first learned to cook. It had a kitchen and one small room containing five tables on the ground floor, a slightly larger dining room upstairs, and a few tables strategically placed outside for the inevitable overflow. Fifine, *la patronne,* and my lost friend, did all the cooking herself, aided by a kitchen staff of one; the service was carried out by family and friends – Josef, ex-fisherman and famous local *pétanque* champion, directed the activities of a team of personable young 'cousins' who waited on table. For those friends of mine who demanded *la grande cuisine,* an impressive décor and impeccable service, my advice was to stay away. For here the service was friendly but often erratic; there was no *cave* of select vintage wines; no flaming *spécialités de la maison,* no fuss, no bother; but the simple rustic dishes of Provence, lovingly prepared by Fifine, were sublime. All Provence was her domain: fennel came from the mountains behind the coast, wild thyme and rosemary from the neighbouring hills; the town's best fishermen arrived at her door several times a day with their latest catch; tomatoes were selected with care from one special *vendeuse* in the open-air vegetable market, fresh *basilic* from another. Eggs and vegetables were delivered daily from a nearby farm.

Fifine loved and excelled in the rustic dishes of Provence and the fruits of her private sea, the Gulf of St Tropez. It was she who taught me the pleasures of the unknown local wines; the special richness of the pure olive oil of Provence; what fish to put into *bouillabaisse*; how to make an *aïoli,* a *rouille,* a *tapénade.*

*Aïoli,* sometimes referred to as *le beurre de Provence,* was originally a sauce made of olive oil and crushed garlic, thickened with fresh breadcrumbs and mashed boiled potato. Today, the *liaison* of this famous sauce is almost always made with raw egg yolk, and modern *aïoli* is really a mayonnaise with a pungent garlic base.

Chez Fifine, *aïoli,* served *sur commande* only and a masterpiece of presentation and high savour, featured salt codfish, fresh sea bream, tiny octopus and a medley of boiled vegetables – carrots, new potatoes, sweet potatoes, courgettes, onions, green beans – as well as hard-boiled eggs, raw tomatoes and fresh basil and parsley, served with the strong *aïoli* sauce from which the dish gets its name.

# Fifine's Aïoli
Serves 4 to 6

| | |
|---|---|
| 450 g/1 pound salt codfish | *Sauce:* |
| 6 potatoes in their jackets | 4 fat cloves of garlic per person |
| 6 sweet potatoes | salt |
| 6 courgettes | 1 egg yolk for each two persons |
| 450 g/1 pound small carrots | olive oil |
| 450 g/1 pound green beans | freshly ground pepper |
| 6 hard-boiled eggs | lemon juice |
| 6 large ripe tomatoes | |
| lettuce and fresh herbs to | |
| decorate serving dishes | |

Soak the codfish overnight in cold water.

The next day, boil the fish and vegetables – white and sweet potatoes in their jackets, whole courgettes and carrots and French beans – separately. All the vegetables should be tender but still quite firm, and on no account overcooked. Serve hot vegetables, hard-boiled eggs in their shells and raw tomatoes on large serving dishes decorated with lettuce and sprigs of fresh herbs. Place the fish in the centre. For best effect, group the well-drained vegetables by colour. Serve with *aïoli* sauce, from which this famous dish gets its name.

**To make the sauce:**  Crush the garlic to a smooth paste in a mortar with a little salt; blend in the egg yolks until the mixture is a smooth homogeneous mass. Now take olive oil and proceed (drop by drop at first, a thin fine trickle later) to whisk the mixture as you would for a mayonnaise. The *aïoli* will thicken gradually until it reaches the proper stiff, firm consistency. The exact quantity of oil is, of course, determined by the number of egg yolks used. Season to taste with additional salt, a little pepper and lemon juice. This sauce is served chilled in a bowl. Guests help themselves.

# Portuguese Codfish
Serves 4

| | |
|---|---|
| 450 g/1 pound salt cod fillets | 4 tablespoons finely chopped |
| 6 tablespoons olive oil | flat-leaf parsley |
| 4 tablespoons wine vinegar | 6 tablespoons olive oil |
| | 2 tablespoons lemon juice |
| *Onion Dressing:* | salt and freshly ground |
| 1 Spanish onion, finely chopped | pepper |

Soak the cod in water overnight.

The next day, drain the cod and place in a saucepan; cover with cold water and bring slowly to the boil. Remove from the heat and allow to steep for 10 minutes.

Drain the cod fillets and sauté gently in the olive oil until golden. Remove from the heat; pour the vinegar over and allow to stand for 5 minutes. Transfer the fish to a warm serving dish and pour the onion dressing over.

**To make the onion dressing:**   Combine the onion and parsley with the olive oil, lemon juice, and salt and pepper, to taste. Whisk until well blended (in a blender, if you like).

## Brandade de Morue
Serves 4

| | |
|---|---|
| **450 g/1 pound salt cod fillets** | **juice and grated zest of ½ lemon** |
| **2 cloves garlic, crushed** | **freshly ground pepper** |
| **6 tablespoons double cream** | **toast triangles fried in olive oil** |
| **150 ml/¼ pint olive oil** | **  or butter, to serve** |

Soak the cod fillets in cold water for at least 12 hours, changing the water often. Place the drained cod fillets in a saucepan, cover with cold water and bring to the boil. Remove from the heat, cover the saucepan and let the cod simmer gently for 10 minutes. Strain the cod, remove the bones and skin, and flake the fish with a fork.

Place the cod flakes in a blender with the garlic, 2 tablespoons cream and 4 tablespoons olive oil and blend, adding the remainder of the cream and olive oil alternately from time to time until completely absorbed and the *brandade* has the consistency of mashed potatoes. When ready to serve, simmer the mixture in a *bain-marie*, or in a saucepan over water; stir in the lemon juice and zest and add pepper to taste. *Brandade de morue* may be served hot or cold. If hot, place in a mound on a warm serving dish and surround with toast triangles fried in olive oil or butter. If the *brandade* is too salty, blend in 1 or 2 boiled potatoes.

## Délices de Sole Lucas Carton
Serves 6

| | |
|---|---|
| **3 sole (450–550 g/1–1¼ pounds each)** | **6–8 tablespoons dry white wine** |
| | **salt and freshly ground pepper** |
| **½ medium Spanish onion, finely chopped** | **2–4 very ripe tomatoes** |
| | **50 g/2 ounces very white button mushrooms, cut into slivers** |
| **1–2 sprigs flat-leaf parsley** | |
| **175 g/6 ounces butter** | **6–8 tablespoons crème fraîche** |

Have the fishmonger fillet the sole, but ask him for the bones, head and fish trimmings to make a fish *fumet*. Soak the fillets and bones in cold water for 1 hour.

To make fish *fumet:* cut the bones in 4 or 5 pieces and simmer gently in a covered saucepan for 6 to 8 minutes with the onion, parsley and 2 tablespoons butter. Moisten with dry white wine and 6 to 8 tablespoons water. Bring to the boil, skim impurities from the surface and simmer for 10 to 12 minutes.

Butter a long flameproof dish and place the fillets of sole in it. Season well with salt and pepper, to taste. Peel, seed and chop the tomatoes and scatter over the fish fillets with the mushrooms. Pour over the *fumet*; cover with buttered paper and bring to the boil; lower the heat to a simmer. Cook for 7 to 8 minutes.

Pour the liquid into a saucepan; stir in the crème fraîche and reduce over a high heat until the sauce is of the desired consistency. Place the sauce in the top of a double saucepan and gradually add the remaining butter in the little pieces, whisking constantly as you would for a *sauce hollandaise*, without letting the water under the pan come to the boil. Cover the fillets with this sauce and glaze under the grill for a few seconds. Serve immediately.

## Filets de Sole Bonne Femme
Serves 4

2 sole (about 450 g/1 pound each)
salt and freshly ground pepper
2 tablespoons finely chopped shallots
2 tablespoons finely chopped mushrooms
150 ml/¼ pint dry white wine
fish stock (made from fish trimmings)
1 *bouquet garni* (bay leaf, thyme, 4 sprigs flat-leaf parsley)
12 button mushroom caps
2 tablespoons butter
1 tablespoon lemon juice
flour
butter

Ask your fishmonger to fillet the sole; keep the heads, bones and trimmings for stock. Season the fillets generously with salt and pepper and put them in the bottom of a buttered earthenware baking dish. Sprinkle with the shallots and mushrooms and add half the dry white wine and just enough fish stock to cover. Add the *bouquet garni*; bring to the boil; cover with a buttered paper and bake in a moderate oven (180°C/350°F/gas 4) for 10 minutes. Sauté the mushroom caps in the butter and lemon juice until tender.

Arrange the poached fillets on a heated serving dish; put the fish liquor into a small saucepan; add the remaining wine and reduce over a brisk heat to two-thirds of the original quantity. Thicken the sauce if necessary with a *beurre manié* (made by kneading equal quantities of butter and flour to a smooth paste). Bring the sauce to the boil and cook until it has the consistency of cream.

Place 3 mushroom caps on each portion of sole; pour the sauce over and glaze for a minute or two under the grill before serving.

## Casserolettes de Filets de Sole 'Lasserre'
Serves 4

2 sole (about 450 g/1 pound each)
butter
2 shallots, finely chopped
4 mushroom stalks, finely chopped
salt and freshly ground pepper
4 individual baked pastry shells
16 asparagus tips
8 button mushrooms, finely chopped
béchamel sauce (page 34)
1 egg yolk
4 slices truffle (optional)
finely chopped flat-leaf parsley

Remove the fillets from the sole and cut each fillet into 3 equal pieces; arrange in a well-buttered gratin dish. Sprinkle with shallots and mushroom stalks, add salt and pepper to taste, and cover with the fish bones. Cover with buttered paper and poach in a hot oven (230°C/450°F/gas 8) for 10 minutes.

In the meantime, garnish the bottom of each baked pastry shell with 4 asparagus tips and finely chopped mushrooms, both sautéed in butter.

Arrange the poached fish in the pastry shells. Reduce the cooking liquid from the sole and add it to a well-flavoured *sauce béchamel* with the yolk of 1 egg and a knob of butter. Fill the pastry shells with this sauce and glaze under grill until golden.

Lasserre tops each tart with a glazed slice of truffle, sprinkles the dish with parsley and fixes a small pastry 'handle' to each one to form a *casserolette*, or little casserole.

## Trout Amandine
Serves 4 to 6

4–6 fresh trout
salt and freshly ground pepper
milk
flour
100 g/¼ pound butter
1 tablespoon olive oil

4–6 tablespoons blanched
    slivered almonds
juice of ½ lemon
2–4 tablespoons finely chopped
    flat-leaf parsley

Season the cleaned trout with salt and a little pepper. Dip them in milk and then in flour, and then sauté in half the butter and 1 tablespoon oil until golden brown on both sides. Drain the fat from the pan and melt the remaining butter. Add the almonds and cook, shaking the pan continuously, until the almonds are golden brown. Add lemon juice and parsley and pour the sauce over the trout on a heated platter.

## Trout Père Louis
Serves 4

4 tablespoons butter
4 fresh trout
6–8 tablespoons crème fraîche
2 tablespoons Grand Marnier

2 tablespoons cognac
salt and freshly ground pepper
2–4 tablespoons slivered toasted
    almonds (see recipe above)

Melt the butter in a thick-bottomed frying pan and sauté the cleaned trout until tender. Heat the crème fraîche, without letting it come to the boil, in a saucepan. Stir in the Grand Marnier and cognac and add salt and pepper to taste. Place the trout on a heated serving dish; pour over the sauce and sprinkle with toasted almonds. Serve immediately.

## Chinese Steamed Fish
Serves 2

**2 whiting (about 350 g/¾ pound each)**
**100 g/¼ pound button mushrooms, thinly sliced**
**1 clove garlic, finely chopped**
**2 chopped spring onions (or 2 tablespoons coarsely chopped onion or shallots)**

**4 tablespoons olive oil**
**2 tablespoons soy sauce**
**1 tablespoon cornflour**
**2 tablespoons dry white wine**
**salt and freshly ground pepper**

Place the cleaned fish in a flat dish large enough to hold them. Add the mushrooms. Combine the garlic, spring onion, olive oil, soy sauce, cornflour, dry white wine and salt and pepper, to taste. Mix well and pour over the fish.

Place the dish in a large steamer, or on a rack in a large saucepan wide enough to hold it, with about 5 cm/2 inches of rapidly boiling water. Cover and steam for 15 minutes. Remove to a hot platter and serve immediately. Steamed rice or steamed sliced carrots, new potatoes and green beans should accompany this dish.

## Truite au Vin Rosé
Serves 4

**4 good-sized trout**
*vin rosé*
**4 shallots, finely chopped**
**150 ml/¼ pint thick *sauce hollandaise* (page 39)**

**4 tablespoons double cream**
**salt and freshly ground pepper**
**8 triangles white bread sautéed in 2 tablespoons butter**
**chopped flat-leaf parsley**

Place the trout in a well-buttered baking dish. Pour in *vin rosé* to cover, add the shallots and cover the dish with buttered paper. Poach the fish in a slow oven (150°C/300°F/gas 2) for about 20 minutes, or until cooked through but still firm. Lay on a dry cloth and carefully remove the skins.

Reduce the liquid in which the fish were poached until there remains only a small amount of slightly thickened sauce. Cool the sauce, strain it, and add the thick *hollandaise* mixed with 4 tablespoons double cream. Add salt and pepper, to taste.

Arrange the trout on a warm platter; spoon the sauce over the fish and serve garnished with triangles of bread sautéed in butter and sprinkled with parsley.

# Chapter 6

# Shellfish

## Lobster à l'Américaine

They are fishing the Mediterranean dry. Voracious hordes of tourists are taking their toll on the sea itself, as well as despoiling the coastline of Southern France. This year, even in the fishing ports, local fish cost more than those brought overland a thousand miles from the Atlantic.

At the end of the war the rocky coves of the Riviera were filled with lobsters. But year by year the French have had to go farther afield to catch them, until now they have virtually deserted the shores of Metropolitan France and are to be found in great numbers only off the coasts of Corsica.

I think the reason the French are eating up their sources of lobster so quickly is that they are not content just to boil them and serve them with mayonnaise or a *sauce verte* as we do in this country. The English have a fixation about the perfection of their raw materials which makes them shy of masking their true flavours. But even the most perfect raw material can be enhanced by skilful blending with other flavours that will develop its subtleties and draw out its delicacy. It is this that the French have done with lobster *à l'américaine*, one of the truly great dishes of the world – or, if you prefer it, lobster *à l'armoricaine*, as it is sometimes described on menus throughout France.

For there are two schools of thought on the lobster argument: certain food snobs claim that the spelling is *à l'armoricaine*, because *armor* was the old Breton name for sea and Brittany was at one time called *Armorica*; according to them, there was no other part of France where you could get better lobsters and so France's greatest lobster dish was at once baptised *à l'armoricaine*. Any other version of this name, they decided, was only a mistake in spelling. The other school of purists claim that this dish could not be Breton because of its use of garlic, tomatoes and cognac in the recipe and that it most nearly resembled lobster cooked in the Provençal manner of Southern France.

They called the dish lobster *à l'américaine*, not because the dish was of American extraction, but because it was created by Pierre Graisse, a Parisian chef recently returned from America, who, following the current vogue for all things American, called his restaurant Peter's and named this dish, his creation, lobster *à l'américaine*.

Legend has it that one evening when the dinner hour was well and truly over and Pierre-Peter was getting ready to close up for the night, a party of guests entered his restaurant and insisted that he serve them dinner. The chef decided that if they had soup and *hors-d'œuvres*, he would just have time to prepare a fish dish for them. But on looking into the depleted stores of the restaurant, he discovered that there was no fish left, just some live lobsters ready for the following morning. He chopped some onions, garlic and shallots, sautéed them gently in butter and olive oil, added tomatoes, fish stock and some dry white wine and when the sauce was bubbling, cut up the lobsters and cooked them in the highly spiced sauce. The result surpassed all expectations and one of the world's most famous dishes was born . . . the product of a moment of necessity and the inspiration of a great cook.

## Lobster à l'Américaine
Serves 4 to 6

**2 live lobsters (1 kg/2 pounds each)**
**100 g/¼ pound butter**
**150 ml/¼ pint olive oil**
**1 carrot, finely chopped**
**1 small onion, finely chopped**
**2 shallots, finely chopped**
**2 cloves garlic, finely chopped**
**300 ml/½ pint dry white wine**
**4 tablespoons cognac**
**600 ml/1 pint canned tomatoes**

**2 tablespoons tomato purée**
**1 bay leaf**
**150 ml/¼ pint fish stock or dry white wine**
**salt and freshly ground pepper**
**1 tablespoon flour**
**1 tablespoon butter**
**lemon juice**
**pinch cayenne pepper**
**finely chopped fresh flat-leaf parsley, chives and tarragon**

Order live lobsters from your fishmonger; drop them into warm water and bring to the boil so that they lose consciousness and die painlessly. Remove from the heat. Working over a shallow bowl to catch the juices, break off and crack the claws. Cut each lobster tail into thick slices. Cut the body shells in half; remove and discard the intestinal tube which is exposed when the body of the lobster is cut open; reserve coral and all the juices left in the bowl.

Combine 3 tablespoons butter and 3 tablespoons olive oil in a thick-bottomed frying pan; add the lobster pieces and sauté for 5 minutes, stirring occasionally. Reserve.

Heat the remaining butter and olive oil in another pan and sauté the carrot, onion, shallots and garlic until the onion is transparent. Place the lobster pieces on a bed of vegetables (reserving the juices in the pan the lobsters were cooked in); pour over the white wine and simmer for 3 minutes. Add the warmed cognac and flame. Add the tomatoes, tomato purée, bay leaf, lobster liquids, fish stock and salt and pepper, to taste. Cover the pan and simmer for 15 minutes.

Remove the lobster; keep warm. Simmer the tomato sauce, uncovered, until slightly reduced. Blend in the coral, creamed with 1 tablespoon each flour and butter, and simmer until thickened; strain the sauce and flavour to taste with lemon juice, salt, pepper and cayenne. Add the lobster pieces and the juice from pan in which the lobsters were cooked and heat through.

Just before serving, sprinkle with finely chopped parsley, chives and tarragon. Serve hot with boiled rice or pilaff.

# Boiled Lobster

One of the best ways to appreciate a sweet, firm lobster, full of the clean taste of the sea, is to eat it freshly boiled. So if a fresh, live lobster comes your way, the best method of cooking is to plunge him into a simple *court-bouillon* (water, salt, freshly ground pepper, bay leaf and thyme) and poach him for 5 minutes for the first pound (450 g) and 5 minutes after for each additional pound (450 g). Remember, the most common error in preparing lobster (and all fish, for that matter) is overcooking.

When the lobster is cooked, allow it to cool in the *court-bouillon*; then remove it, place it on its back on a chopping block and split it lengthwise down the middle with a heavy French knife or kitchen cleaver. Give the knife or cleaver a quick blow with a hammer or mallet so that the shell and meat are severed at the same time; remove the stomach, intestines and the dark vein that runs through the body at the centre. But do not throw away the greyish-green liver or coral-coloured roe; they are delicacies. Crack the claws so that the meat can be easily extracted and serve the lobster hot with hot melted butter and lemon wedges, hot melted butter with fresh lime juice, 3 or 4 fennel seeds and tarragon, or cold with freshly made mayonnaise. Allow 450 to 700 g/1 to 1½ pounds of lobster per portion.

# Grilled Lobster

Grilling a lobster takes a delicate touch. Its succulence depends on many things: the freshness of the lobster, its size, the heat of the grill and, of course, above all on your own judgement. Split the live lobster down through the middle of the body and the tail; remove the roe (black when it is uncooked) and the dark vein that runs through the tail. Grill it for 8 to 10 minutes on the shell side; turn it over, spread with softened butter and grill for 6 to 8 minutes on the flesh side.

Garnish with paprika and melted butter to which a little lemon juice has been added. Serve additional melted butter with each lobster. Allow 1 small lobster per portion.

# Grilled Lobster with Sherry

Serves 4

| | |
|---|---|
| **2 live lobsters (700 g–1 kg/** | **2–4 tablespoons dry sherry** |
| **1½–2 pounds each)** | **cayenne pepper** |
| **salt and freshly ground pepper** | **paprika** |
| **6 tablespoons butter** | |

Plunge the lobsters in warm water to which you have added salt and a generous amount of pepper, and bring gently to the boil. Boil for 1 minute. Drain and halve lengthwise. Keep warm.

Melt the butter lightly in a saucepan, add dry sherry and season to taste with cayenne pepper and paprika. Pour over the lobster and grill until golden.

# Lobster Newburg
Serves 4

4 small cooked lobsters
4 tablespoons butter
4 tablespoons cognac
2 egg yolks, beaten

300 ml/½ pint double cream
salt and freshly ground pepper
cayenne and paprika

Cut the lobsters in half lengthwise. Crack the claws. Remove the lobster meat from the shells; cut into large cubes; sauté in the butter for a few minutes. Add warm cognac and flame.

Combine the egg yolks and cream in the top of a double saucepan and cook over water, stirring continuously, until the mixture coats the spoon. Add the lobster meat and pan juices and heat through, taking care that the sauce does not curdle. Add salt, pepper, cayenne and paprika, to taste. Serve on a bed of rice or in individual *vol-au-vent* cases.

# Quick Lobster Thermidor
Serves 4

4 small cooked lobsters
425 ml/¾ pint cream sauce (page
  35)
dry sherry
1 teaspoon dry mustard
pinch cayenne

Worcestershire sauce
salt and freshly ground pepper
4 tablespoons freshly grated
  Parmesan
paprika
butter

Cut the lobsters in half lengthwise. Crack the claws. Remove the lobster meat from the shells and cut into large cubes. Reserve the shells. Heat the cream sauce; season to taste with a little dry sherry, dry mustard, cayenne pepper, Worcestershire sauce, salt and pepper. Simmer gently for 2 minutes; add the diced lobster meat and heat through.

Fill the lobster shells with the mixture; sprinkle the grated Parmesan over top; dust with paprika; dot with butter and brown under grill.

# Green Lobster Salad
Serves 6

150 ml/¼ pint mayonnaise
6 tablespoons puréed spinach
salt, freshly ground pepper and
  cayenne
juice of 2 lemons
1 lobster, cooked in *court-
  bouillon*

½ cucumber, peeled, seeded and
  diced
2 hard-boiled eggs, diced
3 large, ripe avocado pears
finely chopped tarragon, chives
  and flat-leaf parsley, to
  garnish

Make a *sauce verte* by combining the well-flavoured mayonnaise with the puréed spinach. Season to taste with salt, pepper, cayenne and a little lemon juice, and pass the green mayonnaise through a fine sieve.

Dice the lobster meat; prepare the cucumber and hard-boiled eggs. Slice the avocado pears in half and remove the stone; score the flesh with a sharp knife in even-sized segments about 6 mm/¼ inch square, cutting down to the skin. Be careful not to pierce the skin with the knife while doing so. Remove the avocado segments carefully with a spoon; dice them and marinate in lemon juice. Brush the inside of the avocado shells with lemon juice and reserve.

Combine the drained avocado, cucumber, lobster and eggs in a bowl. Add the *sauce verte*; toss carefully and fill the avocado shells with this mixture. Chill, and just before serving sprinkle with tarragon, chives and parsley.

## Lobster Gratin
Serves 4

2 live lobsters (about 700 g–
  1 kg/1½–2 pounds each)
2 tablespoons butter
2 tablespoons olive oil
1 carrot, 1 onion, 1 stalk celery,
  finely chopped, softened in a
  little butter
1 bay leaf
1 pinch dried thyme
salt and freshly ground pepper
6 tablespoons cognac
150 ml/¼ pint dry white wine

generous pinch cayenne
225 g/½ pound button
  mushrooms, sliced
1 large truffle, diced
150 ml/¼ pint double cream
300 ml/½ pint béchamel sauce
  (page 34)
2 tablespoons finely grated
  Gruyère
knobs of butter
crescents of flaky pastry

Cut the lobsters in two and remove the creamy parts. Reserve. Heat the butter and olive oil in a thick-bottomed frying pan and sauté the lobster halves for 3 minutes on each side. Remove from the pan; place the carrot, onion, celery, bay leaf, thyme, salt and pepper in the pan. Return the lobster halves and place on top of this mixture; sauté for 1 minute. Flame with the cognac; when the flames die out, pour the dry white wine over. Season to taste with salt, pepper and cayenne; cover the pan and simmer gently for 20 minutes.

When cooked, remove the lobster meat from the shells and dice coarsely. Add the mushrooms and truffle to the vegetable mixture in the pan. Stir in the cream and simmer over the lowest heat possible until well blended.

Combine the béchamel sauce with the lobster; season generously and bring to the boil. Remove from the heat; combine with the creamed vegetable mixture and pour into a well-buttered gratin dish. Sprinkle with Gruyère and little knobs of butter and heat under the grill until golden. Serve very hot, garnished with crescents of flaky pastry.

# American Crab Salad
Serves 4

450 g/1 pound cooked crabmeat,
flaked

100 g/¼ pound celery, finely
chopped

2 tablespoons finely chopped red
pepper

juice of 1 lemon

dry mustard

salt, freshly ground pepper and
cayenne

150 ml/¼ pint mayonnaise

lettuce

4 tomatoes

2 hard-boiled eggs

8 black olives

finely chopped flat-leaf parsley

Combine lightly the cold, cooked crabmeat, the celery and pimento. Season with lemon juice, dry mustard, salt, pepper and cayenne, to taste.

Bind the salad with well-flavoured mayonnaise and serve on lettuce leaves. Garnish with quartered tomatoes, hard-boiled eggs and black olives. Top with a little more mayonnaise and dust with finely chopped parsley.

# Devilled Crab
Serves 4

4 tablespoons butter

4 tablespoons flour

425 ml/¾ pint hot milk

4 hard-boiled eggs, chopped

1 tablespoon Dijon mustard

1 teaspoon dry mustard

1–2 tablespoons Worcestershire
sauce

2 tablespoons finely chopped
flat-leaf parsley

1 tablespoon finely chopped
onion

1 tablespoon finely chopped
green pepper

450 g/1 pound cooked
crabmeat

salt and freshly ground pepper

cayenne pepper

2–4 tablespoons freshly grated
Parmesan

Melt the butter in the top of a double saucepan; add the flour and cook over water, stirring continuously until the *roux* is well blended. Add the hot milk gradually, stirring continuously until the sauce begins to thicken. Stir in chopped hard-boiled eggs, mustards, Worcestershire sauce, parsley, onion and green pepper. Simmer the sauce, stirring from time to time, until thick.

Flake the crabmeat and add to the sauce, stirring gently so as not to break the meat. Add salt, pepper and cayenne, to taste, and fill crab shells or ramekins with the mixture. Top with freshly grated Parmesan and bake in a hot oven (230°C/450°F/gas 8) for 20 minutes.

# Crab Tart
Serves 4 to 6

shortcrust pastry for 20-cm/
  8-inch pie tin (page 12)
beaten egg
225 g/½ pound cooked crabmeat
2 tablespoons finely chopped
  flat-leaf parsley

2 tablespoons butter
2 tablespoons dry sherry
4 egg yolks
300 ml/½ pint single cream
salt and freshly ground pepper
grated nutmeg

Line a 20-cm/8-inch pie tin with the shortcrust pastry. Prick the bottom with a fork; chill for at least an hour; brush with a little beaten egg and bake 'blind' at 220°C/450°F/gas 8 for 15 minutes.

Sauté the crabmeat and parsley in the butter; sprinkle with the sherry and put into the pastry shell.

Whisk the egg yolks in a bowl; add the cream and whisk until thick and lemon-coloured. Flavour to taste with salt, pepper and freshly grated nutmeg, and pour over the crabmeat mixture.

Bake in a moderate oven (180°C/350°F/gas 4) for about 30 minutes, or until the custard is set.

# Prawns in Whisky
Serves 4

4 tablespoons butter
4 tablespoons olive oil
2 tablespoons finely chopped
  shallots (or onion)
1 clove garlic, finely chopped
450 g/1 pound fresh shelled
  tiger prawns
2 tomatoes, peeled, seeded and
  chopped
salt and freshly ground pepper

cayenne pepper
6 tablespoons whisky
6 tablespoons dry white wine
1 teaspoon cornflour, diluted in
  2 tablespoons water
4 tablespoons double cream
1 tablespoon finely chopped
  tarragon
1 egg yolk
boiled rice, to serve

Combine the butter and olive oil in a frying pan; add the shallots and garlic, and sauté until transparent. Add the prawns, tomatoes and salt, pepper and cayenne pepper, to taste; sauté gently for a few minutes. Pour over 4 tablespoons whisky and flame.

Add the white wine and simmer for 5 minutes. Remove the prawns and keep warm. Combine the remaining whisky, cornflour and cream; add to the sauce and beat vigorously over a high heat until the sauce comes to the boil. Boil for 1 minute; remove from the heat; add the tarragon and pour a little hot sauce over the egg yolk. Mix well and then stir the egg mixture into the sauce. Pour over the prawns and serve immediately with rice.

# Oysters

The Roman Emperor Tiberius is said to have lived on oysters practically all of his life. Now I am not suggesting you follow suit, but a plate of fresh oysters from Colchester or Whitstable, served on ice with freshly ground pepper and a wedge or two of lemon, is hard to beat.

It is very easy to tell a good oyster from a bad one. The shells of live oysters are tightly closed; those of dead oysters are usually, though not always, a little open. If tapping the shell produces a hollow sound within, it is very likely dead.

Oysters are a fine choice for a late-night supper party, either served on ice with piping hot tiny sausages as they do in northern France; deep-fried in hot oil and butter and served with wedges of lemon, or, if you must, a little *sauce tartare;* or, perhaps my favourite of all, the New Orleans recipe for oysters Rockfeller, so named because they are 'as rich as Rockefeller'.

## Oysters Rockefeller
### Serves 4

4 tablespoons chopped shallots
225 g/½ pound butter
4 tablespoons fine breadcrumbs
1 bunch watercress, leaves finely chopped
4 tablespoons each chopped celery leaves and flat-leaf parsley

1 tablespoon chopped chervil
1 teaspoon finely chopped tarragon
4 tablespoons Pernod
salt, freshly ground pepper and cayenne
rock salt
24 freshly opened oysters

Sauté the shallots in 4 tablespoons of the butter until transparent; add the breadcrumbs and stir over a low heat until lightly browned. Combine in a large bowl or mortar with the watercress, celery, parsley, chervil, tarragon, Pernod, and salt, pepper and cayenne pepper, to taste. Add the remaining butter and pound to a smooth paste. Keep cool until ready to use.

Place a bed of rock salt in a baking tin large enough to hold the oysters comfortably, or in 4 small tins; damp the salt slightly and place the oyster shells, opened, on this bed. Place 1 tablespoon of green herb butter on each oyster and bake in a hot oven (230°C/450°F/gas 8) for 4 to 5 minutes, or until the butter has melted and the oysters are heated through. Serve immediately.

## Fried Oysters
### Serves 4 to 6

2–3 dozen oysters
2 eggs, beaten
4 tablespoons double cream
salt and freshly ground pepper

cornmeal, biscuit crumbs or fresh breadcrumbs
100 g/¼ pound butter
150 ml/¼ pint peanut oil
lemon wedges

Shell the oysters. Combine the eggs and cream in a bowl. Add salt and pepper, to taste. Dip the oysters in the egg mixture, then in the cornmeal or crumbs, and allow to set on aluminium foil for about 5 minutes before cooking.

Melt the butter in a large, thick-bottomed frying pan or deep-fryer. Add the oil; bring to frying temperature and cook the oysters until golden brown. Serve immediately with wedges of lemon.

### Old English Stew'd Oysters
Serves 4

| | |
|---|---|
| **600 ml/1 pint oysters and liquor** | **¼ teaspoon paprika** |
| **1 bay leaf** | **300 ml/½ pint hot milk** |
| **4 tablespoons butter** | **300 ml/½ pint hot cream** |
| **1 teaspoon Worcestershire sauce** | **2–4 tablespoons dry sherry** |
| **salt and cayenne** | **freshly grated nutmeg** |

Place the oysters and their liquor in a saucepan with the bay leaf, butter, Worcestershire sauce, salt, cayenne and paprika, and simmer gently until the oyster edges begin to curl.

Remove the bay leaf; add the heated milk and cream. Stir once, bring to simmering point again; add the sherry; correct the seasoning and pour into individual serving bowls. Just before serving, dust with a little freshly grated nutmeg.

# Moules Marinière

I have never seen a mussel growing on the Mediterranean coast, yet I can hardly remember a restaurant there that does not make a speciality of some delicious manner of serving mussels. There are vast quantities of mussels along the cliffs of Cornwall; but how many of the local restaurants serve even the simplest mussel dish?

*Moules marinière* – one of the world's great dishes – makes the most of mussels, simmered for a few minutes only in dry white wine with a few finely chopped shallots or a small onion or two and a little parsley and thyme. Make this simple and inexpensive dish your own. And then, using this same basic recipe, prepare the mussels in any number of ways for a delicious first course or for a light luncheon or supper dish.

Try mussels *en brochette*, first simmered in dry white wine with aromatics, then stripped of their shells, rolled in egg yolk and breadcrumbs, slipped on metal skewers alternately with cubes of fat green bacon, and grilled or pan-grilled until delicately brown. Or, more simply, fry egg-and-breadcrumbed mussels which you have prepared in this way in deep fat until golden, and serve with lemon wedges or *sauce tartare*. I like mussels, too, prepared as for Moules Marinière, stripped of their shells and folded into a creamy omelette; or served in the half-shell with a cheese or garlic butter dressing.

**To clean mussels:**   Place the mussels in a bowl and wash well under running water. Scrape each shell with a knife, removing all traces of mud, seaweed and barnacles. Discard any mussels with cracked, broken or opened shells; they are dangerous. Rinse again in running water and remove the 'beards'.

**To keep cooked mussels:**   Wrap cooked mussels in a damp towel and put them on one of the lower shelves of your refrigerator. Strained mussel liquor can also be kept in the refrigerator to use the following day for a *sauce velouté* or a *soupe aux moules*.

## Moules Marinière
Serves 4

4 shallots, finely chopped
1 tablespoon butter
300 ml/½ pint dry white wine
2–3 tablespoons finely chopped
   flat-leaf parsley
2 sprigs thyme

1 bay leaf
freshly ground pepper
48–60 cleaned mussels (see
   directions above)
2 tablespoons butter
1 tablespoon flour

**Step 1.**   Sauté the shallots in the butter until transparent but not coloured. Add the dry white wine, parsley, thyme, bay leaf and pepper, to taste, and simmer gently for 10 minutes.

**Step 2.**   Add the mussels to the wine and herb mixture; cover the saucepan and steam, shaking constantly, until the shells open. Remove the top shells from the mussels and arrange the mussels in a large, deep, heated serving platter. Keep warm. Discard any mussels that don't open.

**Step 3.**   Reduce the cooking liquor to half its original volume and thicken by adding a *beurre manié*, made by creaming together the butter and the flour. Correct the seasoning and pour the sauce over the mussels. Sprinkle with a little finely chopped parsley and serve immediately.

## Mussels à l'Ail
Serves 4

Prepare the cleaned mussels as in Steps 1 and 2 above, using half the quantity of wine. Place the mussels in a shallow baking pan or gratin dish. Chop 1 shallot and 4 cloves of garlic finely and sauté in 50 g/2 ounces butter until soft. Do not let the butter take on colour. Add 2 tablespoons finely chopped flat-leaf parsley and spoon the mixture over the mussels. Allow to cool; sprinkle with fresh breadcrumbs and bake in a moderately hot oven (200°C/400°F/gas 6) until the sauce is melted and delicately browned. Serve at once.

## Mouclade
Serves 4

Prepare the cleaned mussels as in Steps 1 and 2 on page 90, using half the quantity of wine. Remove the shells completely and place the mussels in a shallow ovenproof dish. Strain the mussel liquor and reduce over a high heat for 2 to 3 minutes. Add 150 ml/¼ pint cream and simmer for 10 to 15 minutes, stirring from time to time. Pour over the mussels; sprinkle lightly with fresh breadcrumbs and bake in a 200°C/400°F/gas 6 oven until heated through. Serve at once.

## Deep-fried Mussels Béarnaise
Serves 4

| | |
|---|---|
| 48 large cleaned mussels (see directions on page 90) | 225 g/½ pound green bacon (1 piece) |
| 2 tablespoons chopped shallots | freshly ground pepper |
| 2 sprigs thyme | flour |
| 2 sprigs flat-leaf parsley | beaten egg |
| 1 bay leaf | breadcrumbs |
| sea salt | béarnaise sauce (page 38) |
| 150 ml/¼ pint dry white wine | |

Place the mussels in a saucepan with the shallots, thyme, parsley and a bay leaf. Season lightly with salt and moisten with the white wine. Cover the saucepan and steam for 4 to 5 minutes, or until the shells are well opened.

Remove the mussels from their shells; dice the green bacon and place the mussels on small skewers with squares of bacon between them. Season to taste with pepper. Roll in flour; dip in beaten egg and then in dry breadcrumbs. Thread skewers on a piece of string and fry in deep fat until golden. Serve with béarnaise sauce.

## Steamed Mussels in Crock 'Four Seasons'
Serves 4

| | |
|---|---|
| 48 cleaned mussels (see directions on page 90) | 4 sprigs flat-leaf parsley, finely chopped |
| 3 shallots, finely chopped | 150 ml/¼ pint double cream |
| 1 tablespoon butter | salt and freshly ground pepper |
| 150 ml/¼ pint white wine | lemon juice |
| 150 ml/¼ pint bottled clam juice | |

Place the mussels in a fireproof crock with the shallots, butter, white wine, clam juice and parsley. Cover and steam for 5 minutes or until the mussels are all open. Add the cream, salt, pepper and lemon juice, to taste. Bring to the boil again and serve.

# Mussels Victoria

Serves 4

48 cleaned mussels (see
  directions on page 90)
2 tablespoons chopped shallots
2 sprigs thyme
2 sprigs flat-leaf parsley
1 bay leaf
sea salt
150 ml/¼ pint dry white wine

*Beurre d'Escargots:*
225 g/½ pound butter
3 cloves garlic, finely chopped
6 tablespoons finely chopped
  flat-leaf parsley
4 tablespoons finely chopped
  chives

Choose fine fat mussels and place in a saucepan together with the shallots, thyme, parsley and a bay leaf. Season lightly with salt and moisten with the white wine. Steam for 4 to 5 minutes, or until the shells are well opened. Remove 1 half-shell from each; butter the mussels copiously with *beurre d'escargots*; and place the mussels in their half-shells in 4 individual ovenproof dishes. Bake in a hot oven 230°C/450°F/gas 8 for 2 to 3 minutes.

**To make the beurre d'escargots:**  Knead together the butter, garlic, parsley and chives. If chives are unavailable, add more parsley. Chill the butter before using.

# Salade de Moules

Serves 4

48 cleaned mussels (see
  directions on page 90)
2 tablespoons chopped shallots
2 sprigs thyme
2 sprigs flat-leaf parsley
1 bay leaf
sea salt

150 ml/¼ pint very dry white
  wine
wine vinegar
olive oil
freshly ground pepper
4 tablespoons chopped flat-leaf
  parsley

Place the mussels in a saucepan together with the shallots, thyme, parsley and a bay leaf. Season lightly with salt and moisten with the white wine. Simmer until the mussels are well opened. Remove them from their shells.

Prepare a dressing made of one part liquid in which the mussels were cooked, one part wine vinegar and one part olive oil. Add salt and pepper, to taste; pour over the mussels while they are still warm. Sprinkle with chopped parsley. The mussels should be moist, but without excess dressing. Serve cold as an *hors-d'œuvre*.

# Grilled Scallops
Serves 4

8 scallops
butter
salt and freshly ground pepper
4 rounds of hot buttered toast

1 tablespoon finely chopped
    flat-leaf parsley
lemon juice

Wash and trim the scallops; dry carefully. Place on a buttered baking tin; dot with butter; season to taste with salt and pepper. Preheat the grill. Place the scallops about 7.5 cm/3 inches from the heat and grill for 4 to 6 minutes, or until delicately browned.

To serve: place on the rounds of hot buttered toast and sprinkle with parsley and lemon juice.

# Fried Scallops
Serves 4

12 scallops
2 eggs, beaten
4 tablespoons double cream
salt and freshly ground
    pepper

cornmeal, biscuit crumbs or
    fresh breadcrumbs
2 tablespoons butter
2 tablespoons oil
lemon wedges

Wash and trim the scallops; slice in half. Combine the eggs and cream in a bowl. Add salt and pepper, to taste. Dip the scallops in the egg mixture, then in cornmeal or crumbs, and allow to set on aluminium foil for about 5 minutes before cooking.

Melt the butter with the oil in a thick-bottomed frying pan. When the fats are hot, add the scallops and fry until golden brown.

Serve immediately with wedges of lemon.

# Basic Poached Scallops
Serves 4

8–10 scallops
300 ml/½ pint dry white wine
½ onion, chopped

1 *bouquet garni* (flat-leaf
    parsley, thyme, bay leaf)
salt and freshly ground pepper

Wash and trim the scallops; dry carefully. Place in a saucepan with the white wine and enough water barely to cover. Add the onion and *bouquet garni* and season with salt and freshly ground pepper, to taste. Bring slowly to the boil and simmer gently for 5 minutes or until tender. Drain the scallops, straining and reserving the liquor. Slice the scallops if they are large and use as directed in any of the following recipes.

## Baked Scallops Provençal
Serves 4

basic poached scallops
  (page 93)
2 tablespoons butter
2 tablespoons olive oil
1 clove garlic, finely chopped

2 tablespoons finely chopped
  flat-leaf parsley
2 tablespoons freshly grated
  breadcrumbs
salt and freshly ground pepper

Prepare the scallops as above. Heat the butter and olive oil in a heatproof baking dish until the butter sizzles. Slice the scallops thickly and toss in the dish with garlic, parsley and breadcrumbs. Season to taste with salt and pepper, and bake under the grill until the scallops are golden.

## Scallops Mornay
Serves 4

basic poached scallops (page 93)
2 tablespoons butter
2 tablespoons flour
150 ml/¼ pint cream
4 tablespoons grated Gruyère

salt and freshly ground pepper
crushed dried chillies
freshly grated breadcrumbs
freshly grated Gruyère cheese
butter

Prepare the scallops as above. Melt the butter in the top of a double saucepan; stir in the flour and cook over water, stirring continuously, until the *roux* is well blended. Add the cream and enough scallop liquor (about 150 ml/¼ pint) to make a smooth, rich sauce. Stir in the Gruyère and poached sliced scallops and heat through. Season with salt and pepper and a pinch of crushed dried chillies.

Fill scallop shells or individual casseroles with this mixture. Sprinkle with breadcrumbs and more cheese; dot with butter and heat under grill for a few minutes to glaze the top.

## Scallops and Mushrooms in White Wine
Serves 4

basic poached scallops (page 93)
12 button mushrooms, sliced
4 shallots, finely chopped
2 tablespoons finely chopped
  flat-leaf parsley
4 tablespoons butter

2 tablespoons flour
salt and freshly ground pepper
pinch of crushed dried chillies
4 tablespoons double cream
freshly grated breadcrumbs
butter

Prepare the scallops as above. Sauté the mushrooms, shallots and parsley in the butter until golden. Blend in the flour and add the reserved liquor very slowly, stirring constantly. Season with salt, pepper and dried chillies to taste. Stir in the cream and combine the scallops with the sauce in a baking dish. Sprinkle with breadcrumbs, dot with butter and brown under the grill.

# Scallops au Gratin
Serves 4

**8–10 scallops**
**300 ml/½ pint dry white wine**
**2 tablespoons finely chopped**
**shallots**
**4 tablespoons double cream**
**salt and freshly ground pepper**
**2 teaspoons butter**

**2 teaspoons flour**
**2 tablespoons *sauce hollandaise***
**(page 39), or 1 egg yolk**
**4 button mushrooms, sliced and**
**simmered in water with a**
**little lemon juice**

Wash the scallops well in cold water. Separate the coral and remove any membranes still attached. Combine the scallops and coral in a saucepan with the white wine, shallots, cream, and salt and pepper, to taste. Cove ther pan and simmer for 5 minutes.

Remove the meats; add a *beurre manié*, made by combining the butter and flour until smooth, and simmer the sauce until it is well blended and reduced a little. To finish the sauce, stir in 2 tablespoons *sauce hollandaise*, or if this is not available, egg yolk.

Fill scallop shells or individual casseroles with the sliced scallops and coral; add a few slices of simmered mushroom. Pour the sauce over and brown under the grill. Serve immediately.

# Coupe 'Caprice'
Serves 4

**1 small melon**
**225 g/½ pound small cooked,**
**shelled prawns**
**300 ml/½ pint well-flavoured**
**mayonnaise**
**1–2 tablespoons tomato ketchup**
**4 tablespoons double cream**
**2 tablespoons finely chopped**

**green pepper**
**2 tablespoons finely chopped red**
**pepper**
**salt and freshly ground pepper**
**dash of Tabasco**
**1 tablespoon finely chopped**
**fresh tarragon**

Chill the melon and prawns. Combine the mayonnaise, ketchup and cream; stir in the peppers and season to taste with salt and pepper and a dash of Tabasco. Chill. Peel, seed and dice the melon and combine with the prawns and sauce. Spoon into individual salad bowls. Sprinkle with tarragon and serve immediately.

## Chinese Steamed Prawns
Serves 4

700 g/1½ pounds large fresh
  shelled tiger prawns
cornflour
4 shallots, finely chopped
100 g/4 ounces mushrooms,
  finely sliced
50 g/2 ounces cucumber, finely
  sliced

2–4 tablespoons soy sauce
4 tablespoons dry white wine
freshly ground pepper
cooked rice, to serve
tomatoes

Roll the prawns in cornflour and place on a platter in a steamer with the shallots, mushrooms, cucumber, soy sauce and white wine. Season with a little pepper, and cook over 5 cm/2 inches of fast-boiling water, covered so that the platter is entirely confined in steam, until tender.

Serve hot from the steamer on a bed of rice, garnished with fresh tomatoes.

Chapter 7

# Beef

## The Roast Beef of England

When Erasmus described, more than four hundred years ago, the things upon which various nations of the world prided themselves – the Scots their nobility and logical sense, the French their breeding – he said of the English that they 'particularly challenge to themselves Beauty, Music and Feasting'. The excellence of English food had been a byword for centuries before Erasmus wrote, perhaps because the penalties for slapdash cooking were so severe, for Edward I once ordered all the cooks of the inns on the road between London and York to be executed because their dishes were not to his taste.

But even as early as the seventeenth century the English were looking back nostalgically to the good old days when 'poor boyes did turn the spitts and lick't the dripping-pan, and grew to be huge lusty knaves'. The meat they were roasting, the meat of meats for the English, was Beef. The roast was brought to the table on a spit, a servant holding it while the guest cut off a piece, which was eaten with the fingers and often without a plate. Indeed, medieval directions for setting a table often referred to 'trencher pieces' of bread on which guests could lay down their portion of meat.

Nothing can compare with roast beef, charred on the outside, moistly tender within, served with King Edward potatoes baked in their jackets and a melting Yorkshire pudding, happy recipient of the noble juices of the roast.

Accompany this perfection with freshly grated horseradish beaten into whipped cream – a modern touch to an ancient recipe – and a green vegetable: topped and tailed green beans, a purée of green peas or new-born Brussels sprouts swathed in delicately browned, buttered breadcrumbs.

Beef contains the highest form of protein for human consumption in the most palatable, stimulating and digestible form. Its juiciness is due to the presence of a certain proportion of fat both outside and inside the meat. It is the slow melting of this inside fat – the 'marbling', and its penetration into every cell of the roast – that is responsible for its savouriness.

### Five Tips for Roasting Beef

1. Only tender pieces of beef make good roasts.

2. A sirloin or rib roast, like all large pieces of meat, should stand for an hour or two at room temperature before roasting. So, if your beef has been stored in the refrigerator, be sure to take it out at least two hours before roasting.

3. Do not salt beef before putting it in the oven; the salt forms a crust which prevents the meat from colouring uniformly. I like to prepare mine by rubbing it generously with fresh dripping or butter and then dusting it lightly with a mixture of dry mustard, freshly ground pepper and a little browned flour, before leaving it to absorb these flavours for an hour or two at room temperature.

4. Remember to heat the serving dish and, especially, the sauceboat.

5. Do not put sliced beef to warm in the oven; it will dry out and become grey in colour.

## Roast Beef
Serves 8 to 10

1 sirloin or rib roast of beef (2.5–3.5 kg/5–8 pounds)
4–6 tablespoons dripping or butter
1 tablespoon dry mustard
freshly ground pepper

2 tablespoons lightly browned flour
1 flattened piece beef suet, to cover
4–6 tablespoons water or red wine
salt

Spread the beef with the dripping or butter and sprinkle with a mixture of dry mustard, pepper and flour which you have lightly browned in a frying pan or in the oven. Tie a flattened layer of beef suet over the top

When ready to roast, place the meat on a rack over a roasting pan and brown in a preheated, fairly hot oven (425°F/220°C/gas 7) for 15 minutes. Reduce the oven to 170°C/325°F/gas 3; add the warmed red wine or water to the pan and continue to roast, basting frequently, allowing 15 to 18 minutes per 450 g/pound if you like your beef rare, 20 to 24 minutes per 450 g/pound for medium, and 25 to 30 minutes per 450 g/pound if you prefer it well done.

When the meat is cooked to your liking, season to taste with salt and additional pepper; remove to a warm serving platter and let it stand for 15 to 20 minutes at the edge of the open oven before carving. During this time the beef sets, the cooking subsides and the roast is ready for carving. In the meantime, pour off the fat in the roasting pan and use the pink juices that pour from the roast as it sets; stir all the crusty bits into it to make a clear sauce. I sometimes add a little wine, a knob or two of butter and a dash of Worcestershire sauce. Bring to the boil, reduce the heat and simmer for 1 or 2 minutes. Strain and serve in a sauceboat with the roast.

# Sliced Beef in Aspic

Serves 4

8 slices rare roast beef
2–3 sprigs thyme, leaves only
2 tablespoons finely chopped
    basil leaves
salt and freshly ground pepper
carrot slices, cooked
tiny white onions, boiled

leaves of chervil, tarragon or
    flat-leaf parsley
600 ml/1 pint Madeira aspic
    (page 25)
1 teaspoon Worcestershire
    sauce
cayenne pepper

Arrange overlapping slices of cold rare beef in a shallow serving dish. Sprinkle with the thyme, basil, salt and pepper. Garnish with rows of carrot slices and tiny white onions; decorate with leaves of chervil, tarragon or parsley.

Heat the Madeira aspic; add the Worcestershire sauce and a few grains of cayenne pepper; cool until the aspic is syrupy. Pour the aspic over the beef slices and chill in the refrigerator for at least 2 hours, or until the aspic has set.

# Summer Beef Salad

Makes an *hors-d'œuvre* salad for 4

450 g/1 pound cold roast beef
2 eating apples
2 stalks celery
4 shallots, finely chopped
1 small clove garlic, finely
    chopped

4 tablespoons finely chopped
    flat-leaf parsley
6–8 tablespoons olive oil
2–3 tablespoons wine vinegar
salt and freshly ground pepper

Trim and dice the roast beef. Peel, core and dice the apples. Clean and dice the celery. Combine the beef, apples and celery with the shallots, garlic and parsley in a salad bowl. Season to taste with olive oil, vinegar, salt and pepper, and chill.

# Grilled Steak

Serves 4

1 rump steak (about 4 cm/
    1½ inches thick)
freshly ground pepper

2–4 tablespoons softened butter
sea salt

Remove the steak from the refrigerator at least 30 minutes before cooking and slit the fat in several places around the side to prevent the meat from curling during cooking. Preheat the grill for 15 to 20 minutes. Sprinkle both sides of steak the with pepper and spread with butter.

Rub the hot grid with a piece of suet, place the steak on grid and grill for 8 minutes on each side for a rare steak; grill a few more minutes if you prefer steak to be medium rare. Sprinkle with salt to taste.

## Steak à la Bordelaise
Serves 4

Grill the steak as on page 99.

Finely chop ½ Spanish onion and 2 shallots; add 2 tablespoons finely chopped flat-leaf parsley and sauté the mixture in 2 tablespoons olive oil until the onion is transparent. Stir in 1 tablespoon flour; add 150 ml/¼ pint red wine and cook over a high heat, stirring continuously, until the wine bubbles. Then lower the heat and simmer, stirring continuously, until the sauce thickens a little. Poach some thinly sliced beef marrow for 1 minute in hot water; slice thinly or cut into dice and add to the sauce. Pour the sauce over the steak. Sprinkle with sea salt and a little freshly ground pepper and serve immediately.

## Steak alla Pizzaiola
Serves 4

Grill the steak as on page 99 and serve with *pizzaiola* sauce.

Sauté 1 thinly sliced garlic clove in 2 tablespoons olive oil until transparent. Add 1 medium can Italian peeled tomatoes and salt and freshly ground pepper, to taste, and cook over a high heat for 15 minutes. Stir in 2 tablespoons finely chopped flat-leaf parsley and the finely chopped leaves of 2 sprigs of marjoram, and pour the sauce over the steak. Serve immediately.

## Beefsteak au Roquefort
Serves 4

| | |
|---|---|
| 1 fine rump steak (5 cm/2 inches thick) or 4 sirloin steaks | 50 g/2 ounces butter |
| 2 tablespoons melted butter | juice of ½ lemon |
| salt and freshly ground pepper | 2 tablespoons finely chopped flat-leaf parsley, chervil or |
| 25 g/1 ounce Roquefort cheese | chives |

Trim excess fat from the steak. Brush with melted butter and place on a very hot grill. Grill until cooked to your liking. Add salt and freshly ground black pepper, to taste.

While the steak is grilling, cream the Roquefort and butter with the lemon juice, herbs and a little salt and pepper. Serve steak immediately, topped with the Roquefort butter.

## Beefsteak à la Mirabeau
Serves 4

| | |
|---|---|
| 2 tablespoons butter | anchovy fillets, cut in half lengthwise |
| 1 tablespoon flour | |
| 1–2 teaspoons anchovy paste | sliced stuffed olives |
| 4 sirloin steaks | olive oil |
| freshly ground pepper | melted butter |

Mash the butter and flour to a smooth paste; add the anchovy paste and blend well. Spread the anchovy mixture over the steaks; season to taste with freshly ground pepper and grill on one side in the usual manner. Remove the steak from the grill pan, turn it over and make a lattice-work of anchovy fillets on the uncooked side. Fill each square with a slice of olive; brush with olive oil or melted butter and grill until done. Serve with melted butter.

## Steak au Poivre
Serves 4

| | |
|---|---|
| **2–3 tablespoons black peppercorns** | **sea salt** |
| **1 kg/2 pounds rump steak** | **parsley or garlic butter** |
| | **sprigs of watercress** |

Crush the peppercorns coarsely with a rolling pin or with a mortar and pestle. Sprinkle one side of the steak with half the pepper, pressing it into the meat with the flat of your hand. Repeat with other side. Let the steak stand at room temperature for at least 30 minutes to absorb flavours.

Preheat the grill. Cook the steak 7 to 10 cm/3 to 4 inches from the grill until brown; turn and cook the other side for 5 more minutes for a very rare steak. Grill slightly longer for medium rare.

Transfer the steak to a hot serving dish; sprinkle with salt to taste and dot with parsley or garlic butter. Garnish with sprigs of watercress.

## Tournedos
Serves 4

| | |
|---|---|
| **4 *tournedos*** | **4 rounds of bread** |
| **freshly ground pepper** | **butter** |
| **2 tablespoons butter** | **lemon juice** |
| **2 tablespoons olive oil** | **sea salt** |

Ask your butcher to prepare 4 *tournedos* for you – slices cut from the fillet, usually encased in a thin layer of fat. Season with pepper, to taste, and sauté in the butter and olive oil until well browned (2 to 3 minutes on each side) but still pink and moist in the centre. Remove from the pan and keep warm. Sauté the bread in the butter; sprinkle lightly with lemon juice; place a *tournedos* on each slice; season to taste with salt and serve with one of the following garnishes or sauces.

## Tournedos à la Béarnaise
Serves 4

Cook as above and spoon 2 tablespoons béarnaise sauce (on page 38) on each *tournedos*.

## Tournedos Beauharnais
Serves 4

Cook as above and set a small cooked artichoke heart filled with béarnaise sauce (page 38) on each *tournedos*. Sprinkle with finely chopped flat-leaf parsley and tarragon. Pour Madeira sauce (page 37) around the *tournedos*.

## Tournedos Rossini
Serves 4

Cook as above, but place a slice of *pâte de foie gras* on each fried *croûton* before topping with the *tournedos*. Pour Madeira sauce (page 37) around the *tournedos*.

## Bœuf Stroganoff
Serves 4 to 6

**1 kg/2 pounds rump or fillet of beef**
**freshly ground pepper**
**2 tablespoons finely chopped onion**
**4 tablespoons butter**

**225 g/½ pound button mushroom caps, sliced**
**sea salt, freshly grated nutmeg and mace**
**300 ml/½ pint sour cream**

Cut the steak across the grain into slices 1 cm/½ inch thick. Season to taste with pepper and flatten each slice with a wooden mallet.

Sauté the onion in half the butter until it just begins to turn colour; add the sliced beef and sauté for about 5 minutes, turning the pieces so that all the sides are browned. Remove from the pan and keep warm.

Add the remaining butter to pan and sauté the mushroom caps. Return the beef to the pan. Season to taste with salt, nutmeg and mace; add the sour cream and heat through.

## Carbonade de Bœuf
Serves 4

**2 tablespoons olive oil**
**1 kg/2 pounds raw beef steak, cut into 4 thin slices**
**salt and freshly ground pepper**

**2 tablespoons butter**
**4 large onions, thinly sliced**
**1 tablespoon flour**
**1 bottle Guinness**

Heat the olive oil in a thick-bottomed frying pan. Season the beef slices to taste with salt and pepper and brown on both sides. Place the meat in overlapping layers in a small ovenproof casserole.

Add the butter to the frying pan and brown the onions. Sprinkle with the flour and add to the meat in the casserole. Add Guinness to cover; place the lid on the casserole and cook over a low heat for about 2 hours, or until the beef is tender. Correct the seasoning.

Serve with a potato purée or *spätzle* (thick egg noodles).

# Fillet of Beef 'en Chemise'
Serves 6

1 fillet of beef (approximately
  1.2 kg/2½ pounds), prepared
  by your butcher
brandy
100 g/¼ pound mushrooms,
  finely chopped
½ Spanish onion, finely
  chopped

2 tablespoons butter
4 tablespoons *pâté de foie gras*
4 tablespoons softened butter
salt and freshly ground
  pepper
puff pastry
1 egg yolk, slightly beaten

Brush the fillet with brandy; trim it neatly, removing the ends, and let it stand at room temperature for at least 30 minutes. Sauté the mushrooms and onion in the butter until soft.

Roast the fillet in a moderate oven (190°C/375°F/gas 5) for 15 to 20 minutes, or until half cooked. Allow the fillet to cool slightly; remove skewers, cords and fat; spread with a mixture of *foie gras* and softened butter, seasoned to taste with salt and pepper. Spread thinly with the mushroom and onion mixture.

Roll out the puff pastry into a thin sheet and wrap the fillet in it, securing it neatly. Place on a baking tin; brush with cold water and bake in a hot oven (230°C/450°F/gas 8) for 12 to 15 minutes. Brush the pastry with slightly beaten egg yolk and continue baking until the crust is browned.

# Fillet of Beef 'en Cochonailles'
Serves 6

1 fillet of beef (approximately
  1.2 kg/2½ pounds), prepared
  by your butcher
brandy
11 slices cooked ham or boiled
  bacon
225 g/½ pound mushrooms,
  finely chopped

1 Spanish onion, finely chopped
salt and freshly ground pepper
4–6 tablespoons butter
softened butter
puff pastry
1 egg yolk, slightly beaten
béarnaise sauce (page 38)

Brush the fillet of beef with brandy; trim it neatly, removing the ends, and slice it into 12 equal parts without completely separating the slices. Place a thin slice of cooked ham or boiled bacon, cut to fit the fillet, between each slice and spread with some of the mushrooms and onions, which you have seasoned with salt and pepper and sautéed until soft in the butter.

Re-form the fillet; fasten with metal skewers and roast it in a moderate oven (190°C/375°F/gas 5) for 15 to 20 minutes, or until half cooked.

Allow the fillet to cool slightly; remove the skewers, cords and fat; spread with softened butter; season to taste with salt and pepper and spread thinly with the remaining mushroom and onion mixture.

Roll out the puff pastry into a thin sheet and wrap the fillet in it, securing it neatly. Place on a baking tin; brush with cold water and bake in a hot oven (230°C/450°F/gas 8) for 12 to 15 minutes. Brush the pastry with slightly beaten egg yolk and continue baking until the crust is browned. Serve with béarnaise sauce.

## Beef Steak and Kidney Pie
Serves 4 to 6

350 g/¾ pound calf's kidney
2 tablespoons flour
1 teaspoon salt
½ teaspoon freshly ground
  pepper
1 kg/2 pounds thick beef steak,
  cut into large bite-size pieces
4 tablespoons butter, or suet in
  equal quantity
4 shallots, finely chopped
300 ml/½ pint rich beef stock

¼ teaspoon freshly ground
  pepper
1 bay leaf
1–3 teaspoons chopped flat-leaf
  parsley
pinch each powdered clove,
  marjoram
flaky pastry, to cover
1–2 tablespoons dry sherry
1 teaspoon Worcestershire sauce

Clean the kidney, split it, remove the fat and large tubes and soak in salted water for 1 hour. Dry and cut into 6-mm/¼-inch slices. Mix the flour, salt and pepper together, and roll the beef and kidney in this mixture.

Melt the butter or suet in a thick-bottomed saucepan or iron casserole and sauté the shallots until golden. When the shallots have taken on a little colour, add the beef and kidneys and brown them thoroughly, stirring almost constantly. Moisten with the beef stock, add the pepper, bay leaf, parsley, clove and marjoram; stir; cover, and simmer over a low heat for 1 to 1¼ hours or until meat is tender. If the liquid is too thin, thicken with a little flour mixed to a smooth paste with water.

Grease a deep baking dish, place a pie funnel in the centre, add the meats and liquid, and allow to cool. In the meantime, make the flaky pastry crust and place over the meat, moistening and pinching the edges to the dish. Make vents in the pastry to allow steam to escape and bake in a hot oven (230°C/450°F/gas 8) for 10 minutes. Lower the heat to moderate (190°C/375°F/gas 5) and continue baking for 15 minutes, or until the pastry crust is golden brown. Just before serving the pie, insert a small funnel into the centre vent and pour in a mixture of dry sherry and Worcestershire sauce.

## Steak and Kidney Pudding
Serves 4 to 6

700 g–1 kg/1½–2 pounds steak,
  cut into small pieces
225 g/½ pound calf's kidney
2 tablespoons flour

½ teaspoon freshly ground
  pepper
½ teaspoon salt

175 g/6 ounces freshly grated or
  packaged suet
350 g/¾ pound self-raising flour
salt and freshly ground
  pepper
dripping

4 tablespoons finely chopped
  shallot or onion
150 ml/¼ pint rich beef stock
150 ml/¼ pint port wine
2 teaspoons soy sauce
grated rind of ½ lemon

Cut the steak and kidney into rather small pieces and shake well in a bowl containing the flour, pepper and salt, until all the pieces are well coated.

Combine the finely chopped suet with the flour, adding pepper and salt to taste, to make a light suet crust.

Grease a basin with dripping, line it with the crust, put in the seasoned meat and the shallot or onion. Combine the stock, port wine, soy sauce and lemon rind, and fill up the basin with this mixture to near the top; put on the pastry lid, making sure that the edges are well sealed to keep in the steam. Cover the whole pudding with a floured cloth and simmer or steam for 3 to 4 hours. The crust should be rather damp.

## Beef Olives
Serves 4 to 6

100 g/4 ounces fresh breadcrumbs
50 g/2 ounces freshly grated suet
4 tablespoons finely chopped
  flat-leaf parsley
1 teaspoon dried marjoram,
  thyme or winter savory
½ teaspoon grated lemon rind
2 eggs
grated nutmeg
salt and freshly ground pepper
water or white wine, to mix

1 kg/2 pounds top side of beef
  cut into about 12 thin slices
  (approximately 7.5 by 10 cm/
  3 by 4 inches)
1 Spanish onion, finely chopped
100 g/¼ pound mushrooms,
  finely chopped
4 tablespoons butter or olive oil
425 ml/¾ pint beef stock
1 tablespoon flour
1 tablespoon butter

To prepare the forcemeat stuffing: mix the breadcrumbs, suet, parsley, dried herbs, lemon rind and eggs. Season generously with grated nutmeg, salt and pepper. If the mixture seems too dry, add a little water or dry white wine.

Beat the slices of beef well with a rolling pin to flatten and tenderise them. Spread forcemeat mixture on each piece of meat; roll up and secure with very fine string.

Sauté the onion and mushrooms in the butter or olive oil in a flameproof casserole until the onion is transparent. Add the beef olives and brown on all sides. Pour the stock over; cover and simmer until tender, 1½ to 2 hours.

Just before serving, remove the strings and thicken the gravy by stirring in knobs of butter mixed to a smooth paste with flour. Correct the seasoning and serve immediately.

# Bœuf à la Bourguignonne

If one gave stars to the regions of France – as well as to their better restaurants – for the excellence of their cooking, Burgundy would have an unchallenged 'three'. The high quality of its native beef and poultry, allied to the fame of its vintages, makes this one of the most distinctive – if one of the richest – cuisines of France.

Most Burgundian dishes are of the long, slow-cooking variety – superb casseroles of meat, fish and game – guaranteed to make even the least expensive cuts of meat taste delicious. Indeed, food and wine are so closely linked together in Burgundy that it is a toss-up whether it is the famous vintages of the region or *bœuf à la bourguignonne* that has brought Burgundy the greater international fame. For *bœuf à la bourguignonne* – or *bœuf bourguignon* as it is sometimes more simply called – is one of the truly great dishes of the world. Combining tender nuggets of beef bathed in a rich wine-flavoured sauce with crisp *lardons* of green bacon or fat salt pork, tiny white onions parboiled to *al dente* tenderness, and button mushrooms sautéed in butter and lemon juice, this dish is as delicious to eat as it is easy to prepare.

Like many wine-based dishes, *bœuf à la bourguignonne* is better when reheated and served on the following day. Make this world-famous casserole one of your regular party dishes, preceded by a hot clear soup or a cold or hot *hors-d'œuvre* and followed by a crisp green salad, cheese or fruit. Nothing could be simpler or more delicious.

## Bœuf à la Bourguignonne
Serves 4 to 6

**1.3 kg/3 pounds top side or top rump of beef**
**flour**
**4 tablespoons olive oil**
**4 tablespoons butter**
**100 g/¼ pound salt pork, diced**
**salt and freshly ground pepper**
**4 tablespoons cognac, warmed**
**2 carrots, coarsely chopped**
**1 leek, coarsely chopped**
**4 shallots, coarsely chopped**
**1 Spanish onion, coarsely chopped**
**1 clove garlic, coarsely chopped**

**1 calf's foot, split (optional)**
**1 *bouquet garni* (1 sprig thyme, 1 bay leaf, 1 stalk celery, 2 sprigs flat-leaf parsley)**
**½ bottle good red burgundy**
**beef stock or water, to cover**
**1 tablespoon flour**
**1 tablespoon butter**
**18 tiny white onions**
**12 button mushrooms**
**sugar**
**lemon juice**
**chopped flat-leaf parsley**

Cut the beef into large cubes; remove the fat and roll the cubes in flour. Heat 2 tablespoons of the olive oil and 2 tablespoons of the butter in a large frying pan and sauté the salt pork until crisp and brown. Remove the pork from the pan and transfer to a large earthenware casserole. Brown the beef well on all sides in the remaining fat, season to taste with salt and pepper and moisten with warmed cognac. Ignite the cognac; let the flame burn away and add the meat to the casserole.

Cook the carrots, leek, shallots, onion and garlic in the fat remaining in the frying pan, stirring occasionally, until lightly browned, adding a little more butter and olive oil, if necessary.

Transfer the vegetables to the casserole with the meat; add the calf's foot and *bouquet garni*. Pour over all but 4 tablespoons of the wine, and just enough hot water or good beef stock to cover the contents of the casserole. Cover and cook in a very slow oven (140°C/275°F/gas 1) for 1½ to 2 hours.

Remove the fat from the sauce; stir in, bit by bit, 1 tablespoon butter worked with 1 tablespoon flour; cover; continue to cook gently in the oven for about 2 hours or longer.

Brown the onions in 1 tablespoon butter in a saucepan with a little sugar. Add 4 tablespoons red wine, cover and cook over low heat until the onions are almost tender. Keep warm. Sauté the mushroom caps in the remaining oil and butter and a little lemon juice. Keep warm.

When the meat is tender, remove the calf's foot and *bouquet garni;* correct seasoning; add onions and mushroom caps and sprinkle lavishly with parsley.

## Bœuf à la Mode
Serves 8 to 10

| | |
|---|---|
| 1 boned joint of beef (about 1.8–2.3 kg/4–5 pounds), silverside or top rump | pinch of dried thyme |
| | 2 tablespoons lard or dripping |
| salt and freshly ground pepper | 2 tablespoons butter |
| 300 ml/½ pint red or white wine | 2 tablespoons flour |
| 1 Spanish onion, sliced | 300 ml/½ pint beef or veal stock |
| 2 large carrots, sliced | 1 or 2 beef or veal bones |
| 1 clove garlic | 1 small can tomatoes |
| 2 stalks celery, sliced | 6 carrots |
| 2 bay leaves | 24 tiny white onions |
| 4 sprigs flat-leaf parsley | butter |
| 4 tablespoons cognac | sugar |

Have your butcher lard the beef with strips of larding pork. Season it with salt and pepper and put in a porcelain or earthenware bowl (not metal) with the red or white wine, onion, carrots, garlic, celery, bay leaves and parsley. Add the cognac and a pinch of thyme. Let the meat marinate in a cold place in this mixture for 6 hours or more, turning the meat over several times to allow it to absorb the wine.

Remove the meat from the marinade; drain and dry the piece thoroughly. Melt the lard or dripping in a heatproof casserole just large enough to hold the beef; add the meat and brown it on all sides. Pour off excess fat.

Melt the butter in a large saucepan; stir in the flour and cook the *roux*, stirring constantly, until it is browned. Gradually stir in the marinade followed by the beef or veal stock. Bring the sauce to the boil, stirring constantly, and pour it over the meat. Add the beef or veal bones and canned tomatoes.

Cover the casserole closely and braise on top of the stove or in a very slow oven (140°C/275°F/gas 1) for 2 hours.

Cut the carrots into pieces and blanch; glaze the onions in a little butter and sugar. Remove the meat from the gravy and skim off all the fat. Clean the pan and put back the meat with the glazed carrots and onions and strained gravy. Bring back to the boil; reduce the heat and simmer 1½ to 2 hours longer, or until the meat is tender. Correct the seasoning of the gravy, which should have reduced to about half the original quantity. If it has not done so, reduce by boiling it separately over a high heat until you are left with the correct quantity. Skim off any remaining fat.

Slice the meat thinly across the grain so that the larding will show. Serve the sauce separately.

## Bœuf en Daube à la Provençale
Serves 6 to 8

| | |
|---|---|
| **1.8 kg/4 pounds lean beef** | **4 tablespoons olive oil** |
| **2 onions, sliced** | **225 g/½ pound lean bacon, diced** |
| **2 carrots, sliced** | **1 Spanish onion, cut in quarters** |
| **1 *bouquet garni* (thyme, flat-leaf** | **4 cloves garlic** |
| **parsley and bay leaf)** | **1 piece orange peel** |
| **salt and freshly ground pepper** | **300 ml/½ pint hot stock or water** |
| **300 ml/½ pint red wine** | **100 g/¼ pound stoned black** |
| **4 tablespoons cognac** | **olives** |

Cut the beef in 2.5-cm/1-inch cubes and place in a large bowl or earthenware casserole with the onions and carrots, *bouquet garni*, salt, pepper, red wine and cognac, and marinate in this mixture for 5 to 6 hours, stirring occasionally.

Heat the oil in a frying pan; melt the diced bacon in it and brown the onion quarters in the fat. Drain the beef, reserving the juices of the marinade, and sauté with the bacon bits and onions until browned, shaking the pan from time to time. Add the garlic cloves and orange peel; then moisten with the marinade which has been boiled to reduce to half the original quantity. Pour over the hot stock or, failing this, hot water. Cover the pot with greaseproof paper and the lid, and cook in a very slow oven (140°C/275°F/gas 1) for up to 4 hours. Remove from the oven; skim the fat from the surface; add the stoned olives and correct the seasoning. Cook for another 30 minutes. Serve in the casserole.

## Estouffade de Bœuf
Serves 6

| | |
|---|---|
| **225 g/½ pound lean bacon** | **1 bottle red wine** |
| **2 tablespoons butter** | **well-flavoured beef stock, to** |
| **2 tablespoons olive oil** | **cover** |
| **1.3 kg/3 pounds lean beef** | **2 cloves garlic, crushed** |
| **2 tablespoons flour** | **1 *bouquet garni* (thyme, bay leaf,** |
| **6 medium-sized onions,** | **flat-leaf parsley and celery)** |
| **quartered** | **225 g/½ pound mushrooms, sliced** |
| **salt and freshly ground pepper** | **butter** |

Dice the bacon, blanch in boiling water and sauté in butter and olive oil until golden. Remove from the pan. Cut the lean beef into good-sized chunks; sprinkle with flour and brown in the same amalgamation of fats. Add the quartered onions to the meat chunks and cook, stirring constantly, until well browned. Season with salt and pepper. Add the red wine and beef stock to cover, garlic and a *bouquet garni*. Bring to the boil; cover and cook in a very slow oven (140°C/275°F/gas 1) for 2½ to 3 hours.

Drain the *ragoût* in a fine sieve placed over a terrine. Place the beef chunks and bacon cubes in a clean casserole. Sauté the mushrooms in a little butter and add to the meat. Skim the fat from the sauce; reduce over a high heat to the desired consistency and strain it over the meat and garniture. Simmer gently, covered, for 30 minutes or until tender, and serve in the casserole.

## Oxtail Ragoût
Serves 4 to 6

| | |
|---|---|
| 1 medium-sized oxtail | 1 generous *bouquet garni* |
| flour | 2 fat cloves garlic |
| salt and freshly ground pepper | 8 carrots |
| 2 tablespoons butter | 425 ml/¾ pint tomato juice |
| 2 tablespoons olive oil | 425 ml/¾ pint beef stock |
| 100 g/¼ pound fat bacon, diced | 4 turnips |
| 2 Spanish onions, stuck with | 4 leeks |
| cloves | 4 stalks celery |

Get your butcher to cut the oxtail into serving pieces. Soak in cold water for 3 to 4 hours. Put in fresh water and bring to the boil, skimming regularly. Drain, and dry with a clean cloth.

Put some flour, seasoned with salt and pepper, into a large paper bag; add the blanched oxtail pieces and shake well to coat evenly. Heat the butter and olive oil in a large flameproof casserole; add the bacon pieces and sauté until golden. Remove the bacon and brown the oxtail sections in the resulting fat. Then return the bacon; add the onions stuck with cloves, *bouquet garni*, garlic, 4 of the carrots, thickly sliced, and salt and pepper to taste. Combine the tomato juice and beef stock; add to the meat and vegetables and bring slowly to the boil. Cover the casserole; transfer to a very slow oven (140°C/275°F/gas 1) and cook gently for 3 to 4 hours. Cool and skim off the fat.

Forty-five minutes before serving: scrape the remaining carrots and cut them in half lengthwise; scrape and quarter the turnips; clean the leeks and celery carefully. Add the vegetables to the *ragoût* and continue cooking gently until tender.

# Italian Beef Stew
Serves 4 to 6

1 tablespoon lard
1 tablespoon olive oil
225 g/½ pound fat salt pork, diced
1 onion, sliced
2 cloves garlic, chopped
1.2 kg/2½ pounds lean beef, cut
  into bite-sized pieces

salt and freshly ground pepper
1 generous pinch dried
  marjoram
150 ml/¼ pint dry red wine
4 tablespoons tomato purée,
  diluted in water

Combine the lard and olive oil in a thick-bottomed pan or flameproof casse-role; when the fat begins to bubble, add the salt pork, onion and garlic and sauté until golden. Add the pieces of meat seasoned with salt, pepper and marjoram, and cook, stirring frequently, until the meat is well browned on all sides. Now add the dry red wine (one of the rougher Italian ones) and continue cooking until the wine has been reduced to half the original quantity. Add the diluted tomato purée and enough boiling water to cover the meat. Cover the pan and simmer slowly for about 2 hours, or until the meat is tender and the savoury sauce is thick and richly coloured. A tablespoon or two of red wine just before serving will add extra *bouquet* to this dish, which should be served directly from the casserole.

# Sauerbraten
Serves 4 to 6

1.8 kg/4 pounds top round of
  beef
425 ml/¾ pint dry red wine
150 ml/¼ pint wine vinegar
1 teaspoon salt
1 teaspoon crushed black
  peppercorns
2 large onions, sliced
2 large carrots, sliced
2 stalks celery, chopped

½ lemon, sliced
2 bay leaves
4 sprigs flat-leaf parsley
4 allspice berries
4 cloves
6 tablespoons butter
4 tablespoons flour
1 tablespoon brown sugar
dumplings or buttered noodles,
  to serve

Get your butcher to roll the meat and tie it into a round. Wipe with a damp cloth and place in a deep bowl. Make a marinade by combining the wine and wine vinegar with the salt, peppercorns, onions, carrots, celery, lemon, bay leaves, parsley, allspice and cloves. Bring to the boil and pour over the meat; cover and place in the refrigerator for 3 days, turning it once a day.

Remove the meat from the marinade and wipe dry. Heat the marinade. Meanwhile, melt 4 tablespoons of the butter in a deep pot and sear the meat; sprinkle with 2 tablespoons flour and brown on all sides. Pour the hot marinade over it and cover tightly; lower the heat and simmer gently for 2½ to 3 hours, or until the meat is tender. Pour the liquid off the meat to cool, and set the pot with meat aside. Skim the fat from the liquid; strain it. Melt the remaining butter in a saucepan and blend in the remaining flour and the sugar; cook slowly until slightly browned. Gradually add the strained marinade and continue cooking, stirring constantly, until thick and smooth. Pour the sauce over the meat, cover, and simmer for 30 minutes. Serve with dumplings or buttered noodles.

## Grilled Beefburgers
Serves 4

1 kg/2 pounds chopped fresh lean beef

4 tablespoons chopped beef marrow

4 tablespoons thick cream or cold water

4 tablespoons finely chopped onion

salt and freshly ground pepper

2 tablespoons melted butter

Combine the first four ingredients; add salt and pepper to taste and form into 8 patties. Brush the patties with melted butter and grill for 4 to 5 minutes on each side.

# The American Meat Loaf

Among the great dishes of the world, many American specialities take pride of place – New England boiled dinner, clam chowder and Boston baked beans, Southern fried chicken, New Orleans prawn and chicken gumbo, Caesar salad, San Francisco's 'cioppino', Philadelphia's 'pepper pot', lobster Newburg and oysters Rockefeller – to name just a few. But none has captured the heart of the American people so completely as the all-American meat loaf . . . an easy-to-cook, easy-to-serve Sunday night supper that is famous the length and breadth of the land.

Try this interesting meat loaf pâté – a sort of oven-baked hamburger – the next time you want an informal supper dish for the family. It will become a fast favourite, I know.

Shape your meat loaf into a loaf or round to bake on a flat baking tray, or press it into a loaf tin or ring mould and cook in the same fashion.

Ring the changes on the basic recipe. Cut ingredients by half for a 'young family' loaf. Use just beef, or pork and veal, or just veal in the basic recipe. Make a loaf of corned beef or a combination of calf's liver and sausage meat. Try poached chicken, finely ground and blended with a spicy, curry-flavoured béchamel sauce before baking.

Change the flavours at will. Almost anything goes in the world of the American meat loaf. Try dry mustard, Worcestershire sauce and finely chopped savory for a different flavour accent. Give your meat loaf body and softness with fresh breadcrumbs, diced white bread and even cornflakes. For a chunky texture, stir in finely chopped green pepper, celery, crisp bacon or water chestnuts. Onions, garlic, herbs and spices lend flavour. Red wine, dry white wine, brandy, lemon juice, tomato, chilli and Worcestershire sauces give dash and accent. Eggs are used to bind the mixture together.

Serve with tomato sauce, chilli sauce, chilled sour cream, hot curry sauce or red wine sauce *à la bordelaise*.

## American Meat Loaf
Serves 6

6 tablespoons finely chopped onion
6 tablespoons finely chopped celery
2 cloves garlic, finely chopped
2 tablespoons olive oil
2 tablespoons butter
150 ml/¼ pint red wine, plus extra for basting
2–4 slices white bread
450 g/1 pound finely minced beef

225 g/½ pound finely minced veal
225 g/½ pound finely minced pork
100 g/¼ pound beef or pork fat, finely minced
1 teaspoon salt
½ teaspoon freshly ground pepper
ground allspice
½ teaspoon dried thyme
2 bay leaves, crushed
2 eggs, well beaten

Sauté the onion, celery and garlic in the olive oil and butter until transparent. Add the red wine and simmer gently for 5 minutes.

Trim the crusts from the bread; dice; add to the wine mixture and pour the mixture over the minced meats and fat. Mix well and season generously with salt, pepper, allspice, thyme and bay leaves.

Stir in the beaten eggs and put in a well-greased baking dish, or pat into a loaf shape on a greased baking tin or oiled board, and bake in a slow oven (170°C/325°F/gas 3). Baste from time to time with a few tablespoons of heated wine. Cooking time: a minimum of 1 hour. Serve with tomato or chilli sauce.

## Shepherd's Pie
Serves 6

1 Spanish onion, finely chopped
2 tablespoons olive oil
450 g/1 pound cooked roast beef, minced
300 ml/½ pint rich beef gravy or *sauce espagnole* (page 36)
2 teaspoons Worcestershire sauce

1 tablespoon finely chopped flat-leaf parsley
¼ teaspoon mixed dried herbs
salt and freshly ground pepper
6 tablespoons double cream
3 tablespoons melted butter
1 egg, lightly beaten
hot mashed potatoes

Sauté the onion in the olive oil until transparent and soft; add the minced cooked beef, gravy (or *sauce espagnole*), Worcestershire sauce, parsley, mixed herbs and salt and pepper, to taste. Keep warm.

Add the cream, 2 tablespoons melted butter and the beaten egg to the hot mashed potatoes and season to taste with salt and pepper.

Place the meat mixture in the bottom of a deep, well-buttered, ovenproof baking dish. Top with the mashed potatoes; brush with the remaining melted butter and bake for 15 to 20 minutes in a moderately hot oven (200°C/400°F/gas 6) or until the potatoes are golden brown.

# New England Boiled Dinner

New England, the group of Eastern states that formed the Federal Union – with New York, Pennsylvania and Virginia – in the days when the American flag had only thirteen stars, has given us many great dishes.

The Irish cooks of the great New England first families whose fortunes came from the four-masted sailing ships which plied the seven seas prided themselves on their plain, good, substantial and nourishing fare. And this love of hearty food, with no frills or furbelows, has come down to us to this very day.

I like New England clam chowder made with native clams (quahaugs) so fresh that the salty tang of the sea is still with them, combined with crisp bits of bacon, potatoes and onions simmered to pale gold, and bathed in a rich soup of milk, cream and butter; Saturday night suppers of Boston baked beans, cooked with tender salt pork and a touch of dry mustard, sweet with dark molasses and brown sugar, sometimes laced with Jamaican rum. This unctuous dish, Puritan cousin of the French *cassoulet*, is at its succulent best when served with its traditional partner, steamed Boston brown bread, rich and moist.

I like Sunday breakfasts of deep-fried codfish cakes; grilled Maine lobsters with drawn butter; the fabulous outdoor feast that is the New England clam bake – a misnomer really, for clams make up only one item of this outdoor dinner and 'bake' is a relative term, for the clams and their companions – corn on the cob, lobsters, sausages, frankfurters and sweet and white potatoes – are actually pit-steamed between layers of fresh seaweed, heated on a base of white-hot stones.

But best of all, in my estimation, is the New England boiled dinner. There is no misnomer here, for this is indeed a complete meal, a transatlantic echo of the great country dish that has found its way into the cuisine of every great nation – the hot pot of cock and beef of old England, the *pot-au-feu royale* of France, the *olla podrida* of Spain, and the *bollito misto* of Italy. The New England boiled dinner is an earthy concoction of corned brisket of beef, plump boiling fowl and fat salt pork, simmered until fork-tender with a quartered cabbage, carrots, turnips, onions and potatoes, and served with boiled beetroot, horseradish sauce and pickles.

To make this country dish, ask your butcher to 'corn' or 'salt' a brisket of beef in brine and saltpetre for seven days. Silverside prepared in this way makes for very good eating.

# New England Boiled Dinner
Serves 8

1.8–2.3 kg/4–5 pounds corned
  brisket of beef
450 g/1 pound salt pork
2 bay leaves
6 peppercorns
1 large boiling chicken
6 large carrots, scraped
6 medium onions, peeled
6 large potatoes, peeled

2 medium turnips, peeled and
  quartered
1 medium head cabbage,
  quartered
2 medium cooked beetroot,
  quartered
horseradish sauce, to serve
pickles, to serve

Wipe the corned beef with a damp cloth; tie it into shape and put into a large stockpot or heavy-bottomed saucepan. Add enough cold water to cover and bring to the boil. Drain and rinse the beef. Repeat this operation.

Cover the brisket with boiling water; add the salt pork, bay leaves and peppercorns; cover and simmer over low heat for 3 to 5 hours, or until the meat is tender, adding the chicken after first hour.

Cool slightly; skim excess fat and add the carrots, onions, potatoes and turnips. Cook for about 20 minutes, then add the cabbage wedges; cook until the vegetables are crisp and tender.

Serve the beef on a platter garnished with vegetables and with cooked beetroot. Accompany with horseradish sauce and pickles.

# Boiled Beef and Carrots
Serves 6 to 8

1.8–2.3 kg/4–5 pounds round of
  beef
24 carrots, sliced
2 turnips, coarsely chopped
2 Spanish onions, chopped
2 stalks celery, chopped
8 peppercorns
salt

2 cloves
1 *bouquet garni* (bay leaf,
  2 sprigs celery tops, 4 sprigs
  flat-leaf parsley)
onion sauce, to serve
dumplings or buttered noodles,
  to serve

Tie the beef securely and place in a casserole with the vegetables and water to cover. Bring to the boil; lower the heat so the water barely simmers; cover and simmer for 20 minutes. Skim; add the peppercorns, salt to taste, cloves and *bouquet garni*; cover and simmer gently for 3 to 4 hours or until the meat is just tender and the vegetables are soft.

To serve: remove the meat from broth; untie it and place on a heated serving dish; serve the vegetables on another dish. Accompany with onion sauce, dumplings or buttered noodles.

# Chinese Steamed Beef
Serves 4 to 6

1 kg/2 pounds rump steak
225 g/½ pound button
  mushrooms, thinly sliced
4 tablespoons coarsely chopped
  onions
2 tablespoons soy sauce

4 tablespoons light vegetable oil
1 tablespoon cornflour
2 tablespoons dry white wine
freshly ground pepper
steamed rice, to serve

Slice the rump steak thinly across the grain. Put the meat and vegetables in a shallow heatproof dish. Combine the soy sauce, oil, cornflour and white wine and pour over the meat and vegetables. Season to taste with pepper and place the dish in a steamer or on a rack in a large saucepan with about 5 cm/2 inches of rapidly boiling water.

Cover and steam for 15 minutes.

Serve hot from the steamer, accompanied by steamed rice.

# Chapter 8

# Lamb

## Middle East Kebabs

*Kebab* (*kabab* or *kabob*) means 'to grill or broil' in most of the languages in which it appears. *Shish* (Turkish and Middle Eastern) or *sikh* or *seekh* (Indian) means 'skewer'. So that any food skewered and grilled is a *shish* or *sikh kebab*. In Britain, *kebab* commonly means skewered bits of meat, or meat and vegetables, grilled over charcoal, or under a gas or electric grill.

On my first trip to Morocco, I was fascinated by the little stalls in the streets, where cooks grilled small *brochettes* of meat – tiny cubes of beef, lamb or liver – over portable charcoal braziers in the open market-places. The tantalising aroma of these grilled meats with their pungent sauces and spices made my mouth water in every city I visited. The famous *saté* of Java is a similar version of this dish. Made of beef, pork, lamb or chicken, the *saté* consists of nothing but meat, marinated in soy sauce and spices, grilled on thin skewers of bamboo.

But of all the skewered meat dishes in the world, by far the best known – and the most easily translatable in our kitchens – is Turkish *shish kebab*. I like to serve this dish with a rice pilaff or on a bed of shredded lettuce lightly dressed with oil and lemon juice, or with skewered vegetables. Or combine the two for a *shish kebab* with vegetables. Green peppers, tomatoes, poached baby onions, sliced courgettes or aubergines and button mushrooms all lend their flavours and textures to this magnificent dish.

First marinate your meat – the Turks like lamb, cut from the leg; others prefer beef. Let it remain in this mixture for at least 4 hours, or overnight. Then thread the cubed meat on long skewers alternately with the vegetables of your choice. Do not push the pieces of meat and vegetables too closely together. Grill about 10 cm/4 inches from charcoal, or gas or electricity, until the meat is medium brown, basting with marinade juices from time to time.

Nothing beats a rotating spit for *kebabs*. This method ensures even cooking and self-basting of precious juices. And if the weather is too cool for outdoor cookery, *kebabs* can be grilled indoors with ease. Electric or gas-fired grills or 'rotisserie' spits equipped with skewers approximate the outdoor fire. Or simply arrange the skewers under the grill and brown the meat, fish, vegetables or even fruits as you would a steak or chops.

When cooking on a skewer, be careful not to let the skewered meat touch the metal grill. If you do, some of the meat will stick to the hot metal. And when you attempt to turn the skewer, the meat or vegetables may stick to the grid and some pieces may fall into the fire. It is much wiser to suspend the skewers above the flames and away from the hot metal grid. When cooking outdoors, for instance,

I usually place a brick on each end of the grid and place the ends of the skewers on the bricks so that they can be turned easily.

## Turkish Lamb Kebabs
Serves 4

1 kg/2 pounds lamb, cut from leg
4 small green peppers, caps and seeds removed, cut into chunks
4 tomatoes, cut into chunks
4 small onions, poached
2 courgettes, sliced thickly
4 mushroom caps, cut into chunks
rice pilaff (page 221), to serve

*Marinade Sauce:*
6 tablespoons olive oil
4 tablespoons sherry
1–2 cloves garlic, finely chopped
¼ Spanish onion, finely chopped
2 tablespoons finely chopped flat-leaf parsley
1 level teaspoon dried oregano
salt and freshly ground pepper

Combine the marinade ingredients in a mixing bowl. Cut meat into 4-cm/1½-inch squares and place in the marinade mixture, making sure each piece of meat is properly covered. Cover the bowl with a plate and refrigerate for 12 to 24 hours. Turn the meat several times during the marinating period.

When ready to cook, place the meat on 4 large metal skewers alternately with green pepper, tomato, poached onion, courgettes and mushroom caps. Brush the meat and vegetables with the marinade sauce and cook over charcoal or under a hot grill until done, turning the skewers frequently and basting several times during cooking. Serve the kebabs with rice pilaff.

## Moroccan Skewered Lamb
Serves 4

350 g/¾ pound lamb
350 g/¾ pound lamb fat
1 leek, white part only, chopped
½ Spanish onion, chopped
1 tablespoon chopped chervil

1 teaspoon salt
1 teaspoon each of powdered cumin, ginger and paprika
¼ teaspoon crushed dried chillies
4 tablespoons olive oil

Cut the lamb and fat into equal-sized cubes about 1 cm/½ inch square and place in a large bowl. Pound the leek with the onion, chervil and salt in a mortar; add to the meat and sprinkle with the cumin, ginger, paprika, crushed dried chillies and oil. Mix well and let meat marinate in this mixture for at least 2 hours. Thread on to skewers and cook over charcoal, turning frequently until done.

# Russian Skewered Lamb

Serves 4 to 6

700 g/1½ pounds boned lamb
225 g/½ pound green bacon
  (1 piece)
225 g/½ pound raw gammon
  (1 piece)

salt and freshly ground pepper
olive oil
350 g/¾ pound rice
2 tablespoons finely chopped
  flat-leaf parsley

Cut the lamb, bacon and gammon into bite-sized pieces. Blanch the bacon and gammon; drain.

Place the lamb, bacon and gammon alternately on skewers. Season to taste with salt and pepper, brush with olive oil and cook over charcoal or under a hot grill for 10 to 15 minutes, or until done.

Cook the rice in the usual way. Serve the skewers on bed of rice. Sprinkle with parsley.

# Barbecued Lamb Provençal

Serves 6 to 8

6 cloves garlic, finely chopped
6 tablespoons finely chopped
  flat-leaf parsley
6 tablespoons fresh breadcrumbs

6 tablespoons softened butter
juice of 1 lemon
salt and freshly ground pepper
1 leg of lamb (2.3 kg/5 pounds)

Make a smooth paste of the garlic, parsley, breadcrumbs, butter and lemon juice and season to taste with salt and pepper. Wipe the lamb with a damp cloth and spread with this paste, pressing it well in so the seasonings will not fall off during the cooking. Allow the flavour to penetrate for at least 1 hour. Start the fire at least an hour before the cooking time to have a bed of ash-grey coals to cook over. Balance the lamb on the spit, inserting the spit in line with the bone so it can rotate freely and easily. Roast for 1½ to 2 hours for a leg of lamb as pink and juicy as I like it, longer if you like it less rare. Allow the meat to rest on the spit for 10 minutes to retain its juices then remove the spit.

*Note:* A leg of lamb may be roasted on a rack in a roasting pan in a moderately slow oven for 15 to 20 minutes per 450 g/pound. Provençal dressing will give the same wonderful flavour.

Moules Marinière: page 90

Stuffed Peppers: page 196

French Onion Soup (opposite): page 16

Turkish Lamb Kebabs: page 117

Coq-au-Vin (opposite): page 158

# Moussaka

Serves 4 to 6

1 Spanish onion, finely
chopped
1–2 cloves garlic, finely
chopped
4 tablespoons olive oil
450 g/1 pound cooked lamb,
diced, chopped finely or
minced
225 g/½ pound mushrooms,
chopped
4–6 tomatoes, peeled, seeded
and chopped

2 tablespoons finely chopped
flat-leaf parsley
salt and freshly ground
pepper
1–2 tablespoons tomato purée
4–6 tablespoons rich beef or
veal stock
4–6 aubergines, unpeeled
flour
olive oil
4–6 tablespoons grated
Parmesan

Sauté the onion and garlic in the olive oil until transparent. Add the lamb and continue cooking, stirring from time to time, until brown. Add the mushrooms, tomatoes, parsley, and salt and pepper, to taste, and cook until the onion is tender.

Dilute the tomato purée in the stock, add to the meat and vegetable mixture and simmer for 10 minutes.

Slice the aubergines thinly lengthwise; dust with flour and fry on both sides in hot olive oil. Drain on absorbent paper. Line a baking dish with the slices of aubergine; spread a layer of stuffing mixture on them; sprinkle lightly with grated Parmesan; cover with a layer of aubergines and continue this process until the baking dish is full, ending with a layer of aubergines. Sprinkle with grated Parmesan and bake in a moderate oven (190°C/375°F/gas 5) until the top has browned nicely. Serve hot; it is also very good cold and can be successfully reheated.

## Moussaka Variations

1. Add freshly grated Parmesan and freshly grated breadcrumbs to the meat and vegetable mixture and proceed as above.

2. Add freshly grated Parmesan and freshly grated breadcrumbs to the meat and vegetable mixture. Fill the aubergine-lined baking dish with the mixture; pour over a well-flavoured white sauce; top with aubergine slices and grated cheese; bake as above.

3. Beat 2 eggs; blend in 2 tablespoons flour; add 1 small carton yoghurt and whisk to a creamy sauce. Pour this sauce over the meat and vegetable mixture and proceed as above.

4. Dice 1 aubergine; dust with flour; sauté in oil and combine with the meat and vegetable mixture in the original recipe or in any of the variations above.

# Roast Saddle of Lamb

| | |
|---|---|
| 1 saddle of young lamb | 425 ml/¾ pint beef stock |
| softened butter | 1 tablespoon butter |
| salt and freshly ground pepper | 1 tablespoon flour |
| crushed dried rosemary | puréed potatoes and peas, to |
| 150 ml/¼ pint water | serve |

Spread the saddle of lamb with softened butter and sprinkle with salt, pepper and crushed rosemary, to taste.

Place the saddle in a moderately hot oven (200°C/400°F/gas 6); pour the water into the roasting pan and roast the lamb for about 1 hour, basting frequently.

Remove the roast from the oven; discard the fat from the pan; add well-flavoured beef stock and a *beurre manié* (the butter kneaded to a smooth paste with the flour); and cook over a high heat, stirring all the crusty bits from the sides of the pan into the sauce, until the sauce is smooth and thick. Strain and reserve. Serve with puréed potatoes and peas.

# Roast Saddle of Lamb à l'Arlésienne

| | |
|---|---|
| 1 saddle of lamb | cloves of garlic, unpeeled |
| softened butter | olive oil |
| salt and freshly ground pepper | |
| crushed dried rosemary | *Garnish:* |
| 150 ml/¼ pint water | 24 new potatoes, boiled and |
| 425 ml/¾ pint hot beef stock | sautéed in butter |
| 1 tablespoon butter | 6 tablespoons finely chopped |
| 1 tablespoon flour | mushrooms and 2 tablespoons |
| 6 medium-sized courgettes | each finely chopped flat-leaf |
| 6 tomatoes, sliced | parsley and truffles, sautéed |
| 1 Spanish onion, finely chopped | in butter |
| sprigs of thyme | watercress |

Spread the saddle of lamb with softened butter and sprinkle with salt, pepper and crushed rosemary, to taste.

Place the saddle in a moderately hot oven (200°C/400°F/gas 6); pour the water into the roasting pan and roast the lamb for 1 hour, basting frequently.

Remove the roast from the oven; discard the fat from the pan; add the well-flavoured beef stock and a *beurre manié* (the butter kneaded to a smooth paste with the flour) and cook over a high heat, stirring all the crusty bits from the sides of the pan into the sauce, until the sauce is smooth and thick. Strain and reserve.

Slice each courgette lengthwise into 4 or 5 slices, without cutting all the way through, to make a fan shape. Place a thin slice of tomato in each opening. Place the partially roasted saddle of lamb in an oiled baking tin in which you have scattered the finely chopped onion, sprigs of thyme, garlic and salt and pepper, to taste. Surround with stuffed courgettes; sprinkle with a little olive oil and continue to

Deep Dish Apple Pie: page 255

Crêpes Suzette (opposite): page 252

French Raspberry Tart: page 257

roast for about 45 minutes, or until the meat is tender (allow about 15 minutes per 450 g/pound in all).

To serve: place the lamb on a large heated serving dish; place the stuffed courgettes at one end of the dish and the sautéed potatoes at the other. Sprinkle the vegetables with finely chopped mushrooms, parsley and truffles, which you have sautéed in butter. Garnish with watercress.

## Marinated Saddle of Lamb

1 saddle of lamb
2 cloves garlic, finely chopped
4 tablespoons olive oil
4 tablespoons soy sauce

2 tablespoons dry white wine
salt and freshly ground
 pepper

Rub the saddle of lamb with a damp cloth. Combine the garlic, olive oil, soy sauce, white wine and salt and pepper, to taste, in a bowl.

Rub this mixture well into the whole saddle of lamb and allow the flavour to penetrate for at least 1 hour. Just before cooking, rub more of the mixture into the lamb, reserving some for basting.

Place the saddle in a slow oven (170°C/325°F/gas 3) and roast for 15 to 20 minutes per 450 g/pound, basting from time to time, or until the roast is pink and rare.

## Roast Shoulder of Lamb with Herbs

1 shoulder of lamb
2 tablespoons olive oil
salt and freshly ground pepper

6 sprigs each thyme, bay leaves,
 rosemary

Have your butcher bone and trim a shoulder of lamb ready for rolling. Do not have him roll it.

Lay the lamb out flat; brush with the olive oil and sprinkle with salt and pepper, to taste. Place 2 sprigs each of thyme, bay leaves and rosemary on the lamb; roll up neatly and tie securely. Place 4 sprigs each of thyme, bay leaves and rosemary around the lamb and tie securely. Brush with olive oil and roast in a hot oven (230°C/450°F/gas 8) for 20 minutes; lower the heat to moderate (190°C/375°F/gas 5) and cook until tender.

# Roast Leg of Lamb Provençal
Serves 8

1 leg of lamb (about 2.3 kg/
  5 pounds)
1 tablespoon butter
6 cloves garlic
700 g/1½ pounds potatoes,
  peeled and thickly sliced

salt and freshly ground
  pepper
4–6 tablespoons finely chopped
  flat-leaf parsley
300 ml/½ pint rich chicken
  stock

Have your butcher trim and tie a leg of lamb. Butter a shallow flameproof casserole or gratin dish just large enough to hold the leg of lamb comfortably and rub it lightly with a cut clove of garlic. Arrange the potatoes in the bottom of the dish in overlapping rows. Salt and pepper the potatoes generously. Chop the remaining garlic finely and sprinkle over the potatoes along with the parsley. Place the raw lamb on the potatoes and moisten with rich chicken stock.

Roast in a slow oven (170°C/325°F/gas 3) for 1¼ to 1½ hours, or until the lamb is pink and tender. If you prefer lamb less pink, increase the cooking time. Serve as it is.

# Moroccan Steamed Lamb
Serves 6 to 8

1 tablespoon coarse salt
¼ teaspoon powdered saffron
½ level teaspoon powdered
  cumin
2.3 kg/5 pounds lamb (cut from
  shoulder)

freshly ground pepper
4 tablespoons butter
cooked rice, to serve
powdered cumin and salt, to
  serve

Combine the salt, saffron and cumin and rub the lamb with this mixture. Season to taste with pepper.

Wrap the meat in a clean kitchen towel and place in the top section of a large double steamer over boiling water. (The bottom section of the steamer should be three-quarters full.)

Close the steamer hermetically with damp towels and steam the lamb over a high heat for 3 hours without lifting the cover.

Just before serving, sauté the lamb in the butter until golden. Serve with rice, powdered cumin and salt.

# Lamb Chops 'en Cuirasse'
Serves 6

6 lamb chops
6 tablespoons butter
225 g/½ pound mushrooms,
   finely chopped
1 Spanish onion, finely chopped

2 slices ham, finely chopped
salt and freshly ground pepper
flaky pastry
1 egg, beaten
tomato sauce (page 38), to serve

Trim the lamb chops and sauté in a little butter until golden. Remove and allow to cool. Add the remaining butter to the pan and sauté the mushrooms, onion and ham until the vegetables are soft. Season to taste with salt and pepper. Cool.

Spread the mushroom mixture on both sides of each chop. Roll out the pastry into 6 circles (big enough to encase the chops); place 1 chop on each; wrap in pastry, leaving the bone out; moisten the join with water and seal securely.

Place the pastry-wrapped chops on baking sheet, join side down; brush with beaten egg and bake in a hot oven (230°C/450°F/gas 8) for 15 to 20 minutes. Serve with tomato sauce.

# Italian Breaded Lamb Chops
Serves 2 to 3

4–6 baby lamb chops
1 tablespoon olive oil
salt and freshly ground
   pepper
flour

1 egg, beaten
dry breadcrumbs
4–6 tablespoons butter
4–6 tablespoons olive oil
watercress

Brush the lamb chops with the olive oil and season to taste with salt and pepper. Dust the chops with flour; dip in beaten egg and roll in dry breadcrumbs.

When ready to serve, sauté in the butter and olive oil until golden brown. Garnish with watercress.

# Grilled Marinated Lamb Chops – I
Serves 4 to 6

8–10 loin lamb chops
salt and freshly ground pepper
2 bay leaves, crumbled

2 cloves garlic, finely chopped
6 tablespoons olive oil
6 tablespoons dry white wine

Have your butcher trim a loin of baby lamb into 8 or 10 chops. Arrange them in a large, flat dish and season to taste with salt and pepper. Add the bay leaves, garlic, olive oil and white wine and marinate the chops in this mixture, turning them once or twice, for at least 2 hours.

Preheat the grill for 15 to 20 minutes; rub the grid with pieces of suet; place the chops on it and grill for 2 to 3 minutes on each side. Serve immediately.

# Grilled Marinated Lamb Chops – II
Serves 6

6 lamb chops
salt and freshly ground pepper
150 ml/¼ pint lemon juice
150 ml/¼ pint olive oil or corn oil

4 tablespoons finely chopped
mint
1–2 teaspoons grated lemon zest
2 cloves garlic, finely chopped

Season the chops on both sides with salt and pepper. Combine the remaining ingredients in a small bowl and blend well. Place the lamb chops in a flat dish just large enough to hold them and pour the marinade mixture over them. Marinate the chops for 2 to 4 hours, turning occasionally. When ready to serve, grill over charcoal for 5 minutes; turn and grill 5 minutes longer, or until the chops are cooked through. Brush the chops with the marinade mixture during cooking time.

# Rognons Flambés 'Lasserre'
Serves 4

4 lamb kidneys
4 tablespoons butter
1–2 teaspoons Dijon mustard
salt and freshly ground pepper
2–4 tablespoons port

Armagnac
2–4 tablespoons *pâté de foie
gras*
1–2 tablespoons lemon juice
boiled new potatoes, to serve

Skin the kidneys and sauté quickly in half the butter to allow them to 'stiffen' and brown while still remaining practically raw.

Dice the kidneys; melt the remaining butter in a thick-bottomed frying pan and add the diced kidneys, Dijon mustard and salt and pepper, to taste, and stir well over a high heat for a minute or two before adding the port.

Sprinkle the kidneys with Armagnac and ignite, allowing the flames to die down and the alcohol to disappear, stirring continuously.

Mash the *pâté de foie gras* with a fork until well blended; stir into the sauce; cook for a minute or two more until the sauce is unctuous and the kidneys are tender. Do not allow the sauce to boil at any time during its preparation. Just before serving, stir in lemon juice to taste. Serve with boiled new potatoes.

# Blanquette d'Agneau

I first became interested in French casserole cookery when I lived in Paris and Naomi came from her native Burgundy in answer to my advertisement in the daily press for a housekeeper. As soon as I saw her I knew that hire her I must. She was a trim, white-haired, little old lady with fat rosy cheeks, dressed in a strict blue suit and cream flannel blouse, with a narrow black tie that exactly matched the ribbon on her pince-nez.

Naomi had been a *cordon bleu* cook for a famous Marquis and as such was qualified for the highest of positions, but age and recurrent attacks of migraine had taught her to avoid the heavy responsibilities of *haute cuisine* and hire herself out as cook and maid of all work. I engaged her on the spot and for the five long years that I remained in Paris I never regretted the day. For Naomi proved to be a treasure such as I have rarely known, a superb cook, a wonderful housekeeper and a true friend.

Most of Naomi's dishes were of the long, slow-cooking variety – the superb casseroles of meat, fish and game for which France is so famous. And she was an expert in the art of making even the least desirable cuts of meat taste delicious. Sometimes she would marinate the meat in wine, olive oil and herbs to tenderise it before it was cooked. Other times she would 'seize' it in a little butter or olive oil, flavour it with aromatic herbs and a touch of garlic, and then simmer it for hours in a sauce made rich with stock, wine or cream.

I soon learned, however, that long cooking alone cannot ensure perfect results. Naomi taught me to watch the pot to make certain it cooked so gently that it hardly bubbled, for it was only in this way that meat could be kept from going stringy and tough; to add crisp *lardons* of streaky bacon or fat salt pork, along with tiny white onions parboiled to *al dente* tenderness, and button mushrooms sautéed in butter and lemon juice, to lend contrast in texture and flavour to my dishes. And she taught me to give casserole dinners. For Naomi had one failing only – a hangover from her days in the household of the Marquis – she disliked waiting on table, preferring the anonymity of her kitchen to facing the battery of guests in the dining-room. So together we evolved the perfect plan for easy entertaining: one superb casserole dish cooked to perfection, preceded by a cold or hot *hors-d'oeuvre*, and followed by a crisp green salad, cheese and fruit. Nothing could be simpler or more delicious. And nothing moved my circle of Paris friends to more heartfelt thanks than one of Naomi's casseroles.

*Navarin de mouton* and *blanquette d'agneau* were two of her favourites – and to anyone who once tasted Naomi's versions of these famous dishes, no ordinary lamb stew would ever be the same again. A boned shoulder or breast of young lamb was the secret here, poached in a light stock with an onion studded with a clove, carrots, leek and a good-sized *bouquet garni.*

Naomi always added poached tiny white onions and sautéed button mushrooms to her *blanquette* just before serving so that the vegetables would offer texture and flavour contrast to the meltingly tender lamb.

# Blanquette d'Agneau

Serves 4 to 6

1.2 kg/2½ pounds shoulder or
   breast of lamb
1.2 litres/2 pints veal stock
   (or stock and water)
1 teaspoon salt
freshly ground pepper
1 Spanish onion, studded with a
   clove
2 carrots, roughly chopped
1 leek, roughly chopped
1 *bouquet garni* (2 or 3 sprigs
   flat-leaf parsley, 1 sprig thyme,
   1 bay leaf, 1 stalk celery)

12 tiny white onions
12 button mushrooms, and
   enough butter and lemon
   juice in which to simmer
   them
2 tablespoons butter
2 tablespoons flour
2 egg yolks
150 ml/¼ pint cream
lemon juice
freshly grated nutmeg

Cut the shoulder or breast of lamb, or a combination of the two, into small pieces, and let soak for 12 hours in cold water with a little lemon juice. Change the water 2 or 3 times.

Place the blanched lamb pieces in a deep flameproof casserole with enough light veal stock (or stock and water) to cover, add salt and pepper and bring to the boil. Remove any scum that forms on the surface with a perforated spoon as you would for a *pot-au-feu*.

Add the onion studded with clove, carrots, leek and *bouquet garni*. Cover the casserole and simmer gently over a very low heat or in a low oven for 1½ hours, or until tender.

Cook the tiny onions in a little water until just firm. Drain and keep warm. Simmer the mushroom caps in a little butter and lemon juice and keep warm.

Make a white *roux* by combining the butter and flour in a saucepan. Add 600 ml/1 pint of stock from the lamb and stir well over a high heat until the sauce is smooth and creamy. Lower the heat and simmer for 15 minutes, stirring from time to time. Remove the saucepan from the heat and 'finish' the sauce by stirring in the egg yolks, the cream and the juice of half a lemon.

Drain the lamb pieces from the remaining stock (removing bits of bone and fat which have separated from the meat in cooking). Clean the casserole; return the lamb pieces to it and strain the sauce through a fine sieve over the meat. Stir the mushroom caps and onions carefully into the *blanquette*; season with a little grated nutmeg and cover and keep warm in the oven until ready to serve. A little more fresh cream and a squeeze of lemon may be added just before serving.

# Italian Lamb Stew
Serves 4 to 6

1 tablespoon lard
1 tablespoon olive oil
225 g/½ pound fat salt pork,
    diced
1 Spanish onion, sliced
2 cloves garlic, chopped
1.2 kg/2½ pounds boned lamb,
    cut into bite-sized pieces

salt and freshly ground pepper
1–2 sprigs marjoram, leaves
    only
1–2 sprigs rosemary, leaves
    only
150 ml/¼ pint dry red wine
4 tablespoons tomato purée,
    diluted in water

Combine the lard and olive oil in a thick pan or flameproof casserole; when the fat begins to bubble, add the salt pork, onion and garlic and sauté until golden. Add the pieces of meat seasoned with salt, pepper, marjoram and rosemary and cook, stirring frequently, until the meat is well browned on all sides. Now add the dry red wine (one of the rougher Italian ones) and continue cooking until the wine has reduced to half the original quantity. Add the diluted tomato purée and enough boiling water to cover the meat. Cover the pan and simmer slowly for about 2 hours, or until the meat is tender. A tablespoon or two of red wine just before serving will add extra *bouquet* to this dish, which should be served directly from the casserole.

# Scots Hotch Potch
Serves 4 to 6

1.3 kg/3 pounds neck of lamb
2.4 litres/4 pints water or stock
2 Spanish onions, coarsely
    chopped
salt and freshly ground pepper
celery salt
450 g/1 pound peas

225 g/½ pound broad beans
4–6 young carrots
4–6 young turnips
1 small cauliflower
4 tablespoons finely chopped
    flat-leaf parsley

Place the neck of lamb in a saucepan with the water or stock, onion, and salt, pepper and celery salt, to taste. Bring slowly to the boil and skim carefully. Add half the quantity of peas with the beans, carrots and turnips. Bring to the boil again; skim carefully; lower the heat and simmer slowly, covered, for 3 hours.

Wash the cauliflower well and separate into florets. Half an hour before serving, add the cauliflower and remaining peas and continue cooking until the vegetables are tender. Just before serving, remove the lamb; cut into serving pieces and return to the saucepan with the vegetables. Add the finely chopped parsley, correct the seasoning and serve immediately.

# Daube de Mouton
Serves 6

1.3 kg/3 pounds boned shoulder
  of mutton
thin strips pork fat
thin strips green bacon
2 onions, sliced
4 carrots, sliced
1 *bouquet garni* (thyme, flat-leaf
  parsley and bay leaf)
salt and freshly ground
  pepper
600 ml/1 pint red wine

4 tablespoons olive oil
100 g/¼ pound green bacon,
  diced
1 Spanish onion, sliced
1 clove garlic, finely chopped
600 ml/1 pint hot stock
2–4 tablespoons tomato
  purée
2 tablespoons finely chopped
  flat-leaf parsley

Cut the mutton into 6.5-cm/2½-inch cubes; lard each piece with pork fat and green bacon and place in a large bowl or earthenware casserole with the onions and carrots, a *bouquet garni*, salt and pepper, to taste, and red wine. Marinate the meat in this mixture for 5 or 6 hours, stirring occasionally.

Remove the lamb from the marinade; drain. Heat the olive oil in a frying pan; sauté the diced green bacon and the onion until the onion is transparent. Add the lamb and sauté with the bacon and onion until browned, shaking the pan from time to time. Add the chopped garlic; moisten with the marinade which has been boiled to reduce it to half the original quantity. Pour over the hot stock mixed with the tomato purée.

Cover the casserole with greaseproof paper and the lid, and cook in a slow oven (170°C/325°F/gas 3) for 3 to 4 hours. Remove from the oven; skim the fat from the surface, sprinkle with parsley and serve in the casserole.

# Curried Lamb Loaf
Serves 4 to 6

1 kg/2 pounds boned lamb,
  minced
1 tablespoon curry powder
¼ teaspoon each powdered
  ginger, turmeric and
  coriander
⅛ teaspoon each paprika and
  cayenne
1 tablespoon flour
coarse salt and freshly ground
  pepper
1 egg, lightly beaten

*Court-Bouillon:*
900 ml/1½ pints water
2 tablespoons finely chopped
  coriander
generous pinch dried thyme

*Sauce:*
½ Spanish onion, finely
  chopped
butter
salt and freshly ground pepper
¼ teaspoon paprika
¼ teaspoon powdered coriander
150 ml/¼ pint yoghurt

Combine the minced lamb, curry powder, ginger, turmeric, coriander, paprika, cayenne, flour, and salt and pepper, to taste. Add 1 egg; mix well and form the meat mixture into a loaf.

Place the loaf in a buttered gratin dish just large enough to hold it.

To steam the loaf: combine the water, coriander and thyme; bring to the boil, place the gratin dish in the top of a steamer and steam the loaf for 20 to 30 minutes.

**To make the sauce:**  Sauté the onion in butter until soft; sprinkle with salt, pepper, paprika and coriander, to taste; pour in the juices from the loaf; stir in the yoghurt and heat through. Pour over the loaf.

## Lamb Curry
Serves 4 to 6

**1.2 kg/2½ pounds boned lamb**
**4 tablespoons butter**
**2 tablespoons olive oil**
**1 large Spanish onion, finely**
**chopped**
**1 clove garlic, finely chopped**
**1 green pepper, finely**
**chopped**
**2 stalks celery, finely chopped**
**150 ml/¼ pint canned coconut**
**milk**
**300 ml/½ pint well-flavoured**
**stock**
**50 g/2 ounces seedless raisins**

**6 tablespoons yoghurt**
**boiled rice, to serve**
**curry condiments, to serve**
**(see method)**

*Kari Blend:*
**2 tablespoons curry powder**
**½ teaspoon each ginger and**
**turmeric**
**¼ teaspoon each paprika and**
**cayenne**
**1 tablespoon flour**
**coarse salt**
**freshly ground pepper**

Cut the lamb into cubes 4 cm/1½ inches in diameter and sauté in the butter, turning with a wooden spoon to preserve the juices, until golden. Remove the meat from the pan; add the olive oil and sauté the onion, garlic, green pepper and celery until the vegetables are soft.

Mix the *kari* blend thoroughly in a bowl and stir into the vegetable mixture. (*Note:* If this is your first curry, stir in half the mixture; check the flavour of the sauce after you have added the coconut milk and stock and add more *kari* until the sauce is of the desired pungency.) Add the coconut milk and stock to the vegetables and spices. Cover and simmer for 15 minutes. Add the meat and raisins and continue cooking over a low heat until the meat is tender, stirring occasionally.

Remove from the heat, stir in the yoghurt; correct the seasoning and serve with boiled rice and traditional curry condiments: mango chutney, apple chutney, preserved *kumquats*, etc.

# Chapter 9

# Veal

## Osso Buco

Why can't restaurants write menus that really help? First of all, most menus are too full. To offer a choice of forty different dishes is not really helpful to the diner. Nobody's taste could be so jaded that they could not select a meal they want from a dozen or so alternatives. This *embarras du choix*, in fact, defeats all but the most practised, for the majority of people if faced by too wide a selection (and this is proved by statistics) embarrassedly still plump for prawn cocktail and steak . . . or risotto and a pan-seared fillet of salmon, sea bass or John Dory.

I cannot see why at least some of the main dishes on each menu cannot be described in some detail. The White Tower in London and the Forum of the Twelve Caesars in New York have made quite a thing out of their poetic descriptions of the day's specialities. But even a straightforward description of what is in a dish and how it is cooked would prove invaluable. So many people seem to be nervous of betraying their ignorance of what something is, particularly when they are young, that they stick to the same dreary things they have had before every time they eat out. And yet everyone has to eat a dish for the first time some time.

I remember seeing a much travelled sixty-year-old American – knowledgeable beyond belief about the intricacies of Russian and Chinese cooking – tripped by *osso buco*. Much to the scorn of the waiter, she left the marrow. To me it seems that it was the waiter who showed his ignorance in not telling her that the marrow was the climax of the dish, instead of just whisking it away with a distinct sneer.

Because I am always trying something new, some dish I have only heard of before, I am never shy about asking. I discuss constantly with waiters what they mean by the international phrases they use so loosely (and to most waiters, remember, French is as foreign a language as it is to us). They never seem to mind this cross-examination; in fact, they seem rather to like it – at least you are showing an interest in their work and, as Dale Carnegie never tired of pointing out, there is no better way to win friends, etc.

But back to *osso buco*: what other dish hides its most succulent treats so secretly? How on earth, if you had not had it explained to you, could you be expected to know how to enjoy it? I like to serve *osso buco* accompanied by saffron rice as the main course for a summer luncheon with an Italian flavour. It is a sturdy country dish – rich and full-bodied – that fairly cries out to be eaten in the sun. This is definitely not a dish for dieters; it should be savoured to the very last mouthful.

Serve the lightest of *antipasti* before it and follow with a tossed green salad and a choice of cheeses – Italian, of course – or perhaps a fresh fruit salad macerated in Chianti. Chianti or Bardolo Rosso is the perfect liquid accompaniment.

# Osso Buco
Serves 4

4 thick slices shin of veal
flour
salt and freshly ground pepper
2 tablespoons olive oil
2 tablespoon butter
2 cloves garlic, finely chopped
½ Spanish onion, finely chopped
150 ml/¼ pint boiling water or
  light stock

150 ml/¼ pint dry white wine
2–4 tablespoons tomato purée
1 anchovy fillet, finely
  chopped
4 tablespoons chopped flat-leaf
  parsley
grated zest of ½ lemon
saffron rice

Choose shin of veal with plenty of meat and have it sawn into 4 pieces 5 cm/ 2 inches thick. Dredge the pieces with flour; season with salt and pepper and brown them in the olive oil and butter. Add half the garlic and the onion; add the boiling water or light stock, white wine and tomato purée; cover the pan and simmer for 1½ hours. Then add the anchovy fillet and the remaining garlic. Blend thoroughly, heat through and serve sprinkled with parsley and lemon zest, and accompanied by saffron rice.

# Blanquette de Veau
Serves 4 to 6

1.3 kg/3 pounds shoulder or
  breast of veal
freshly squeezed lemon juice
1.2 litres/2 pints veal stock
  (or stock and water)
1 teaspoon salt
freshly ground pepper
1 Spanish onion, studded with
  a clove
2 carrots, roughly chopped
1 leek, roughly chopped

1 *bouquet garni* (2 or 3 sprigs
  flat-leaf parsley, 1 sprig thyme,
  1 bay leaf, 1 stalk celery)
12 tiny white onions
12 button mushrooms (and a
  little butter)
2 tablespoons butter
2 tablespoons flour
2 egg yolks
150 ml/¼ pint double cream
lemon juice
freshly grated nutmeg

Cut the shoulder or breast of veal, or a combination of the two, into small pieces and let soak for 12 hours in cold water with a little of the lemon juice. Change the water 2 or 3 times.

Place the blanched veal pieces in a deep flameproof casserole with enough light veal stock (or stock and water) to cover; add salt and pepper and bring to the boil. Remove any scum that forms on the surface with a perforated spoon as you would for a *pot-au-feu*.

Add the onion studded with a clove, carrots, leek and *bouquet garni*. Cover the casserole and simmer gently over a very low heat, or in a very slow oven (150°C/ 300°F/gas 2), for 1½ hours, or until tender.

Cook the tiny onions in a little water until just firm. Drain and keep warm. Simmer the mushroom caps in a little butter and lemon juice and keep warm.

Make a white *roux* by combining the 2 tablespoons of butter with the flour in a saucepan. Add 600 ml/1 pint of stock from the veal and stir well over a high heat until the sauce is smooth and creamy. Lower the heat and simmer for 15 minutes, stirring from time to time. Remove the saucepan from the heat and 'finish' the sauce by stirring in the egg yolks, cream and a tablespoon of the lemon juice.

Drain the veal pieces from the remaining stock (removing bits of bone and fat which have separated from the meat in cooking). Clean the casserole; return the veal pieces to it and strain the sauce through a fine sieve over the meat. Stir the mushroom caps and onions carefully into the *blanquette*; season with a little nutmeg and cover and keep warm in the oven until ready to serve. A little more fresh cream and lemon juice may be added just before serving.

## Zéphires de Ris de Veau 'Planson'
Serves 6

3 pairs calf's sweetbreads
dry white wine
water
450 g/1 pound fillet of veal, diced

salt and freshly ground pepper
4 egg whites
600 ml/1 pint double cream
*sauce béarnaise* (page 38)

Soak the sweetbreads briefly in iced water and then parboil for 15 minutes in dry white wine and water to cover. Drain; cool and cut them slantwise in 2 or 3 rather thick slices; arrange them in the centre of a veal mousse made in the following manner.

Put the veal through the finest blade of your mincer; then force through a fine sieve. Add salt and pepper, to taste. Place the meat in a bowl set in a bowl of ice; stir in the egg whites, little by little; then add the double cream to this mixture, little by little, beating with a wooden spoon until the mixture is light and smooth.

Butter a ring mould and line it with the veal mousse. Lay slices of sweetbread in the mould, filling up any empty spots with mousse, and top with the remaining mousse mixture. Cover with buttered paper. Set the mould in a pan of water and bake in a slow oven (170°C/325°F/gas 3) for 20 to 30 minutes, or until firm. Unmould and serve with *sauce béarnaise.*

## Maître Paul's 'Blanquette de Veau Menoigère'
Serves 4 to 6

1.3 kg/3 pounds shoulder or breast of veal
2–4 tablespoons butter
12 small onions
1 tablespoon flour
1 *bouquet garni*

salt and freshly ground pepper
2 egg yolks
juice of ½ lemon
4–6 tablespoons double cream
cooked rice or steamed new potatoes, to serve

Cut the veal into 5-cm/2-inch squares and sauté until golden in the butter with the small onions in a thick-bottomed flameproof casserole. Sprinkle with the flour and add just enough water to cover the meat. Add a *bouquet garni* and salt and pepper, and simmer the veal gently for about 1½ hours. Cool for a few minutes, then remove the meat pieces and onions to a hot serving bowl and keep warm.

Thicken the sauce in the following manner: whisk the egg yolks, lemon juice and cream in a bowl. Whisking vigorously, add a ladle of boiling sauce from the veal. Pour this *liaison* into the sauce and bring it to the boil, whisking well until thick and creamy. Pass the sauce through a fine sieve over the meat and onions and serve immediately, accompanied by rice or steamed new potatoes.

## Gourmandise 'Brillat-Savarin' Lasserre
Serves 4

4 slices fillet of veal (about
   100 g/¼ pound each)
4 tablespoons butter
salt and freshly ground pepper
12 button mushrooms
2 teaspoons very finely chopped
   shallots

3–4 tablespoons dry sherry
4 thin pancakes (15–20 cm/
   6–8 inches in diameter)
butter
2–4 tablespoons freshly grated
   Gruyère cheese

Sauté the slices of veal fillet in the butter until well coloured and three-quarters cooked. Season to taste with salt and pepper. Remove and keep warm.

Thinly slice the mushrooms and sauté quickly in the butter which you have used for cooking the veal fillet, together with the shallots. Add the dry sherry, salt and pepper, to taste, and cook, stirring constantly, until the sherry is reduced.

Spoon an eighth of the mushroom-shallot mixture on one side of each pancake; place a nearly cooked fillet on top, and cover with the remaining mushroom-shallot mixture. Close the pancake as if folding a package and place on a buttered dish; put a knob of butter on top of each and sprinkle with Gruyère.

Place in a hot oven (230°C/450°F/gas 8) for 5 minutes then serve immediately.

## Côte de Veau Normande 'Bocage Fleuri'
Serves 4

4 veal chops
salt and freshly ground pepper
2 tablespoons butter
100 g/¼ pound mushrooms
4 tablespoons Calvados

3 tablespoons fresh cream per
   chop
2 tart eating apples, peeled,
   quartered and sautéed in
   butter, to garnish

Season the veal chops with salt and pepper and sauté in the butter until golden on both sides. Slice the mushrooms, add to the veal and simmer for 10 minutes. Add the Calvados; flame; stir in the cream. Reduce the sauce, stirring continuously, until smooth and thick. Serve the veal chops in cream, garnished with sautéed apples.

## Escalopes 'Viscayennes'

Serves 4

1 Spanish onion, finely chopped
6 cloves garlic, finely chopped
2 tablespoons butter
2 tablespoons olive oil
4 green peppers, sliced
8 tomatoes, coarsely chopped
pinch sugar

salt and freshly ground pepper
4 veal escalopes
butter
4–6 tablespoons dry white wine
150 ml/¼ pint double cream
butter
finely chopped flat-leaf parsley

Sauté the onion and garlic in the butter and oil until transparent. Add the green pepper, then the tomatoes, and cook, stirring continuously, for a minute or two. Season to taste with sugar, salt and pepper and simmer for 30 minutes.

Sauté the veal escalopes in a little butter in a frying pan until cooked through. Arrange on a hot serving platter and keep warm. Stir the white wine into the pan juices and cook over a high heat until the sauce is reduced by half. Add the tomato, pepper and onion mixture; pour in the cream and simmer the sauce gently for 5 minutes. Whip butter into the sauce and pour over the escalopes. Sprinkle with parsley and serve immediately.

## Escalopes de Veau à la Vallée d'Auge

Serves 4

4 veal escalopes
salt and freshly ground pepper
2–4 tablespoons butter
2–4 tablespoons Calvados

2 tablespoons dry white wine
175 g/6 ounces sliced button
    mushrooms, sautéed in butter
150 ml/¼ pint double cream

Season the escalopes to taste with salt and pepper and sauté in the butter until tender. Pour over warmed Calvados and flame. Remove from the pan and keep warm. Add the white wine to the pan juices. Cook over a high heat, stirring in all the crusty bits from the sides of the pan. Add the sautéed mushrooms and the cream. Season to taste with salt and pepper. Simmer for 2 or 3 minutes; return the escalopes to the pan and heat through in the sauce. Serve immediately.

## Côte de Veau Coupole

Serves 4

4 veal chops
salt and freshly ground pepper
4 tablespoons butter
1–2 tablespoons finely chopped
    shallots

6 tablespoons cream
4 tablespoons port
12–16 button mushrooms, sliced
4 tablespoons finely chopped ham
sautéed potatoes, to serve

Season the veal chops to taste with salt and pepper and sauté in the butter; when cooked, sprinkle with the shallots. Remove from the pan and keep warm. Stir the cream and port into the juices in the pan; add the mushrooms; heat through and pour the sauce over the veal.

Sprinkle with finely chopped ham. Serve with sautéed potatoes.

## Veal Chops 'en Papillote'

Serves 4

| | |
|---|---|
| 4 veal chops | 1 clove garlic, crushed |
| salt and freshly ground pepper | 150 ml/¼ pint dry white wine |
| 6 tablespoons butter | 2 tablespoons tomato purée |
| 2 tablespoons chopped shallots | 2 tablespoons grated breadcrumbs |
| 225 g/½ pound mushrooms, | 2 tablespoons chopped flat-leaf |
| finely chopped | parsley |
| 1 tablespoon lemon juice | 8 thin slices *prosciutto* |

Season the veal chops with salt and pepper and sauté gently in 4 tablespoons of the butter until golden on both sides (5 to 10 minutes). Remove and keep warm. Prepare a mushroom *duxelles* sauce as follows: add the remaining butter to the pan and cook the shallots and mushrooms with the lemon juice and crushed garlic. Add the white wine, tomato purée, salt and pepper, to taste, grated breadcrumbs and chopped parsley, and cook until a soft paste results.

Cut 4 sheets of greaseproof paper into heart shapes big enough to enclose the chops when folded over; oil them the uppermost side, and place the hearts on the table in pairs. Place a slice of *prosciutto* on one side of each sheet. Coat this with the *duxelles* paste. Place a veal chop on this; coat with more paste and cover with another piece of *prosciutto*. Fold over the paper to enclose the chop, and roll and pinch the edges together very firmly. Fry these *papillotes* in hot oil until they swell up like balloons; transfer to a baking sheet and bake in a moderately hot oven (200°C/400°F/gas 6) until the meat is tender (about 20 to 25 minutes).

## Aïllade de Veau

Serves 4 to 6

| | |
|---|---|
| 1 kg/2 pounds lean veal | salt and freshly ground pepper |
| 4 tablespoons olive oil | 150 ml/¼ pint dry white wine |
| 2 tablespoons fresh breadcrumbs | 4–6 tablespoons water |
| 10 fat cloves garlic, blanched | cooked rice, to serve |
| 4 tablespoons tomato purée | |

Cut the veal into pieces 2.5 cm/1 inch square and sauté them in the olive oil until golden; add the breadcrumbs, blanched garlic and tomato purée. Cook over a gentle heat, stirring continuously, for 5 to 7 minutes. Season to taste with salt and pepper. Moisten with the white wine and water and simmer gently over the lowest of heats for 1 hour. Serve with rice.

# Veau au Vin Blanc
Serves 6 to 8

1 shoulder or loin of veal
(1.3–2.2 kg/3–5 pounds)
2 Spanish onions, thinly sliced
4 large carrots, thinly sliced
4 tomatoes, peeled, seeded and
coarsely chopped
100 g/¼ pound butter

salt and freshly ground
pepper
2 bay leaves
1 large clove garlic
4–6 sprigs flat-leaf parsley
300 ml/½ pint dry white wine

Ask your butcher to bone, roll and tie your roast. Sauté the vegetables in half the butter for about 3 minutes. Remove from the pan and brown the veal on all sides in the pan juices and remaining butter until golden. Season thoroughly with salt and pepper.

Return the vegetables to a casserole, making them into a bed for the veal. Add the bay leaves, garlic and parsley. Place the veal on this bed; moisten with warmed white wine; cover and roast in a 150°C/300°F/gas 2 oven for 2½ to 3 hours, or until tender.

Remove the vegetables; keep the veal warm; skim the fat from the juices and purée the vegetables in a blender. Stir into the vegetables enough of the remaining pan juices to make a gravy of the consistency you require. Serve the veal with the gravy.

# Saltimbocca alla Romana
Serves 4

8 thin slices of veal
8 sage leaves
freshly ground pepper
8 thin slices *prosciutto*
butter

2 tablespoons Marsala or dry
white wine
green beans, peas or *croûtons* of
fried bread, to serve

Flatten the veal into thin pieces about 10 by 12 cm/4 by 5 inches; place 1 sage leaf on each slice, and add pepper to taste (no salt, the *prosciutto* will flavour the meat). Cover each slice of veal with *prosciutto* cut to the same size; make each into a small roll and secure with a toothpick. Cook these little rolls in melted butter until they are golden on all sides, and then add the Marsala or white wine. Let them cook for a moment, then cover the pan and simmer gently until the veal and ham rolls are quite tender. Remove the toothpicks and transfer to a hot dish, surrounded by green beans, fresh peas in butter, or simply with *croûtons* of fried bread.

# Vitello Tonnato

It is almost impossible to eat badly in Rome. Italians have always regarded cooking as an art and you have only to visit a Roman street market in mid-morning to see some of the most beautiful raw foods in existence. Great platters of fish in all the colours of the rainbow; fruits and vegetables spilling from the stalls almost to the pavement; golden yellow cheeses; minute purple artichokes; milk-fed lambs and young kid no bigger than hares; tender young leaves of spinach, cabbage and red cabbage, picked when they are hardly more than sprouts, just right to be included raw, along with crisp pink radishes, in the salads so appreciated by the Romans.

Italian fishermen bring back a great variety of excellent fish and shellfish fresh from the nearby sea. Fresh young trout come from the neighbouring hillside streams. And even the wines from the Alban hills – the famous *castelli romani*, which are not castles at all, but little mountain villages – even the wines are young.

You, like every visitor, will soon have your favourite little *trattoria* where on Fridays they make the most delicious *zuppa di pesce* in the world – one of these intimate little places where the inexpensive local wine has the warmth and colour of the sun, and where the company is as good as the food. These restaurants, scattered throughout the city, are for the most part quite cheap for lunch, which includes a bottle of *vino locale* from the hills behind Rome. They are small and usually crowded. The décor with few exceptions is modest, sometimes nonexistent. But the food is uniformly excellent.

There are many Italian specialities that are particularly Roman in origin. Begin your meal with the famous *fettuccine all' uove*, freshly made thin egg noodles served with country butter and finely grated Parmesan cheese; or try *lasagne alla romana*, wide ribbons of *pasta* dough arranged in alternate layers with *ricotta* and *mozzarella* cheese, minced pork and veal, and slices of hard-boiled egg, the whole bathed with two unctuous sauces – a rich *béchamel* and a special *ragù alla romana*.

Then there are the spaghettis: *alla carrettiera*, cooked *al dente* and served with an aromatic sauce of tuna fish, mushrooms and herbs; *alla matriciana*, with a sauce flavoured with chopped bacon and onions; *all' arrabbiata*, a special sauce made hot with chillies and flavoured with herbs and tomatoes; and *alla carbonara*, served with fried *pancetta* or *prosciutto* and a sauce of finely grated Parmesan, butter and the yolks of eggs.

*Carciofi alla romana* – fresh young artichokes cooked in Roman style – are also on the list of specialities not to be missed. They are utterly delicious in Rome, where they pick them early in the season when they are not much bigger than a baby's fist. The sharp tips of the leaves are cut off, the centre is opened and the whole is baked in oil and herbs. There's no need to remove the 'choke' in the Italian artichoke; all of the plant may be eaten, including the stem.

Romans are not, as a rule, overfond of roasts, steaks or chops. But Rome's own *abbacchio* – milk-fed lamb – is an exception. *Abbacchio* is wonderfully tender and delicate in flavour whether it is cooked *al forno*, in the oven with a breath of rosemary, or *alla cacciatora*, hunter's style with tomatoes, peppers, garlic, wine and herbs. *Saltimbocca alla romana* is a perfect way of giving much-needed flavour to veal.

Here the Roman cook combines thin pieces of tender veal with slices of *prosciutto*, flavours them with sage and fries them in butter.

One of my favourite Italian summer dishes is *vitello tonnato*, lightly poached veal bathed in a rich tuna fish and anchovy sauce. Try Italian 'tunnied veal' as the cold first course for a company dinner, or as the refreshing main course for an outdoor luncheon in the sun. Serve a chilled wine with it and follow with a crisp green salad.

## Vitello Tonnato
Serves 6 to 8

1 leg of veal (1.2–1.3 kg/2½–3
   pounds when boned and
   trimmed)
6 anchovy fillets
several bay leaves
1 Spanish onion, sliced
2 carrots, sliced
2 stalks celery, sliced
4 sprigs flat-leaf parsley
2 cloves
salt and freshly ground
   pepper

300 ml/½ pint dry white wine
   (optional)

*Tuna Fish Sauce:*
150 ml/¼ pint well-flavoured
   mayonnaise (opposite)
175 g/6 ounces tuna fish
6 anchovy fillets
1 tablespoon small capers
2 tablespoons lemon juice
freshly ground pepper
lemon slices

Have your butcher bone and tie the leg of veal. Cut the anchovy fillets into small pieces; pierce holes in the surface of the meat and insert pieces of anchovy fillet. Top the roast with bay leaves. Then place the rolled meat in a flameproof casserole with the onion, carrots, celery, parsley, cloves and salt and pepper, to taste.

Pour in dry white wine and add just enough water to cover the meat (or use water only); bring it slowly to the boil, turn down the heat, cover the casserole, and simmer the veal for 1½ to 2 hours. When the veal is tender, remove the cord and skewers and allow it to cool in the stock.

When cold, drain well and place in a bowl, and cover with tuna fish sauce; cover the bowl and let the meat marinate in the sauce overnight.

Three hours before serving, remove the veal from the sauce; slice thinly; arrange the slices on a serving dish and cover with the sauce which you have thinned with a little of the veal stock or olive oil. I blend mine in the blender. Refrigerate until ready to serve. Serve with sliced lemon.

**To make the tuna sauce:** Make a thick mayonnaise (see opposite). Pound the tuna fish, anchovy fillets and capers with lemon juice and pepper until smooth. Combine with the mayonnaise in a blender and blend (adding a little veal stock if too thick) until the sauce is smooth and creamy.

**Note:** The remainder of the veal stock can be used as the base for a delicious vegetable soup.

*Mayonnaise for Vitello Tonnato:*
2 egg yolks
¼–½ teaspoon dried mustard

salt and freshly ground pepper
lemon juice
300 ml/½ pint olive oil

Combine the egg yolks with the mustard, a pinch or two of salt and pepper and a little lemon juice in a bowl; mix well; then add the olive oil slowly, drop by drop, whisking all the time with a fork or beater until the mayonnaise is of a good thick consistency. Add more lemon juice and salt and pepper to taste. This will make a more than sufficient quantity for the above recipe.

## Hungarian Veal Gulyas
Serves 6 to 8

2 Spanish onions, finely chopped
2 cloves garlic, finely chopped
2 tablespoons lard
1.2 kg/2½ pounds boned veal
2 tablespoons paprika
½ teaspoon caraway seeds
1 bay leaf
1–2 generous pinches each dried
   marjoram and thyme

salt and freshly ground
   pepper
450 g/1 pound button
   mushrooms, sliced
2 red peppers, diced
2 green peppers, diced
1 can Italian peeled tomatoes
300 ml/½ pint sour cream

Sauté the onions and garlic in the lard in a large flameproof casserole until transparent. Cut the veal into 5-cm/2-inch cubes; add to the casserole and sauté until golden on all sides. Sprinkle with paprika and caraway seeds; add the bay leaf and herbs and simmer gently for 10 minutes.

Season to taste with salt and pepper. Top with the mushrooms, peppers and tomatoes. Cover the casserole; bring gently to the boil and simmer in a very slow oven (150°C/300°F/gas 2) for at least 2 hours, or until tender. Serve with the sour cream.

## Roast Loin of Veal

1 loin of veal
salt and freshly ground pepper
chopped rosemary leaves

2–4 tablespoons softened
   butter
150 ml/¼ pint dry white wine

Have your butcher bone and trim the loin of veal. Season to taste with salt, pepper and rosemary leaves. Spread with the softened butter and roast the meat in a moderate oven (190°C/375°F/gas 5) for about 18 to 20 minutes per 450 g/pound, or until it is well done, basting frequently. Add a little hot water if the fat tends to scorch during cooking. Remove the veal from the oven; add the white wine to the roasting pan and make a thin sauce in the usual manner.

## Roast Breast of Veal
Serves 6 to 8

1.3–1.8 kg/3–4 pounds breast of
  veal
lemon juice
salt and freshly ground pepper
225 g/½ pound sausage meat
½ Spanish onion, finely chopped
2 tablespoons butter
2 tablespoons finely chopped
  flat-leaf parsley

1 beaten egg
225 g/½ pound spinach, chopped
  and sautéed in butter
salt, pepper and spices
flour
2 tablespoons butter
2 tablespoons olive oil

Wipe the veal on both sides with a damp cloth; sprinkle with lemon juice and season to taste with salt and pepper.

Combine the following ingredients in a large mixing bowl: sausage meat, onion which you have sautéed in the butter until transparent, parsley, egg, spinach, and salt, pepper and spices, to taste. Mix well. Lay this stuffing in the centre of the veal; make into a neat roll and sew up with fine string.

Dust the veal roll with flour; place it in a roasting pan with the butter and olive oil and roast it in a slow oven (170°C/325°F/gas 3) for about 1½ to 2 hours, basting frequently with fat.

## Poached Breast of Veal
Serves 6 to 8

1 breast of veal, stuffed as
  above
2 Spanish onions, cut in halves
6 small leeks, trimmed
6 carrots, peeled and trimmed

6 small turnips, peeled and
  trimmed
1 *bouquet garni*
water or light stock
salt and freshly ground pepper

Stuff the breast of veal as in the recipe above; combine with the prepared vegetables – onions, leeks, carrots and turnips – and poach gently with *bouquet garni* in salted water or a light stock until tender. Just before serving, season with salt and pepper to taste and serve surrounded by the vegetables.

## Veal Parmigiana
Serves 4

4 thin veal escalopes
1 beaten egg
50 g/2 ounces breadcrumbs
3 tablespoons freshly grated
  Parmesan cheese
salt and freshly ground pepper

2 tablespoons olive oil
butter
300 ml/½ pint hot tomato sauce
  (page 38)
*mozzarella* cheese, in strips

Dip the escalopes in beaten egg, then in breadcrumbs mixed with grated Parmesan cheese and seasoned to taste with salt and pepper. Let the breaded escalopes stand for 10 minutes.

Sauté the escalopes in the olive oil until cooked through; then place them in a shallow, well-buttered gratin dish. Pour over the tomato sauce; top with thin strips of *mozzarella* cheese and bake in a moderate oven (190°C/375°F/gas 5) for 10 to 15 minutes, or until the cheese melts and browns.

## Sautéed Veal Patties
Serves 4

450 g/1 pound raw veal
50 g/2 ounces cooked ham
50 g/2 ounces sausage meat
½ Spanish onion, finely chopped
1 clove garlic, finely chopped
2 tablespoons butter
1–3 teaspoons chopped thyme
2 tablespoons finely chopped
  flat-leaf parsley

salt and freshly ground pepper
1 cupful stale breadcrumbs
150 ml/¼ pint milk
1 beaten egg
flour
olive oil
butter
dry white wine or stock

Put the raw veal, cooked ham and sausage meat through the finest blade of your mincer 3 times. Sauté the onion and garlic in butter until transparent. Combine the minced meats and sautéed vegetables in a large mixing bowl; add the thyme, parsley, and salt and pepper, to taste.

Soak the breadcrumbs in the milk for 5 minutes; press out as much of the milk as you can and add the crumbs to the meat mixture. Stir in the beaten egg and mix well.

Form patties of the veal; dredge with flour and sauté in olive oil and butter for 2 to 3 minutes on each side. Pour off excess fat; cover the pan and simmer gently for 15 minutes, turning the patties from time to time. Serve with the pan juices, to which you have added a little dry white wine or stock.

## Moroccan Brochettes
Serves 4

450 g/1 pound calf's liver
225 g/½ pound beef fat
salt and freshly ground pepper

powdered cumin
crushed dried chillies

Cut the liver into cubes about 2 cm/¾ inch square; cut the fat into slightly smaller cubes. Thread the meat and fat on skewers alternately. Just before grilling over charcoal or under the grill, sprinkle with salt, pepper, cumin and chillies, to taste. Turn the skewers frequently during the cooking time.

# Sauté de Veau
Serves 4 to 6

1.3 kg/3 pounds boned shoulder
  of veal
flour
salt and freshly ground pepper
1 teaspoon paprika
2 tablespoons butter
2 tablespoons olive oil
2 onions, finely chopped
1 clove garlic
1 *bouquet garni*

300 ml/½ pint veal stock
150 ml/¼ pint dry white wine
12 small white onions
4 small carrots, sliced
1 tablespoon butter
1 tablespoon flour
2 tablespoons chopped flat-leaf
  parsley
buttered noodles or boiled new
  potatoes, to serve

Cut the veal into 5-cm/2-inch cubes; dredge the meat with the flour; season
with salt, pepper and paprika and sauté in hot butter and olive oil until browned
on all sides. Add the onions and garlic; allow to cook a little; then add the
*bouquet garni*, veal stock and white wine. Cover the pan and simmer gently for
45 minutes.

Add the onions and carrots; cover the pan and simmer until the vegetables are
tender and the meat cooked through. Remove the herbs, and if you like the sauce
to be a little thick, add a *beurre manié* (the flour and butter kneaded together and
stirred, bit by bit, into the stew until the liquid is thick and smooth). Sprinkle with
parsley and serve with buttered noodles or boiled new potatoes.

# Sauté de Veau Marengo
Serves 4 to 6

1.3 kg/3 pounds boned shoulder
  of veal
flour
salt and freshly ground pepper
2 tablespoons butter
2 tablespoons olive oil
2 onions, finely chopped
1 clove garlic, finely chopped
300 ml/½ pint veal stock

1 strip orange peel
1 *bouquet garni*
2–3 tablespoons tomato purée
150 ml/¼ pint dry white wine
1 tablespoon flour
1 tablespoon butter
2 tablespoons finely chopped
  flat-leaf parsley

Cut the veal into 5-cm/2-inch cubes; dredge the meat with the flour; season to taste
with salt and pepper. Sauté the veal in hot butter and olive oil until browned on
all sides. Add the onions and garlic; simmer for a few minutes.

Bring the veal stock to the boil; add the orange peel, *bouquet garni*, tomato
purée and white wine and pour over the veal pieces; cover the pan and simmer
until the meat is cooked through. Remove the herbs, and stir in a *beurre manié*
(the flour and butter, kneaded together and stirred, bit by bit, into the stew until
the liquid is thick and smooth). Sprinkle with parsley.

# Ris de Veau Truffé à la Crème
Serves 4

2 pairs calf's sweetbreads
juice of ½ lemon
*court-bouillon* (equal quantities
  of white wine, veal stock and
  water)
300 ml/½ pint hot béchamel
  sauce

1–2 tablespoons finely chopped
  truffle
1–2 tablespoons Madeira
salt and freshly ground pepper
cooked rice or vol-au-vent cases,
  to serve

Soak the sweetbreads in acidulated cold water (water and juice of ½ lemon) for 1 hour, changing the water when it becomes tinged with pink. Blanch them for 15 minutes in a simmering *court-bouillon*. When cool, trim and cut into slices 5 cm/2 inches thick. Add the sweetbreads to the hot *sauce béchamel* and heat thoroughly without letting the sauce boil. Add the truffle and Madeira to the sauce; season to taste with salt and pepper and serve in a ring of rice or in individual *vol-au-vent* cases.

Chapter 10

# Pork

## Choucroute Garnie

*Choucroute garnie* is the beginning and end of all informal party meals: perfect for informal parties, beer gatherings and any other hospitable occasion when appetites are keen. Do not attempt to make this dish unless you know seven hearty trenchermen to share it with you. For *choucroute* (sauerkraut) *garnie* (with all the trimmings) is not for the timid, for the wary or for the ubiquitous watchers of weight. This great country dish from Alsace is definitely for those who like to eat and prefer to wash down their hearty fare with generous quantities of chilled lager or dry white wine.

To me, making *choucroute garnie* is as enjoyable as eating it. For when you cook sauerkraut you do not just lump it into a pot. You cook it in a low oven or over a gentle, slow fire, tossing it from time to time with a long fork until it is soft.

For flavour embellishments: you add a little sliced onion, garlic and apple, perhaps a little grated potato, a few caraway seeds, or juniper berries if you have them, and instead of water, stock or dry white wine.

All sorts of changes can be rung upon the accessories cooked with or added to *choucroute* just before serving. Build your *choucroute garnie* on a flavoursome base of sauerkraut and add your choice of the following: salt pork, smoked ham, a wing or two of goose or partridge, a loin of pork or pork chops, and a combination of every type of sausage you can get your hands on ... *Bratwurst*, *Knockwurst*, Frankfurt or Vienna sausages, *saucisses de Toulouse* or just plain 'bangers'. In France, a hot, spicy Lorraine sausage is one of the highlights of the feast. I often add a *cotechino* sausage stripped of its casing, cooked with the sauerkraut and then cut into fat slices just before serving.

Serve your sauerkraut on your largest platter and dress it with cooked meats and sausages, ham and floury boiled potatoes. Serve with mustard, pickles and lashings of chilled lager or dry white wine. *Choucroute garnie* is a party feast you will long remember.

### Choucroute Garnie
Serves 8, royally

pork fat, thinly sliced
2 Spanish onions, sliced
2 cooking apples, cored and sliced
4 cloves garlic, coarsely chopped

1.3 kg/3 pounds sauerkraut, well washed
225–350 g/½–¾ pound salt pork
freshly ground pepper
6–8 juniper berries, crushed
dry white wine, to cover

1 boned loin of pork
1 large garlic sausage
8–16 sausages (*Bratwurst*,
   Toulouse, *Knockwurst* or

frankfurters)
8 boiled potatoes, to serve
8 slices cooked ham (optional),
   to serve

Line a deep earthenware casserole or stockpot with the pork fat; add half the onions, apples and garlic. Place a thick layer of well-washed and drained sauer-kraut on top with a piece of salt pork. Grind plenty of black pepper over it; sprinkle with juniper berries and add the remaining onions, apples and garlic. Place the remaining sauerkraut on top and add just enough dry white wine to cover. Put on the lid and cook in a 150°C/300°F/gas 2 oven for 4 to 6 hours. The longer it cooks the better.

A loin of pork, fresh or smoked, is excellent with *choucroute*. Add it to the *choucroute* about 2½ hours before serving. Half an hour later add a large garlic sausage and a selection of small sausages as available. To serve, heap the *choucroute* in the middle of a platter and arrange the slices of meat, garlic sausage and other sausages around it.

Serve with boiled potatoes and, if desired, slices of cooked ham.

# Bauernschmaus

In cooking, sometimes the simple things are best. When at home, Henri Soulé, the celebrated owner of New York's Pavillon and Côte Basque restaurants, loved to serve *brandade de morue*, a delicious purée of salt cod. Mario Gallati, the guiding light behind three famous London restaurants, the Caprice, the Empress and the Écu de France, liked nothing better than a huge plate of chicken-wing tips. René Hure, proprietor of the Hostellerie de la Poste in Avallon, one of France's greatest restaurants, used to serve his favourite guests an earthy *pot-au-feu* of beef, pork and chicken, simmered in beef stock, when he entertained at home.

One of my favourite peasant dishes (worthy, I think, to take its place among the Great Dishes of the World) is *Bauernschmaus* (a delectable concoction of boiled meats and sauerkraut, graced by the magisterial presence of a huge dumpling), an Austrian speciality famous from Salzburg to Vienna.

It was at the Vienna Culinary Festival held at the Carlton Tower that I renewed my happy acquaintance with this homely dish. Master chef Karl Duch and his team of Viennese experts prepared many delicious meals for us during his stay here: *Leberknödelsuppe* (strong consommé with calf's liver dumplings), *Tafelspitz 'alt Wiener Art* (the specially cut, slow-simmered beef so beloved by the Viennese) served with a chive and horseradish sauce and a beetroot salad, and *Paprikahuhn 'Franz Lehar'* (poached chicken in a paprika cream sauce), served with *spätzle* (home-made Viennese egg noodles). But it was the *Bauernschmaus* that I returned to sample time and time again.

*Bauernschmaus* is very simple to make in our English kitchens and very simple to serve. You will need a loin of pork, a piece of back bacon, sauerkraut, fresh or tinned, and some delicious bread dumplings flavoured with parsley and nutmeg.

# Bauernschmaus
Serves 6

1 loin of pork (cut into chops)
1 kg/2 pounds sauerkraut, with
    juices
beer or water, to cover
1 teaspoon cumin seeds
1–2 cloves garlic
salt and freshly ground pepper

crushed dried chillies
2 large potatoes, grated raw
2 Spanish onions, sliced
50 g/2 ounces lard
1 piece back bacon (sliced)
12 frankfurter sausages

Simmer the pork with the sauerkraut, beer, cumin seeds, garlic, and salt, pepper and crushed dried chillies, to taste, for 1½ hours. Stir in the raw potatoes, moistened with a little cold water. Cook for 2 to 3 minutes more.

Sauté the onions in the lard until transparent, add to the sauerkraut with the back bacon and frankfurters and simmer for 1 hour longer, adding water or more beer if necessary.

While the meat and sauerkraut are cooking, prepare and cook the dumplings.

To serve: drain the sauerkraut, reserving the juices, and pile on a large wooden platter. Surround with the 3 kinds of meat; garnish the platter with large dumplings and serve the gravy separately, seasoned to taste.

*Dumplings:*
6 bread rolls
150 ml/¼ pint milk
2 eggs, beaten

2 tablespoons finely chopped
    flat-leaf parsley
salt, freshly ground pepper and
    grated nutmeg
25–50 g/1–2 ounces sifted flour

Break up the rolls into small pieces and soak in the milk. Add the eggs, parsley and salt, pepper and nutmeg, to taste. Then add some of the flour and work the mixture into a dough with your hands, adding more flour if the dough is too moist to handle.

Shape the dough into 6 balls and drop them into a large saucepan of boiling salted water. Boil for 12 to 15 minutes, uncovered, until the dumplings rise to the surface. Skim the dumplings from water and drain well.

# Sauerkraut and Frankfurters
Serves 4

4 tablespoons butter
2 medium-sized Spanish onions,
    sliced
1 clove garlic, finely chopped
1 large jar undrained sauerkraut
    in white wine
300 ml/½ pint beer
2 tablespoons brown sugar

1 bay leaf
½ teaspoon celery (or caraway)
    seeds
salt and freshly ground pepper
8 frankfurters
paprika
mustard

Melt half the butter in a thick-bottomed frying pan and sauté the onion and garlic until lightly browned. Add the undrained sauerkraut, beer, sugar, bay leaf, celery (or caraway) seeds, and salt and pepper, to taste. Stir well, cover and simmer for about ¼ hour, stirring from time to time.

Slash the frankfurters diagonally to prevent bursting; dust with paprika and brown in the remaining butter. Serve with the sauerkraut and mustard.

## Roast Loin of Pork
Serves 6 to 8

| | |
|---|---|
| **1 loin of pork (7–8 cutlets)** | **salt and freshly ground pepper** |
| **4 tablespoons softened butter** | **crushed dried chillies** |
| **crumbled dried thyme and bay** | **flour** |
| **leaf** | **butter** |
| **Dijon mustard** | **watercress, to garnish** |

Have your butcher remove the rind from the loin without removing the fat. Mix the softened butter, thyme, bay leaf and mustard to a smooth paste and rub well into the pork several hours before roasting. Sprinkle to taste with salt, pepper and crushed dried chillies and let stand at room temperature to absorb flavours. Arrange the meat, fat side up, and brown in a hot oven (230°C/450°F/gas 8) for 15 minutes. Reduce the heat to slow (180°C/350°F/gas 4) and continue to roast until the meat is done, about 1¼ to 1½ hours.

Remove excess fat from the pan and thicken the pan drippings with a little flour kneaded with an equal amount of butter. Garnish with sprigs of watercress.

## Carré de Porc à la Bonne Femme
Serves 6 to 8

| | |
|---|---|
| **1 loin of pork (7–8 cutlets)** | **18 peeled small new potatoes** |
| **4 tablespoons softened butter** | **18 glazed small white onions** |
| **crumbled dried thyme and bay** | **18 sautéed mushroom caps** |
| **leaf** | **1 *bouquet garni*** |
| **salt and freshly ground pepper** | **2 tablespoons finely chopped** |
| **crushed dried chillies** | **flat-leaf parsley** |
| **2 tablespoons olive oil** | |

Have the butcher remove the rind from the loin, leaving the fat. Mix the softened butter, thyme and bay leaf to a smooth paste and rub well into the pork several hours before roasting. Sprinkle to taste with salt, pepper and crushed dried chillies, and let stand at room temperature to absorb flavours.

Place the pork, fat side up, in an ovenproof casserole; add the olive oil and roast in a slow oven (180°C/350°F/gas 4) for 1 hour or until half cooked. Place the new potatoes, small white onions and mushroom caps around the pork; add the *bouquet garni*, and continue cooking, basting frequently, until tender. Sprinkle with finely chopped parsley and serve from the casserole.

# Boiled Salt Pork with Pease Pudding
Serves 6 to 8

| | |
|---|---|
| 1 shoulder or breast of salt pork | **Pease Pudding:** |
| | 450 g/1 pound split peas |
| 6 large carrots | 1 Spanish onion, thinly sliced |
| 2 Spanish onions, each stuck with 1 clove | 100 g/¼ pound butter |
| | 3 eggs, beaten |
| 6 small leeks | salt, freshly ground pepper and |
| 6 parsnips | grated nutmeg |

Place the salt pork in water; bring to the boil; skim; add the vegetables; bring to the boil and skim again. Then lower the heat and simmer the pork and vegetables gently until tender. Place the pork on a heated serving dish; surround with the accompanying vegetables and serve with pease pudding.

**To make the pease pudding:**  Soak the peas in cold water overnight. Place in a saucepan with the onion; cover with water and simmer gently for 2 to 4 hours, or until cooked. Purée. Combine the purée of split peas, the butter and beaten eggs, and season to taste with salt, pepper and grated nutmeg. Mix well, put into a buttered pudding basin and cook in the oven, in water, until done; or place in a scalded, buttered and floured cloth, tie up and cook in the pot with the pork.

# Carré de Porc à la Provençale
Serves 6 to 8

| | |
|---|---|
| 1 loin of pork (7–8 cutlets) | olive oil |
| 8–12 sage leaves | 6 tablespoons water |
| salt and freshly ground pepper | 6 tablespoons dry white wine |
| crumbled dried thyme and bay leaf | 6 tablespoons olive oil |
| | 2–3 cloves garlic |

Have the butcher bone and tie the loin of pork. Pierce the pork with the point of a sharp knife and insert the sage leaves. Season to taste with salt, pepper, thyme and bay leaf. Sprinkle with a little olive oil and allow to stand for at least 12 hours to absorb the flavours.

Place the pork in an ovenproof casserole; add the water, white wine and olive oil; crush the garlic cloves with the flat of your hand and add them to cooking liquid. Roast the pork in a slow oven (180°C/350°F/gas 4) until tender, about 35 to 40 minutes per 450 g/pound.

## Pork Chops à la Charcutière

Serves 4

4 thick pork chops
2–4 tablespoons melted butter
breadcrumbs
salt and freshly ground pepper
puréed potatoes

*Charcutière Sauce:*
¼ Spanish onion, finely
  chopped
1 tablespoon butter

4–6 tablespoons dry white wine
1 tablespoon wine vinegar
300 ml/½ pint brown sauce
  (page 36)
1–2 tablespoons tomato purée
mustard
1–2 tablespoons finely chopped
  pickles
1–2 tablespoons finely chopped
  flat-leaf parsley

Trim excess fat from the pork chops; brush with melted butter; dip in breadcrumbs, pressing them well in, and season to taste with salt and pepper. Grill the chops until tender and cooked through. Serve with puréed potatoes and a *charcutière* sauce.

*To make charcutière sauce:* Sauté the onion in the butter until golden. Add the wine and vinegar and cook until the sauce is reduced to half its original quantity. Add the brown sauce; stir in the tomato purée and simmer, uncovered, stirring from time to time, for 15 minutes. When ready to serve, stir in mustard, to taste, and finely chopped pickles and parsley.

## Pork Chops 'Ardennaise'

Serves 4

4 thick pork chops
salt and freshly ground pepper
2 tablespoons butter
1 tablespoon lard
6 tablespoons dry white wine
2–3 crushed juniper berries
6 tablespoons beef stock

1 tablespoon butter
1 tablespoon flour
sautéed potatoes, mixed with
  bacon bits and finely chopped
  onion sautéed in butter, to
  serve

Trim excess fat from the pork chops; season with salt and pepper, to taste, and sauté in the butter and lard until tender. Remove the chops and keep warm.

Skim the excess fat from the pan and add the wine, stirring the crusty bits from the sides of the pan into the sauce. Add the juniper berries, beef stock and a *beurre manié* (made by kneading the butter and flour to a smooth paste). Bring to the boil; boil for a few minutes; correct the seasoning and pour over the chops. Serve with sautéed potatoes mixed with bacon bits and finely chopped, sautéed onion.

## Côtelettes de Porc au Sauge
Serves 4

1–2 tablespoons finely chopped
  onion
1–2 tablespoons finely chopped
  flat-leaf parsley
generous pinch crumbled dried
  sage (or about 2 leaves,
  chopped)
1 egg

salt and freshly ground pepper
4 thick pork chops
fresh breadcrumbs
olive oil or lard, for frying
sautéed sliced apples, to serve
sautéed sliced potatoes, to
  serve

Combine the onion, parsley, sage and egg in a bowl. Beat well; season to taste with salt and pepper. Trim excess fat from the pork chops and dip in this mixture several times. Drain well and dip in fresh breadcrumbs, pressing them well in. Allow to stand for 30 minutes. Fry the breaded chops in oil or lard. Serve immediately with sautéed apples and potatoes.

## Pork Chops in Wine
Serves 4

4 thick pork chops
sifted flour
2 tablespoons butter
1 tablespoon olive oil
salt and freshly ground pepper

2 tablespoons finely chopped
  shallots
150 ml/¼ pint dry white wine
2 tablespoons finely chopped
  flat-leaf parsley

Trim excess fat from the pork chops and blanch in boiling water for 1 minute. Drain; dry well and dust with sifted flour. Sauté the chops in butter and olive oil in a thick-bottomed frying pan until golden on both sides. Season to taste with salt and pepper. Add the shallots; then pour the wine over and simmer until it is reduced and the chops are tender.

Place the pork chops on a heated serving dish; pour the sauce over and sprinkle with parsley.

## Pork Chops 'Auberge du Grand Saint Pierre'
Serves 4

4 thick pork chops
2 tablespoons olive oil
1 tablespoon butter
salt and freshly ground pepper

100 g/¼ pound Gruyère cheese,
  finely grated
1–2 teaspoons strong mustard
double cream

Trim excess fat from the pork chops and sauté them gently with a little oil and butter in a thick-bottomed frying pan; season to taste with salt and pepper.

When cooked, spread with a *pommade* made of finely grated Gruyère (about 6 tablespoons) mixed with mustard and just enough cream to make a smooth mixture of spreading consistency.

Spread the chops generously with the cheese *pommade* and glaze quickly under the grill until the sauce is golden. Serve immediately.

### Jambon Chaud Mode d'Ici
Serves 4

4 shallots, finely chopped
150 ml/¼ pint dry white Chablis
1 sprig fresh tarragon, leaves
  only, finely chopped
150 ml/¼ pint rich beef stock
4 tablespoons tomato purée
sea salt and crushed dried
  chillies

150 ml/¼ pint crème fraîche
2 tablespoons diced butter
4 thick ham slices, heated
  through
finely chopped flat-leaf parsley,
  to serve

Make a good *sauce piquante* with a reduction of the shallots, Chablis and tarragon leaves. Moisten with the beef stock. Add the tomato purée; cover and simmer gently for an hour on a very low heat. Season with sea salt and a pinch of crushed dried chillies.

Whisk in the crème fraîche and simmer for 10 more minutes. Pass through a fine sieve; whisk in the diced butter and pour over the hot ham slices. Sprinkle with parsley and serve immediately.

# Chinese Pork and Prawn Balls in Sweet and Sour Sauce

Just how far back good cooking actually goes in China is hard to determine, but the Chinese were early discoverers of fire, and have been farmers for well over four thousand years. In the course of their long history they have evolved a high sense of harmony in the delicate blending of tastes and textures.

Few cooks now believe that Chinese food is too exotic to be attempted in the home kitchen. They know that – with a wok – nothing could be further from the truth. No other special utensils are needed and soy sauce and the few special extras – fresh ginger, bean sprouts, bamboo shoots, tiny hot chillies and water chestnuts – can now be purchased throughout the country.

Chinese dishes are inexpensive, quick to prepare and fun to cook. Using an electric frying pan, or a more traditional chafing dish, you can even cook Chinese food right in the dining room in front of your guests. A Chinese dinner served in true Oriental fashion assures an informal and happy evening. And for those who like an authentic atmosphere, Chinese serving dishes and chopsticks are inexpensive and easily obtainable.

## Serving a Chinese Meal

Rice is the staple food of the Chinese, the centre, the focal point, of a Chinese meal, but ringed with a dozen different dishes, each blending perfectly with it and with each other. According to Chinese food authority Kenneth Lo, an average Chinese meal consists of one or two soups – vegetable soup and a chicken or beef-based soup – one or two meat dishes, an egg or fish dish and one or two vegetable dishes, served in conjunction with the rice. In wealthier families, when up to a dozen separate dishes are served during each meal, rice merely acts as a 'buffer' to the rich and tasty dishes, which may be served course by course or all at the same time.

The one supreme meat for the Chinese is pork. Those Chinese who can afford it eat it almost every day, poorer Chinese dream about it, and even the poorest try to save up a few coins to buy some with which to celebrate the New Year.

Sweet and sour conveys the Orient to our Western palates. Here are two classic recipes for serving pork and prawn balls with this favourite sauce.

## Pork in Sweet and Sour Sauce
Serves 4

550 g/1¼ pounds minced pork
1 small clove garlic, minced
2 tablespoons sake (or 1
   tablespoon each water and
   dry sherry)

1–2 tablespoons soy sauce
salt and crushed dried chillies
oil for frying
sweet and sour sauce (see recipe
   below)

Combine the minced pork and garlic. Season with sake, soy sauce and salt and a pinch of crushed dried chillies, and form into small balls the size of a walnut. Sauté the pork balls in hot oil for about 5 minutes on each side. Remove the pork balls to a serving dish and keep hot. Just before serving, pour the hot sweet and sour sauce over them.

## Prawns in Sweet and Sour Sauce
Serves 4

450 g/1 pound shelled tiger
   prawns (or tiger prawns
   and fish)
100 g/¼ pound pork, not too
   lean, diced
1 dessertspoon cornflour
1–2 tablespoons mirin

(or 1 tablespoon each dry
   sherry and water)
1 tablespoon soy sauce
¼ teaspoon salt
1–2 teaspoons sugar
oil for frying
batter

Using a food processor process the prawns in short bursts. Add the diced pork and process again. Add the cornflour (dissolved in 4 tablespoons of water), mirin, soy sauce, salt and sugar. Make the paste into balls the size of large walnuts.

Heat the oil in a wok (or thick-bottomed frying pan) until very hot. Then reduce the heat; dip the balls in batter (see below) and place in the hot oil. Fry for about 5 minutes, turning from time to time so they are cooked to a golden brown on all sides.

This dish is best when served hot from the pan, but may be put in an oven to crisp for 5 minutes before serving.

**Batter:** 8 tablespoons ice-cold water

**1 egg** 8 tablespoons sieved flour

Stir the egg in a small bowl, but do not whip or beat. Add the ice-cold water and mix well; then sprinkle with sieved flour. Do not beat, just stir lightly to mix the ingredients. Do not worry about lumps in the batter. If you stir too much, the batter becomes sticky and will not react properly.

**Sweet and Sour Sauce:**
**1 small can pineapple chunks** | **1 tablespoon brown sugar**
**2 small carrots, thinly sliced** | **2–3 teaspoons soy sauce**
**1 green pepper, seeded and sliced** | **2 tablespoons peanut oil**
**1 tablespoon cornflour** | **2–3 tablespoons rice vinegar**
**4 tablespoons water** | **3–4 sweet pickles, sliced**

Drain the pineapple chunks. Reserve the juice. Simmer the carrots and pepper gently in the pineapple juice for 5 minutes, or until tender. Mix the cornflour, water, brown sugar, soy sauce, oil and vinegar together smoothly and stir into the stock. Cook for 3 minutes. Add the pineapple chunks and sliced pickles to the sauce. Pour over the pork and prawn balls and serve hot.

## Chinese Sweet and Sour Pork
Serves 6

**2 tablespoons soy sauce** | **1 onion, finely sliced**
**2 tablespoons cornflour** | **1 green pepper, cut in thin strips**
**2 tablespoons *sake* (or 1 table-** | **2 small carrots, finely sliced**
**spoon each dry sherry and** | **12 thin slices fresh ginger root**
**water)** | **1 tablespoon brown sugar**
**1 kg/2 pounds boned pork, cut in** | **3 tablespoons rice vinegar**
**20-cm/¾-inch cubes** | **6 tablespoons water**
**crushed dried chillies** | **1 tablespoon cornflour**
**oil for deep frying** | **salt**
**1 clove garlic, finely chopped**

Combine the soy sauce, cornflour and *sake* (or dry sherry and water), add the pork, season with crushed dried chillies and mix well. Let stand for 10 minutes. Fry the pork in oil until golden brown (about 10 minutes). Drain.

Heat 2 tablespoons oil in a frying pan and sauté the garlic, onion, green pepper, carrots and ginger root for 2 minutes. Mix the sugar, vinegar, water, cornflour and salt, to taste. Add to the vegetables, stirring steadily until the mixture comes to the boil. Return the pork to the pan. Cook over a low heat for 3 minutes.

## Chinese Braised Pork with Spinach (or Bok Choy)

Serves 6

2–4 tablespoons lard
1 kg/2 pounds boned pork, in
2.5-cm/1-inch cubes
4 tablespoons light soy sauce
2 tablespoons *sake* (or dry
sherry)
6 tablespoons water

1 teaspoon finely chopped ginger
1 clove garlic, finely chopped
1 generous pinch sugar
freshly ground pepper
2 tablespoons oil
450 g/1 pound baby spinach
leaves or bok choy

Heat the lard in a wok or deep frying pan; add the pork and sauté, stirring constantly, until golden brown. Combine the soy sauce, *sake* (or dry sherry), water, ginger, garlic, sugar and pepper, to taste, and pour over the pork. Bring the mixture to the boil; lower the heat, cover and simmer gently for 1 hour.

Heat the oil in a saucepan; add the washed drained spinach or bok choy and cook, stirring constantly, for 5 minutes. Drain well and serve with the pork.

# Italian Sausage

The humble sausage – esteemed worthy meat only for a country breakfast or a family supper of 'bangers and mash' in Britain today – was considered a great delicacy by the early Greeks and Romans.

The very word sausage comes from the Latin *salsus*, salty proof indeed that the sausage was a method of preserving as well as a type of food, a very necessary adjunct to good living in the days before refrigerators. And Italians today are as fond of the sausage as they were in Pliny's time.

A well-known Italian sausage, now so popular throughout the world that it is also produced in Germany, Hungary and the United States, is *salame*, generally made of lean pork, fat pork and beef, finely ground and highly seasoned, coloured with red wine and pickled in brine before it is air-dried. There is seemingly no end to the varieties of *salame* to be found in Italy today. Some are highly flavoured with garlic, others are mild; some are eaten fresh and others are considered to be at their best when they are most mature. A visit to any busy, crowded little *salumeria* in Rome – pungent-smelling shops with sausages of all sorts piled high in the windows and hung in stacks like church candles from the ceiling – will give you an immediate idea of the immense variety of *salame*, smoked and raw hams and sausages available.

Perhaps the most familiar to us in this country are the *crespone* or *salame de Milano*, about 6 cm/2½ inches in diameter, red-hued and granite-grained, with a very spicy flavour, and the *salame de Cremona*, a larger, slightly coarser-grained version of the Milan sausage. Try, too, the *salame casalinga*, a rough-marbled sausage with a more distinctive flavour; look for the deep cherry-red of the meat and the white waxiness of the fat which indicate that it is fresh.

*Salame fiorentino* – and its anise-flavoured brother, *salame finocchiona* – I have only had in Italy, but I am assured that they are available in this country from time to time. Both these sausages, specialities of Tuscany, are larger than the Milan sausage and made of pure lean pork and fat.

Good, too, for the *antipasti* platter are the silver-wrapped *cacciatora* and *turisto* sausages on sale here. They both keep well and are to be recommended for travellers and for picnics.

One of my favourite Italian sausages is the large, round, rosy-fleshed *mortadella*, a smooth-tasting sausage studded with square white chunks of fat. Italian-made *mortadella* is produced in Florence and Bologna from the flesh of pigs which feed on the chestnuts and acorns in the surrounding forests. Seasoned with wine, garlic and spices, it is very good for cooking.

The best sausages for culinary purposes are, of course, the ones specially made for this purpose . . . the *cotechino* sausage, a large sausage made of lean pork, fat salt pork, white wine and spices, is often served in Italy with brown lentils or white beans, the robust, country flavour and fat juiciness of this sausage providing the perfect complement to the mealy vegetables. Try slices of *cotechino*, too, with cooked spinach, a speciality of the Cotechino restaurant in Rome. *Cotechino* and the sausage-stuffed pig's trotter from Modena called *zampone* are often used interchangeably in the famous Italian dish *bollito misto*, mixed boiled meats. I first tasted this noble dish at Rome's glamorous Capriccio restaurant, which was located just off the Via Veneto. Capriccio's recipe combined lean beef, fat beef, veal, chicken, a calf's head and a *cotechino* sausage, simmered in salted boiling water with onions, celery, carrots and parsley. Very much like the French *pot-au-feu*, *bollito misto* is served with a *salsa verde* or a spicy tomato sauce.

Other Italian culinary sausages available in this country are the *salsicce negroni*, fat mottled sausages with a rustic flavour, and the thinner, finer *chipolate* sausages. The *negroni* are best poached in water until tender; make sure you prick several holes in each before placing in water; then dry them carefully and sauté gently in oil and butter until done. This method keeps sausages from splitting and yet assures that they are cooked through without taking on too much colour. The *chipolate* are cooked in the usual manner.

## Bean and Sausage Platter
Serves 4

| | |
|---|---|
| 8 **Italian sausages** | 6–8 **tablespoons cold water** |
| 2 **tablespoons olive oil** | 450 g/1 **pound dry white beans,** |
| 2 **tablespoons butter** | **soaked and cooked** |
| 6–8 **tablespoons tomato purée** | **salt and freshly ground pepper** |

Prick holes in the sausages with a fine skewer or the point of a sharp knife; place in a frying pan just large enough to hold them and cover with water. Cook over medium heat until the water evaporates. Remove the sausages and brown in a little oil with butter, turning them from time to time until they are cooked through and well coloured on all sides (20 to 30 minutes). In this way the sausages will be well cooked, will remain soft and keep their skins intact. Remove the sausages. Add the tomato purée to the fat in the pan. Cook for a minute or two, stirring; then add the cold water and simmer gently for 10 minutes.

Add the cooked and drained white beans, season with salt and pepper and simmer gently for a few minutes to allow the beans to absorb the flavour. Return the sausages to the pan and heat through. Serve the beans on a serving platter, topped by sausages.

## Cotechino with Lentils
Serves 4

| | |
|---|---|
| 1 *cotechino* sausage | 1 tablespoon olive oil |
| 350 g/¾ pound brown lentils | 1 tablespoon butter |
| salt | salt and freshly ground |
| ½ Spanish onion, chopped | pepper |
| 2 stalks celery, chopped | 1–2 tablespoons finely chopped |
| 50 g/2 ounces fat salt pork, diced | flat-leaf parsley |

Prick holes in the skin of the *cotechino* with a fine skewer or the point of a sharp knife. Put the *cotechino* in cold water in a pan just large enough to hold it and bring slowly to the boil. Turn down the heat and let the water barely bubble for about 2 hours. While still hot, remove the skin gently and allow the sausage to cool. Reserve the liquid. When the sausage is cool, cut it into fairly thick slices.

Wash the lentils well, picking out any impurities; cook in salted boiling water with the onion and celery for about 1½ hours. When the lentils are soft, drain thoroughly. Sauté the fat salt pork in the olive oil and butter until golden, in the bottom of a flameproof casserole. Add the drained lentils and moisten with a little of the liquid from the *cotechino*. Season to taste with salt and pepper; bring to the boil and then simmer gently for a few minutes until the lentils have absorbed all the liquid. Place *cotechino* slices on top; heat through. Sprinkle with parsley and serve in the casserole.

## Saucisses au Vin Rouge
Serves 4 to 6

| | |
|---|---|
| 2 tablespoons butter | 300 ml/½ pint good red wine |
| 450 g/1 pound Toulouse sausages | salt and freshly ground pepper |
| 2 tablespoons dry breadcrumbs | powdered thyme and bay leaf |

Melt the butter in a frying pan and sauté the sausages over a low heat until golden on all sides, turning them from time to time with a wooden spoon. Add the breadcrumbs, turn up the heat and let the breadcrumbs take on colour. Add the wine;

bring to the boil; lower the heat and simmer gently for 10 minutes. Add salt and pepper, a pinch of thyme and a bay leaf, and simmer for 5 to 10 minutes more.

## Home-made Sausage Patties

Serves 4 to 6

**700 g/1½ pounds lean pork**
**350 g/¾ pound fat salt pork**
**1 clove garlic, crushed**
**1 teaspoon salt**
**1 bay leaf, crushed**
**¼–½ teaspoon ground allspice**
**½–¾ teaspoon ground coriander seeds**
**1 teaspoon coarsely ground pepper**

**1 pinch crushed dried chillies**
**1 egg**
**1 Spanish onion, finely chopped**
**1 teaspoon dried thyme**
**4 tablespoons finely chopped flat-leaf parsley**
**2 tablespoons butter**
**2 tablespoons olive oil**
**soft scrambled egg, to serve**

Put the meat through the finest blade of your mincer, or have it ground by your butcher. Combine the garlic, salt, bay leaf, allspice and coriander, to taste, with coarsely ground pepper and crushed dried chillies in a mortar, and pound to a smooth paste. Add this mixture to the ground meat with the egg, onion, thyme and parsley. Mix thoroughly and form into patties. Sauté in the butter and olive oil until cooked through but not dry. Serve with soft scrambled eggs.

# Chapter 11
# Poultry and Game

## Coq-au-Vin

I made my first contact with *coq-au-vin*, one of the undisputed glories of French cuisine, when I was eighteen. The place – a little French restaurant on New York's West Side, one of those little *bistros* run by a French family, where you could eat inexpensively yet wonderfully well.

Maman served smilingly behind the bar in the small front room with its three or four tables. Papa cooked the specialities of France in the back dining-room-cum-kitchen, separated from his clients only by a low counter, and their daughter served at table. Each night had Papa's favourite speciality: Monday was a creamy *blanquette de veau*; Tuesday, a hearty sausage-and-game-filled *cassoulet*; Wednesday, a majestic *pot-au-feu*; Thursday, *navarin de mouton*, garnished with Papa's own vegetables; Friday was *bouillabaisse* night. But best of all, for me at least, was Saturday, for that was the night they served *coq-au-vin*.

Papa's *coq-au-vin* was a simple affair – chicken simmered in red Burgundy and chicken stock, thickened with a *beurre manié*, garnished with *lardons* of fat salt pork, tiny white onions and baby new potatoes – and I returned there as often as I could after that first visit to enjoy this great country dish.

If that *coq-au-vin* was my first, it was certainly not my last, for this famous dish has travelled from its native Burgundy throughout the length and breadth of France. I do not know of a restaurant in all France that at some time does not feature a version of it. I have enjoyed chicken cooked in red wine, white wine, and even in champagne; I have had it garnished with button mushrooms, tiny white onions, *lardons* of fat salt pork or green bacon, *croûtons* of fried bread or golden pastry crescents, and even with soft-textured cockscombs as it is served today at the Restaurant La Bourgogne in Paris.

Here is my favourite recipe for this famous dish.

### Coq-au-Vin
Serves 4 to 6

| | |
|---|---|
| 1 1.3-kg/3-pound chicken | 12 small white onions |
| 3 tablespoons butter | 12 button mushrooms |
| 2 tablespoons olive oil | flour |
| 100 g/¼ pound green bacon in 1 | salt and freshly ground pepper |
| piece, diced | 2 cloves garlic, finely chopped |

1 sprig thyme
2 bay leaves
2 sprigs flat-leaf parsley
4 tablespoons cognac
½ bottle good red wine

1 lump sugar
1 tablespoon butter
1 tablespoon flour
2 tablespoons finely chopped
flat-leaf parsley

Cut the chicken into serving pieces. Heat the butter and olive oil together with the green bacon in a heatproof casserole. When the bacon begins to turn golden, add the onions and cook for a minute or two, and then add the mushrooms. Sauté this mixture gently until the onions begin to turn transparent and the mushrooms to brown; remove from the casserole and keep warm.

Roll the chicken pieces in seasoned flour and sauté in the same fat for about 5 minutes, or until they turn golden on one side. Then, without piercing, turn the chicken pieces over to brown on the other side. As each of the pieces begins to 'stiffen', remove and put it in a covered dish in a warm oven. Next, return the onions, bacon, mushrooms, chicken segments and their juices to the casserole. Add salt, pepper, garlic, thyme, bay leaves and parsley; cover the casserole and cook in a moderate oven (190°C/375°F/gas 5) until almost tender. Remove the chicken pieces, bacon and vegetables from the casserole and keep warm. Skim off the excess fat from the juices in the casserole. Set the casserole on a high heat, pour in the cognac, warmed in a soup ladle, and ignite it. Allow to burn for a minute or two and then extinguish by pouring in the red wine. Add the sugar; bring to the boil and reduce the sauce over a quick heat to half the original quantity. Thicken with a *beurre manié* made of the tablespoon each of butter and flour. Strain the sauce into a clean casserole; return the chicken pieces, bacon and vegetables to the casserole; cover and allow to simmer in a very slow oven until ready to serve. Garnish with parsley.

## Chicken en Cocotte
Serves 4

1 tender chicken
salt and freshly ground pepper
2 tablespoons butter
2 tablespoons olive oil
100 g/¼ pound fat bacon in 1
piece, diced
4 shallots, coarsely chopped

2 carrots, coarsely chopped
4 tablespoons cognac
4 tomatoes, peeled, seeded and
chopped
1 *bouquet garni*
300 ml/½ pint red wine

Cut the chicken into serving pieces and season to taste with salt and pepper. Heat the butter and oil in an iron *cocotte* or heavy casserole and sauté the bacon pieces until golden. Remove the bacon; add the shallots and carrots and cook, stirring constantly, until the vegetables 'soften'; then add the chicken pieces and brown them on all sides. Return the bacon bits to the pan; pour over the cognac and flame. Then add the tomatoes, *bouquet garni* and red wine. Cover the casserole and let the chicken simmer over a low heat until it is very tender. Add more wine or chicken stock if the sauce reduces too quickly while cooking.

# Poulet François 1er
Serves 4

1 1.6-kg/3½-pound chicken
4 tablespoons butter
225 g/½ pound button mushrooms, quartered
225 g/½ pound small white
   onions

4 tablespoons Calvados
150 ml/¼ pint fresh cream
1 *bouquet garni* (flat-leaf
   parsley, thyme and celery)
salt and freshly ground pepper
fried bread triangles, to garnish

Cut the chicken into quarters and sauté in the butter until golden. Add the button mushrooms and onions, and simmer gently for 5 minutes.

Pour the warmed Calvados over and flame, shaking the pan until the flames die out. Moisten with the cream; add the *bouquet garni* and salt and pepper, to taste, then cover the casserole and cook in a slow oven (170°C/325°F/gas 3) for 45 minutes, or until the chicken is tender.

To serve: place the chicken on a heated serving dish, correct the sauce for seasoning and pour over. Garnish with fried bread triangles and serve immediately.

# Mediterranean Chicken
Serves 4

1 1.6-kg/3½-pound chicken
225 g/½ pound fat bacon in 1
   piece, diced
2 tablespoons butter
2 tablespoons olive oil
225 g/½ pound green olives,
   pitted

225 g/½ pound button
   mushrooms
salt and freshly ground pepper
6 tablespoons cognac
450 g/1 pound diced sautéed
   potatoes
4 tomatoes, sliced

Sauté the whole chicken and the diced green bacon in the butter and olive oil in a flameproof casserole until the chicken is golden on all sides.

Add the green olives, which you have previously soaked in hot water for 15 minutes to remove excess salt, and the button mushrooms. Season the chicken to taste with a little salt and pepper. Moisten with the cognac. Cover the casserole and cook in a slow oven (170°C/325°F/gas 3) for 45 minutes. Add the sautéed potatoes and the tomatoes and simmer gently for another 15 minutes, or until the chicken is tender. Serve in the casserole or on a serving dish.

# Italian Chicken Casserole
Serves 4

225 g/½ pound cooked ham in 1
   piece, diced
4 tablespoons fresh breadcrumbs
2 cloves garlic, finely chopped

2 tablespoons finely chopped
   flat-leaf parsley
1 beaten egg
freshly ground pepper

1 1.6-kg/3½-pound chicken
2 tablespoons butter
2 tablespoons olive oil
150–300 ml/¼–½ pint chicken
   stock

2 tablespoons tomato purée
finely chopped flat-leaf parsley,
   to garnish
cooked rice, to serve

Combine the ham, breadcrumbs, garlic and parsley in a bowl and mix well. Moisten with the beaten egg; season to taste with pepper and stuff the chicken with this mixture.

Melt the butter and olive oil in a thick-bottomed, flameproof casserole and sauté the chicken until golden on all sides. Combine the chicken stock and tomato purée and pour over the chicken. Cover the casserole and simmer gently on top of the stove or in a slow oven (170°C/325°F/gas 3) for about 1 hour, or until the chicken is tender. Correct the seasoning; garnish with parsley and serve with rice.

## Chicken à la Grecque
Serves 4

1 Spanish onion
2 large carrots
2 stalks celery
2 tablespoons butter
2 tablespoons olive oil
1 1.6-kg/3½-pound chicken
150–300 ml/¼–½ pint well-
   flavoured chicken stock
6 tablespoons dry white wine
cooked rice, to serve

*Stuffing:*
6 tablespoons finely chopped
   shallots

2 tablespoons butter
100 g/¼ pound toasted breadcrumbs
2 cloves garlic
2 stalks celery, finely sliced
2 tablespoons finely chopped
   flat-leaf parsley
grated rind of ½ lemon
salt and freshly ground
   pepper
pinch dried rosemary
4 tablespoons cognac

Cut the onion, carrots and celery into thin strips. Combine the butter and olive oil in a saucepan; add the vegetables and cook, stirring continuously, until soft, about 5 minutes. Transfer to a casserole.

To prepare the stuffing: cook the shallots in the butter until transparent. Mix with the remaining stuffing ingredients; fill the cavity of the bird and close the opening with small skewers. Place the bird on top of the vegetables; cook in a preheated oven (230°C/450°F/gas 8) for 20 minutes. Pour the chicken stock over. Cover the casserole; reduce the heat to 170°C/325°F/gas 3 and cook until the chicken is tender, about 30 minutes.

To serve: arrange the drained vegetables and chicken on a hot serving dish. Garnish with cooked rice. Pour the white wine into the stock in the casserole; cook rapidly for several minutes to reduce slightly. Strain and serve with the bird.

# Chicken in Champagne Oasis

Serves 4

1 tender chicken (about 1.3 kg/
   3 pounds)
4–6 tablespoons butter
2 tablespoons finely chopped
   onion
salt and freshly ground pepper

1 tablespoon flour
½ bottle champagne
300 ml/½ pint crème fraîche
4 egg yolks
2 tablespoons crème fraîche

Cut the chicken into serving pieces and simmer in the butter in a flameproof casse-role with the onion and salt and pepper, to taste. Turn the chicken pieces several times; cover the casserole and let them steam at the lowest possible heat for 10 minutes. The chicken should not take on colour.

Sprinkle the chicken pieces with the flour; turn several times and then pour the champagne over. Cover the casserole and simmer gently for 15 minutes more, or until the chicken is tender.

Arrange the chicken pieces on a warm serving dish; cover and keep warm in a low oven. Reduce the pan juices in which the chicken was cooked to a quarter of the original quantity over a high heat. Whisk in the crème fraîche and continue cooking, stirring from time to time, until the sauce is reduced by half.

Whisk the egg yolks and 2 tablespoons crème fraîche until well blended; add a little of the hot sauce to this mixture; blend well and pour the mixture into the hot sauce. Simmer the sauce over a very low heat, or over water, until thick and smooth. Do not allow it to boil. Correct the seasoning and strain over the chicken through a fine sieve. Serve very hot.

# Summer Chicken Casserole

Serves 4

1 1.3-kg/3-pound chicken
2 tablespoons butter
2 tablespoons olive oil
12 small white onions
1 tablespoon flour
salt and freshly ground
   pepper

1 *bouquet garni* (flat-leaf
   parsley, thyme, bay leaf)
24 button mushrooms
2 tablespoons butter
juice of 2 lemons
2 egg yolks
300 ml/½ pint double cream

Cut the chicken into 8 serving pieces and sauté in the butter and oil with the onions until they just begin to turn colour. Sprinkle with the flour and add just enough water to cover the chicken. Season to taste with salt and pepper; add the *bouquet garni*, cover the casserole and cook for about 1½ hours, or until the chicken is tender. Remove the chicken and onions to a deep serving dish or shallow casserole. Reserve the stock.

Sauté the mushrooms in the butter and the juice of 1 lemon until tender, then add to the chicken and onions. Whisk egg yolks, juice of 1 lemon and half the double cream in a bowl. Bring the stock to the boil, and, whisking vigorously, add a ladle of boiling stock to the cream and egg mixture. Pour the mixture into the hot stock and bring gently to the boil, whisking well until the sauce is thick and creamy. Strain the sauce through a fine sieve into a clean bowl and allow it to cool. When it is cool, whisk the remaining cream into it; correct the seasoning and pour over the chicken and vegetables. Toss well. Chill.

## Roast Chicken with Moroccan Flavours
Serves 4

2 tablespoons chopped flat-leaf parsley
2 tablespoons chopped coriander leaves
1 Spanish onion, chopped
1 clove garlic, finely chopped
4–6 tablespoons butter
½ teaspoon sea salt

1 teaspoon powdered cumin
½ teaspoon paprika
¼ teaspoon each saffron and ginger
generous pinch crushed dried chillies
1 roasting chicken

Pound the chopped parsley, coriander, onion and garlic in a mortar. Add the butter, salt, spices and chillies and pound to a smooth paste.

Spread the chicken with this mixture and roast in the usual manner, basting with the sauce from time to time.

## Moroccan Chicken with Chickpeas
Serves 6 to 8

1 chicken (about 1.8 kg/ 4 pounds)
salt
¼ teaspoon paprika
¼ teaspoon powdered cumin
freshly ground pepper
350 g/¾ pound Spanish onions, sliced
75 g/3 ounces butter
¼ teaspoon powdered saffron

100 g/¼ pound chickpeas, soaked overnight
well-flavoured chicken stock
4 tablespoons finely chopped flat-leaf parsley
4 sprigs coriander or 2 sprigs lemon thyme
225 g/½ pound rice, cooked in salted water with butter
2 tablespoons butter
lemon juice

Cut the chicken into serving pieces; season to taste with salt, paprika, cumin and pepper, and sauté with the onions in the butter in a casserole until golden.

Sprinkle with saffron; add the chickpeas and enough good chicken stock to cover, and simmer gently for 1 to 1½ hours, or until the chicken is tender. Just before serving, add the parsley and coriander or lemon thyme.

To serve: spoon half of the rice into a heated serving dish; place the chicken pieces on it; pour over the saffron sauce; add the remaining rice and sprinkle with lemon juice.

## Chicken Braised in White Wine
Serves 4

1 tender 1.8-kg/4-pound chicken
2 tablespoons butter
2 tablespoons olive oil
100 g/4 ounces fat bacon in 1
  piece, diced
4 shallots, coarsely chopped

2 carrots, coarsely chopped
2 tablespoons cognac
1 *bouquet garni*
salt and freshly ground pepper
300 ml/½ pint dry white wine
150 ml/¼ pint chicken stock

Heat the butter and oil in an iron *cocotte* or a heavy heatproof casserole just large enough to hold the chicken. Dice the bacon pieces and sauté in fat until golden. Remove the bacon; add the chopped shallots and carrots and cook, stirring constantly, until the vegetables 'soften'; then add the chicken and brown on all sides.

Return the bacon bits to the pan; pour over the cognac and flame. Then add the *bouquet garni*, salt and pepper, to taste, and the dry white wine and chicken stock. Cover the bird with a piece of buttered paper cut to fit the casserole, with a small hole in the centre to allow steam to escape. Cover the casserole and simmer gently over a very low heat until tender (1 to 1¼ hours). Add more wine or a little chicken stock if the sauce reduces too quickly during the cooking.

## Oven-fried Chicken
Serves 4

1 tender 1.2-kg/2½-pound frying
  chicken
50 g/2 ounces flour
1 teaspoon salt
½ teaspoon black peppercorns,
  crushed
2 tablespoons finely chopped
  flat-leaf parsley
1 teaspoon dried tarragon,
  crushed

1 teaspoon dried rosemary,
  crushed
grated zest of 1 lemon
1 egg, beaten
milk
4 tablespoons butter
4 tablespoons olive oil
thin triangles of bread, for
  frying

Cut the chicken into serving pieces.

Combine the flour, salt, pepper, parsley, tarragon, rosemary and lemon zest in a bowl. Combine the egg and a little milk in another bowl. Dip the chicken pieces into the egg mixture and then into the seasoned flour. Chill.

Place the butter and oil in a shallow baking dish and heat in a moderately hot oven (200°C/400°F/gas 6) until the butter sizzles. Place the chicken pieces in the dish; spoon butter over them and cook for 45 to 50 minutes, or until the chicken is tender and brown, turning the pieces once or twice during the cooking time.

Serve the chicken pieces on thin slices of toast sautéed in butter until crisp. Accompany with the pan juices.

# Poule-au-Pot Henri IV
## Good King Henry's Chicken in the Pot

Serves 4 to 6

**1 fine fat chicken**
**(1.6–2.5 kg/3½–4½ pounds)**

*Court-Bouillon:*
**1 veal knuckle**
**1 teaspoon salt**
**freshly ground pepper**
**2 carrots**
**2 leeks**
**2 turnips**
**2 potatoes**
**few cabbage leaves, if available**
**1 Spanish onion, stuck with 2**
**cloves**
**1 *bouquet garni* (celery, flat-leaf**
**parsley, bay leaf)**

*Stuffing:*
**100 g/¼ pound green bacon**
**100 g/¼ pound fresh pork**
**2–3 cloves garlic**
**100 g/¼ pound dry breadcrumbs**
**milk, to moisten**
**2–3 tablespoons finely chopped**
**flat-leaf parsley**
**½ teaspoon dried tarragon or**
**chervil**
**generous pinch mixed spice**
**2 eggs**
**salt and freshly ground pepper**

**To make the court-bouillon:**  Combine the gizzard, heart, wing tips, neck and feet of the chicken with the veal knuckle, salt, pepper, vegetables and *bouquet garni* in a large saucepan. Add 3.4 litres/6 pints of water and bring to the boil. Skim, lower the heat and simmer, covered, for 1 hour.

**To make the stuffing:**  Put the chicken liver, bacon, pork and garlic through the finest blade of the mincer. Moisten the breadcrumbs with milk; combine with the minced meats and add the parsley, dried herbs, mixed spice, eggs and salt and pepper, to taste. Mix well, adding more milk if necessary to make a fairly loose mixture.

Stuff the chicken; sew up the openings and truss the bird. Poach, covered, in the *court-bouillon* for approximately 1 hour, or until tender. If there is any stuffing left over, tie it in cabbage leaves and poach with the chicken for the last 20 minutes of cooking time.

**To serve:**  For a family luncheon: the hot broth is served first, followed by the chicken surrounded by freshly poached vegetables ... choose among carrots, turnips, onions, green beans and potatoes.

For a company dinner: place the chicken on a heated serving dish and surround with individual pastry shells filled with glazed carrots, onions or French-style peas. Just before serving, spoon a little chicken *velouté* sauce (see page 35) over the chicken and serve the remaining sauce separately.

# Poulet à la Crème
Serves 4

1 1.2-kg/3½-pound chicken
100 g/¼ pound butter
1 medium onion, finely
    chopped

salt and freshly ground pepper
hot water, to cover
300 ml/½ pint cream
4 egg yolks

Cut the chicken into 8 serving pieces. Melt the butter in a large, heavy-bottomed frying pan or flameproof casserole and sauté the chicken pieces gently without letting them colour.

Add the onion, salt and pepper, to taste; cover with hot water and simmer gently until tender.

Just before serving, combine the cream and egg yolks and pour over the chicken. Heat through for 5 minutes, stirring continuously, taking care that sauce never comes to the boil. Correct the seasoning and serve immediately.

# Poule au Riz au Safran
Serves 4

1 fat chicken
1 Spanish onion, stuck with 2
    cloves
2 large carrots
1 *bouquet garni*
1 stalk celery
2 cloves garlic
1 glass dry white wine
1.2 litres/2 pints white stock
    (chicken or veal, or both)
salt and white peppercorns

*Saffron Rice:*
2 tablespoons butter

1 Spanish onion
225 g/½ pound rice
½ quantity of the chicken stock,
    strained
salt and freshly ground pepper
freshly grated nutmeg
1 generous pinch saffron

*Chicken Velouté Sauce:*
2 tablespoons flour
2 tablespoons butter
remainder of the chicken stock
2 egg yolks
juice of 1 lemon

Clean, singe and truss the chicken; place in a casserole with the onion; add the carrots, *bouquet garni*, celery and garlic, and moisten with white wine and good white stock. Season to taste with salt and a few white peppercorns, and simmer gently for about 1½ hours, or until the chicken is tender. Remove the chicken and keep warm. Strain the chicken stock and use for saffron rice and for the chicken *velouté* sauce.

**To make the saffron rice:**  Melt the butter in a saucepan; add the onion and stir for a minute over the heat until transparent. Stir in the rice; add half of the strained chicken stock and salt, pepper, a little nutmeg and saffron, to taste, and simmer very gently, covered, for about 25 minutes, or until the rice is tender but not mushy.

**To make the chicken *velouté* sauce:** Make a white *roux* with the flour and butter; add the remaining chicken stock and bring slowly to the boil, stirring constantly. Simmer, stirring from time to time, until thick and smooth. Correct the seasoning and just before serving add the egg yolks and lemon juice.

# The Festive Duck

The duck is a festive bird. It is ideal for a special occasion. I am always disappointed when I hear cooks in this country recommending that it should be served 'plain roast with green peas and sauce'. I far prefer the Continental methods – French, Italian and Greek – of dealing with this delicious bird, half-way in flavour between poultry and game. It is rich, meltingly tender when young and fairly cries out to be simmered with wine, herbs and brandy in the Provençal manner. It can be filleted raw, marinated in Madeira and herbs and encased with the remainder of the meat, pounded and mixed with truffles and fat salt pork, in a terrine or *pâté en croûte*, or stuffed with rice or wheat and pine nuts and herbs *à la grecque*, before being roasted in the oven.

I remember delicious country meals in France at which duck was the star performer: duck *en gelée*, the duck simmered in a rich stock with carrots, onions and celery, cooled in its own liquids and then served whole in its own jelly, surrounded by young vegetables; duck *en casserole*, the duck cut into serving pieces and marinated overnight in wine and brandy, flavoured with garlic, herbs, onions and carrots, and then simmered in the marinade juices until tender. I also remember duck stuffed with diced green bacon, sauerkraut and diced green apples and roasted in the oven, bathed in dry white wine and its own juices.

But perhaps best of all, I like to roast my ducks to the half-way mark and then finish them with a variety of sweet and savoury ingredients. Duck goes wonderfully with oranges, olives, apples, cherries, herbs and spices, sauerkraut, wild rice, wines, cognac and gin.

Be imaginative with duck at your next dinner party. One 2.5–3-kg/5–6-pound duck, or two smaller ones, will serve 4 to 8 people easily.

## Duck Notes

Ducks mature rapidly and reach their prime about 9 to 12 weeks after they hatch, when they weigh around 2.5 to 3.5/5 to 7 pounds.

You can judge the age of a duck by pressing its beak with your finger. A young duck's beak should be soft and flexible, while an older bird's beak will be hard and firm. A duck is a very fat bird so you will not need to add additional fat when roasting. I usually cut all visible fat from openings before cooking and pour off excess fat occasionally as it accumulates in the pan. This fat – like goose fat – makes an admirable cooking medium for the best fried, sliced potatoes you've ever tasted.

# Roast Duckling
Serves 4 to 8

**Preparation:**  Trim the wing tips and cut off the neck of a 2.5–3-kg/5–6-pound duckling. Wipe the bird with a damp clean cloth inside and out, and sprinkle the cavity with salt and pepper. Rub the cavity with lemon juice or brandy and fill it with ½ sliced onion, ½ peeled and sliced apple and a few celery leaves.

**Preliminary roasting:**  Prick the skin of the bird with a fork; rub with a cut clove of garlic and sprinkle with salt and freshly ground pepper. Place the duckling, breast side up, on a rack in a roasting pan and cook in a moderate oven (190°C/375°F/gas 5) for ½ hour. Remove duck and keep warm.

**To finish the bird:**  Skim the excess fat from the pan, add 300 ml/½ pint dry white wine and continue to roast the bird until tender, basting frequently and allowing about 20 minutes cooking time to 450 g/pound.

# Duckling with Olives
Serves 4 to 8

**Preparation:**  As above.

**Preliminary roasting:**  As above.

**To finish the bird:**  Pour off all but 2 tablespoons of fat from the pan. Stir in 1 tablespoon flour and cook, stirring continuously, until the flour is golden. Add 150 ml/¼ pint chicken stock and 150 ml/¼ pint dry white wine and cook, stirring, until the sauce is smooth and slightly thickened. Transfer the sauce to an oven-proof casserole large enough to hold the duck; season to taste with salt and freshly ground pepper, and add a *bouquet garni* (3 sprigs flat-leaf parsley, 1 bay leaf, 1 stalk celery, 1 sprig thyme).

Place the duck in the casserole and cook, covered, for about 1 hour, or until the duck is tender. Pit 24 green olives and poach them in water for 5 minutes to remove excess salt. Place the duck on a heated serving platter; add the drained olives to the sauce and pour it over the bird. Serve immediately.

# Duckling with Oranges
Serves 4 to 8

**Preparation:**  As above.

**Preliminary roasting:**  As above, but continue roasting, basting from time to time, until the duck is tender, allowing about 20 minutes cooking time to 450 g/pound. Remove the duck from the pan and keep warm.

**To finish the bird:**  Skim the fat from the pan juices and add 150 ml/¼ pint chicken stock, scraping in all the crusty bits from the bottom and sides of the pan.

Stir in the juice of 2 Seville oranges and 1 lemon, and 2 tablespoons cognac. Blend 4 tablespoons each of sugar and water in another pan and cook until the sugar turns to caramel. Add this to the sauce, season with salt, freshly ground pepper and a pinch of crushed dried chillies, and simmer gently until it is reduced by half.

Carve the duckling; place on a heated serving platter; pour the sauce over it and sprinkle with the zest of 2 Seville oranges cut into thin strips and blanched in boiling water. Garnish with fresh orange segments and watercress.

## Duck en Daube
Serves 4

1 tender duck
salt and freshly ground pepper
1 stalk celery, chopped
2 carrots, sliced
2 large onions, sliced
120 ml/4 fluid ounces cognac
425 ml/¾ pint dry red wine

100 g/¼ pound fat bacon in 1
 piece, diced
1 tablespoon olive oil
1 *bouquet garni*
1 clove garlic
225 g/½ pound mushrooms,
 sliced

Cut the duck into serving pieces and place in a porcelain or earthenware bowl. Add salt and pepper, the celery, carrots, sliced onions, cognac and red wine, and marinate the duck in this mixture for at least 2 hours.

Remove the duck from the marinade; drain and dry with a clean cloth. Sauté the bacon in olive oil until golden. Remove the bacon bits and brown the duck pieces in the resulting fat. Place the bacon bits and duck pieces with the pan juices in a large ovenproof casserole and cook, covered, for 20 minutes.

Add the marinade, *bouquet garni*, garlic and mushrooms. Cook over a low heat for 1½ hours, or until the duck is tender. Remove the *bouquet garni*; skim the fat; correct the seasoning and serve in the casserole.

## Duck with Sauerkraut and Apple Stuffing
Serves 4

175 g/6 ounces fat salt pork
1 large onion, coarsely chopped
2 cooking apples, peeled, cored
 and diced
2 tablespoons brown sugar

salt and freshly ground pepper
crushed dried thyme
1 teaspoon caraway seeds
700 g/1½ pounds sauerkraut
1 tender duck

Dice the salt pork and heat in a frying pan until transparent. Add the onion and fry until transparent. Add the apples and toss with the onion and salt pork. When the apples and onion are golden, add the brown sugar, salt, pepper, thyme and caraway seeds. Remove from the heat. Drain the sauerkraut and toss with the apple and onion mixture.

Wash the duck inside and out. Rub the cavity with a little salt and pepper. Stuff with the apple-sauerkraut and truss. Prick well with a fork and place on a rack over a roasting pan. Roast in a slow oven (180°C/350°F/gas 4) for about 2½ hours, pricking the duck from time to time to allow the fat to escape. When the leg joint moves freely, the bird is done.

## Roast Goose

| | |
|---|---|
| **1 fat goose (3.6–4.5 kg/8–10 pounds)** | **flour seasoned with salt and freshly ground pepper** |
| | **dry breadcrumbs** |

Stuff and tie the goose and sprinkle lightly with seasoned flour. Roast in a fairly hot oven (220°C/425°F/gas 7) for 15 minutes; reduce the heat to 180°C/350°F/gas 4 and continue roasting until the goose is tender (about 25 minutes per 450 g/pound if stuffed).

Do not baste the goose during cooking time as it is already fat enough. Remove the fat from the pan several times during cooking. It will keep indefinitely in a cool place and is great for frying potatoes.

If you cover the goose with aluminium foil, remove the foil at least ¼ hour before the end of the cooking time. Then, 15 minutes before the end of the cooking time, sprinkle the goose lightly with dry breadcrumbs; raise the oven heat to 220°C/425°F/gas 7 and cook for a final 15 minutes.

## Austrian Stuffing for Goose or Turkey

| | |
|---|---|
| **1 Spanish onion, finely chopped** | **juice of ½ lemon** |
| **lard** | **thyme and marjoram** |
| **225 g/½ pound sausage meat** | **salt and freshly ground pepper** |
| **2 tablespoons finely chopped flat-leaf parsley** | **225 g/½ pound poultry livers, chopped** |
| **4–6 anchovy fillets, finely chopped** | **50–75 g/2–3 ounces dry bread-crumbs** |
| **2 eggs** | |

Sauté the onion in lard until transparent. Add the sausage meat and sauté until the onion is golden. Combine the onion and sausage mixture in a bowl with the parsley, anchovy fillets, eggs, lemon juice, and thyme, marjoram, salt and pepper, to taste. Sauté the poultry livers in the remaining fat until browned on the outside; add the breadcrumbs and toss until golden. Combine with the other ingredients and stuff the bird.

## Stuffed Goose Neck

| | |
|---|---|
| 1 goose neck | salt and freshly ground pepper |
| 4–6 tablespoons brandy | crushed dried chillies |
| 2 cloves garlic, finely chopped | 450 g/1 pound sausage meat |
| 2 tablespoons finely chopped | 1 duck's liver, chopped |
| flat-leaf parsley | 2 truffles, coarsely chopped |
| 2 good pinches powdered | ½ teaspoon powdered mace |
| cinnamon | 6–8 tablespoons dry white wine |
| 1 good pinch powdered cloves | goose fat or lard, for frying |

Remove the skin from the fat goose neck by separating the skin from the neck at one end with a sharp knife. Peel back the skin and pull it off, inside out, as you would a glove.

Marinate the skin overnight in brandy seasoned with garlic, parsley, cinnamon, cloves and pepper and crushed dried chillies, to taste.

Make a stuffing of the sausage meat, duck's liver and truffles, and season to taste with mace, salt and pepper. Moisten with white wine and the marinade juices and mix well. Turn the skin right side out and stuff with the mixture; then tie or sew it firmly at both ends so that the stuffing cannot fall out during cooking.

Sauté the stuffed neck in goose fat or lard over a low heat until the dressing is cooked through and the neck is brown. Serve the stuffed goose neck hot or cold.

## Confit d'Oie
### Preserved Goose

| | |
|---|---|
| 1 fat goose | 1–2 pinches crushed dried chillies |
| 1 teaspoon salt | salt |
| 1 teaspoon powdered mixed | 2 glasses water |
| spices | melted lard, to cover (if |
| ¼ teaspoon crushed dried | necessary) |
| thyme | |

Cut the goose into 8 or 10 pieces, reserving all the goose fat. Pound the salt, spices, thyme and crushed dried chillies in a mortar; mix well and rub into the goose pieces. Place the pieces in a large casserole and add 20 g/¾ ounce salt per 450 g/pound of goose. Mix well and leave in a cool place for 24 to 36 hours.

Dice the reserved goose fat; combine with the water in a large saucepan or heat-proof casserole, and melt the fat gently over a low heat. When melted, add the goose pieces, from which you have brushed the salt, and simmer gently for 2½ hours, or until the goose is tender.

Wash deep earthenware or Pyrex containers with boiling water; dry well and arrange pieces of preserved goose in them. Continue to cook the fat until froth forms on the surface; skim thoroughly; remove the fat from the heat and cook for 10 minutes.

Pour the fat through a fine sieve to cover the goose pieces. If there is not enough fat to cover all the pieces, melt enough fresh lard to cover them completely. Allow to cool; seal the container with greaseproof paper and tie it securely. A well-prepared *confit* will keep in the refrigerator or in a cool place for several months, to be used little by little, either by itself (served hot with puréed potatoes) or as one of the star ingredients in a *cassoulet*.

## Roast Turkey

| | |
|---|---|
| **1 medium turkey** | **crushed dried chillies** |
| **strips of pork fat or green bacon** | **225 g/½ pound butter, melted** |
| **salt and freshly ground pepper** | **juice of 1 lemon** |

Place the turkey, breast side up, in a roasting pan and cover the breast with thin strips of pork fat or green bacon. Season to taste with salt and pepper and crushed dried chillies, and roast in a fairly hot oven (220°C/425°F/gas 7) for 15 minutes; then reduce the temperature to 180°C/350°F/gas 4 and cook until the juices run clear when the turkey is stuck with a skewer at the leg joint (10 to 15 minutes per 450 g/pound or 20 minutes per 450 g/pound if stuffed), basting frequently with melted butter and lemon juice.

If the turkey has not become golden towards the end of cooking time, bring the heat up to 220°C/425°F/gas 7 again and roast for 10 or 15 minutes more.

## Pintadeau Rôti et Flambé à la Riche
Serves 4 to 6

| | |
|---|---|
| **2 guinea fowl** | **100 g/¼ pound butter** |
| **300 ml/½ pint burgundy** | **100 l/¼ pound *pâté de foie gras*** |
| **grated zest of 1 lemon** | **1–2 tablespoons lemon juice** |
| **4–6 tablespoons cognac** | **salt and freshly ground pepper** |
| **Dijon mustard** | |

Roast the guinea fowl in a moderately hot oven (200°C/400°F/gas 6) for 25 to 30 minutes, or until almost cooked. Cut the birds into serving pieces.

Reduce the wine with the lemon zest to a third of its original quantity. Add the birds to the pan and heat through. Flame with warmed cognac. Stir in mustard, to taste, and continue to simmer for a few minutes, turning the birds from time to time.

Mix the butter and *foie gras* to a smooth paste and add to the pan, stirring in all the juices. Add the lemon juice. Stir pieces of guinea fowl into the sauce, making sure they are well covered. Season to taste with salt and pepper and serve immediately.

# Magdalen Venison

Most of us imagine that a medieval banquet would have consisted of a series of great set pieces like Sir Osbert Sitwell's recipe: 'You first captured a swan – having previously been granted, of course, the necessary royal permission – and then stuffed it with a peacock, inside which you had placed a pheasant, which contained a partridge, and so *ad infinitum.*' But the first written recipes in English, produced by Richard II's cooks in 1391, have an amazingly modern ring about them. I was surprised by the variety of fruits and vegetables available; the number of ways of preparing fish, both salt and 'green'; the different recipes for meat and game; the imaginative use of seasonings, wines and herbs; and the great variety of the recipes themselves. One, for example, advocates the use of grapes to stuff a chicken, together with garlic, parsley and sage.

But the modern ring of these ancient dishes is not so surprising. The High Tables of the Plantagenet kings and of the great houses of the Tudor nobility have their direct descendants in the High Tables at Oxford and Cambridge, where the rulers of the college still dine on a raised dais, separated from the commoners below them.

Famous feasts linger long in the memory of a place like Oxford. Gaudies and Bump Suppers, banquets to royalty and to visiting statesmen, even ordinary fish and flesh days, all have given rise to recipes that are handed down throughout the years from chef to chef in the college kitchens ... the Christmas Boar's Head at Queen's, the legendary Cherry Pie at All Souls, the superb Meringues of Christ Church, and at Magdalen, the seventeen-day ritual of Magdalen Venison.

One of Oxford's greatest dishes, Magdalen Venison, which has been served for two and a half centuries at the yearly Restoration Dinner, is a saddle of venison from the College's own herd, marinated for days, braised in Château wine, garnished with glazed chestnuts, glazed onions and sautéed mushrooms, and served with a heady port wine sauce.

Tradition has it that there should be only as many deer in the park as there are Fellows in College ... and so every year at the Restoration Dinner venison is served.

According to a centuries-old recipe, 'second year' beasts are selected from the herd, killed, blooded and stripped, dusted with rock salt and powdered ginger, and allowed to hang for at least ten days. Then the choicest bits – the saddle, leg or haunch – are cut for High Table and marinated for three days to one week to improve the flavour and tenderise the meat.

# Magdalen Venison
Serves 8 to 10

saddle of venison (2.2–3.2 kg/
  5–7 pound)
4 tablespoons butter
4 tablespoons olive oil
225 g/½ pound diced salt pork

*Marinade:*
1 Spanish onion, sliced
2 carrots, sliced
2 tablespoons butter or olive oil
1 bottle Château wine, either
  burgundy or claret
3 sprigs flat-leaf parsley
1 sprig thyme
1 bay leaf

2 cloves garlic
4–5 black peppercorns
2–4 crushed juniper berries

*Sauce:*
marinade juices, reduced
*beurre manié* (1 tablespoon each
  butter and flour)
1 wineglass of port
2–4 tablespoons redcurrant jelly

*Garnish:*
glazed chestnuts
glazed small white onions
sautéed button mushrooms

**To make the marinade:** 'Sweat' the onion and carrots gently in a little butter or olive oil, then place them in a china or earthenware casserole, not metal. Add the wine, parsley, thyme, bay leaf, garlic, peppercorns and juniper berries. Soak the venison in this mixture for 3 days to a week in a cool place, turning 3 or 4 times a day so that all surfaces of the meat are evenly exposed to the marinade and keep well moistened. The longer the meat is marinated, the gamier the flavour.

**To cook the meat:** Combine the butter and olive oil in a heavy-bottomed metal pan or iron casserole with a tight cover. Add the salt pork and sauté until crisp and golden. Then drain the venison from the marinade, wipe it dry with a damp cloth, and brown it lightly in the fats.

Boil down the juices of the marinade to half the original quantity, and strain the sauce over the seared venison. Cover and cook in a moderately slow oven (170°C/325°F/gas 3) until tender.

When the meat is tender, remove it from the casserole to a warm serving platter and keep it in a warm place.

**To make the sauce:** Reduce the sauce to half the original quantity again by cooking over a high heat. Thicken, if necessary, with a *beurre manié* made by combining flour and butter. Add the port and the redcurrant jelly, to taste, and blend all together, taking care to dislodge all the crusty bits at the sides of the pan. Taste the sauce and correct seasoning, adding a little more port and redcurrant jelly to enrich the sauce if desired.

Strain the sauce, which should be dark and rich, over the venison and serve garnished with alternate clusters of glazed chestnuts, glazed onions and sautéed button mushrooms.

# Venison in Port

Serves 8 to 10

150 ml/¼ pint olive oil
100 g/¼ pound butter
2 carrots, sliced
1 Spanish onion, sliced
2 cloves garlic
1 sprig thyme
1 bay leaf
1 saddle of venison
salt and freshly ground pepper
½ bottle port

1 tablespoon butter
1 tablespoon flour
2 tablespoons redcurrant jelly

*Garnish:*
glazed chestnuts
glazed small white onions
mushroom caps sautéed in
  butter
fried *croûtons*

Combine the olive oil and butter in a braising pan. Add the carrots, onion, garlic, thyme and bay leaf. Place the saddle of venison, seasoned with salt and pepper, on this bed of aromatics. Cover the pan and cook in a moderate oven (190°C/375°F/gas 5) until the saddle begins to brown. Pour the good port over the roast and cook, basting continually with meat and wine juices, until tender.

Remove the saddle to a serving platter and keep in a warm place. Skim away the fat from the pan and strain the sauce into a small saucepan. Reduce the sauce by boiling down to half the original quantity; thicken it with a *beurre manié* (made by kneading the butter and flour to a smooth paste), and add the redcurrant jelly. Correct the seasoning.

Carve the saddle and serve on the bone, surrounded with glazed chestnuts, glazed onions and sautéed mushroom caps. Just before serving, strain the sauce over the venison and surround with fried *croûtons*.

# Venison Steaks

Serves 4

1.3 kg/3 pounds leg or loin of
  venison
fat salt pork, for larding
100 g/¼ pound butter
salt and freshly ground pepper
crushed juniper berries
dried rosemary

1 Spanish onion, grated
150 ml/¼ pint rich beef stock
150 ml/¼ pint red burgundy
150 ml/¼ pint thick sour cream
100 g/¼ pound mushrooms,
  sliced
redcurrant jelly

Have the leg or loin of venison cut into 4 thick steaks. Lard with thin strips of fat salt pork; trim off the larding ends into a thick-bottomed frying pan and add the butter (reserving 1 tablespoon for later use), salt, pepper, crushed juniper berries and dried rosemary (a good pinch per steak). Heat; then add the steaks and brown until done on both sides, about 5 minutes per side, or until tender. Remove the steaks and keep warm. Cut the heat down to a simmer; add the onion, beef stock and red wine to the pan. Mix well, scraping in all the crusty bits from the sides of the pan. Reduce gently until the sauce is rich and thick; add the sour cream; simmer and strain. Clean the pan and sauté the mushrooms in the remaining butter until tender; add the steaks to the pan and pour the sauce over them. Heat through and serve with redcurrant jelly.

## Pigeons Confits aux Raisins
Serves 4

4 pigeons, cleaned
salt and freshly ground pepper
4–6 tablespoons cognac
150 ml/¼ pint melted chicken fat
  or lard
few drops water
4 oval pastry cases or
  rectangular canapés (each
  large enough to hold a pigeon)

1 small can *mousse de foie
  gras*

*Garnish:*
black truffles
peeled and seeded white
  grapes
aspic jelly

Season the pigeons with salt and pepper and flame with the cognac.

Melt the chicken fat with a few drops of water over a low heat. As soon as the fat is nearly melted, add the pigeons; bring the fat to a moderate boil and simmer for 45 minutes to 1 hour.

Remove the pigeons from the fat; place them in a stone or earthenware crock, cover with the strained fat and cool.

Prepare 4 oval-shaped pastry cases and bake in the usual manner, or use 4 rectangular *canapés*. Spread with the *mousse de foie gras* and place 1 pigeon (from which you have removed the fat) in the centre of each. Decorate the pigeons with small pieces of black truffle, surround each bird with 6 large peeled and seeded white grapes and glaze with aspic jelly.

## Rabbit in Cream
Serves 4

1 rabbit or hare, skinned and
  cleaned
100 g/¼ pound lean bacon, thinly
  sliced
100 g/¼ pound fat salt pork,
  thinly sliced
fresh herbs, such as tarragon,
  thyme, rosemary

2 tablespoons butter
6 tablespoons *fine champagne*
salt and freshly ground
  pepper
425 ml/¾ pint fresh cream
stock or dry white wine

Cut the rabbit (or hare) into serving pieces. Line an earthenware casserole, just large enough to hold the rabbit, with alternating thin strips of lean bacon and fat salt pork. Cover this bed with aromatic herbs; sauté the rabbit pieces in the butter until golden; place on the bed of herbs and pour the *fine champagne* or other quality brandy over. Season to taste with salt and pepper.

Place the casserole on a heat diffuser and start cooking on a low heat. After 30 minutes cover the rabbit pieces with fresh cream and a little stock or dry white wine. Cover the casserole and simmer for about 3 hours. Serve from the casserole.

# Vintner's Stew of Rabbit or Hare
Serves 4 to 6

**1 rabbit or hare, skinned and cleaned**

*Marinade Mixture:*
**1 Spanish onion, sliced**
**2 carrots, sliced**
**2 cloves garlic**
**300 ml/½ pint red burgundy**
**4 sprigs flat-leaf parsley**
**1 sprig thyme**
**salt and freshly ground pepper**
**1–2 pinches crushed dried chillies**
**4 tablespoons olive oil**

*For Cooking:*
**salt and freshly ground pepper**
**2 tablespoons flour**
**4 tablespoons olive oil**
**300 ml/½ pint beef stock**
**600 ml/1 pint red burgundy**

*Garnish:*
**12 button mushrooms**
**12 glazed onions**
**100 g/¼ pound fat salt pork, diced**
***croûtons***
**2 tablespoons chopped flat-leaf parsley**

Cut the rabbit (or hare) into serving pieces. Combine the ingredients for the marinade and cover the rabbit with the mixture. Marinate the rabbit for 2 days, turning the pieces several times each day so that they will be well marinated.

Dry the rabbit pieces with a damp cloth; season well with salt and pepper and sprinkle liberally with flour. Sauté the pieces in hot olive oil until golden; skim the fat and add the marinade mixture, beef stock and enough red wine, as necessary, to cover the meat. Bring to the boil, skim and allow to simmer slowly for about 1½ hours, by which time the meat should be almost done. Remove the meat to a serving platter and keep warm. Strain the sauce into a clean casserole; skim the fat and correct the seasoning.

Add the rabbit pieces, button mushrooms, glazed onions and sautéed diced fat salt pork to the sauce and cook for ½ hour more, or until the rabbit pieces are tender. Serve with *croûtons* and parsley.

## Rabbit aux Deux Moutardes
Serves 4

1 fat tender rabbit, cleaned
2 tablespoons flour
salt and freshly ground
  pepper
2 tablespoons olive oil
2 tablespoons butter
100 g/4 ounces fat bacon in 1
  piece, diced and blanched

4 shallots, chopped
1 bouquet garni
150 ml/¼ pint dry white wine
150 ml/¼ pint chicken stock
1 teaspoon Dijon mustard
1 teaspoon English mustard
300 ml/½ pint double cream

Cut the rabbit into serving pieces; roll the pieces in flour, add salt and pepper and sauté until golden in the olive oil and butter with the bacon. Add the shallots and *bouquet garni*; moisten with the white wine and stock, and cook gently, covered, until the rabbit is tender.

Drain the rabbit pieces; keep them warm. Skim the fat from the sauce; whisk the Dijon mustard and English mustard thoroughly with the cream and add to the sauce in the pan. Correct the seasoning; adding a little more mustard, salt and pepper, if desired. Add the rabbit pieces; heat through and serve in the casserole.

## Casseroled Pheasant
Serves 6 to 8

2 young pheasants, cleaned
175 g/6 ounces cooked ham,
  finely chopped
6 tablespoons cooked rice
6 tablespoons cognac
1 egg
salt and freshly ground pepper
powdered thyme and marjoram
fat salt pork

4 tablespoons butter
4 tablespoons olive oil
2–4 shallots, finely chopped
2 tablespoons cognac
450 g/1 pound button
  mushrooms, sliced
2 cloves garlic, chopped
juice of ½ lemon

Stuff the birds with the following mixture: finely chopped pheasant livers combined with the ham and rice, moistened with the cognac and egg and flavoured to taste with salt, pepper, thyme and marjoram.

Truss the birds firmly; wrap them in fat salt pork and brown them on all sides in a flameproof casserole with 2 tablespoons each of the butter and olive oil and the shallots. Pour over the warmed cognac and ignite. When the flames die down, cover the casserole and simmer the pheasants on a low heat or in a slow oven until almost done, adding a little more liquid if necessary.

Sauté the mushrooms and garlic in the remaining butter and oil. Season well and pour over the birds. Finish cooking on a heat diffuser or in a low oven and just before serving, sprinkle with lemon juice.

# Normandy Pheasant
Serves 6 to 8

2 plump pheasants, cleaned
4 tablespoons butter
2 large tart apples
1 wineglass Calvados

300 ml/½ pint fresh cream
juice of ½ lemon
salt and freshly ground pepper
pinch of crushed dried chillies

Truss the pheasants and sauté in half the butter in a heavy-bottomed frying pan until nicely browned on all sides. Remove and keep warm.

Peel, core and slice the apples and sauté them in the remaining butter until golden. Place in the bottom of an earthenware casserole; arrange the pheasants on top; baste with the pan juices of the pheasants thinned down with Calvados and cook in a moderate oven (190°C/375°F/gas 5) for about 30 minutes.

Add the cream and lemon juice and season to taste with salt, pepper and a pinch of crushed dried chillies. Return the casserole, covered, to the oven and cook until the birds are tender and the sauce is thick and creamy.

# Pheasant with Green Apples
Serves 4

1 pheasant, cleaned
salt and freshly ground pepper
100 g/¼ pound green bacon,
   diced
½ Spanish onion, finely
   chopped

1 clove garlic, finely chopped
2 tablespoons butter
2 tablespoons olive oil
4 small cooking apples
4 tablespoons Cointreau
300 ml/½ pint cream

Season the pheasant generously with salt and pepper. Sauté the green bacon, onion and garlic in the butter and oil in a flameproof casserole until golden. Remove the bacon and vegetables; reserve. Then brown the pheasant on all sides in the resulting mixture of fats. Remove the pheasant and keep warm.

Peel, core and slice the apples thickly and sauté in the remaining fat until they start to turn golden. Pour the Cointreau over. Remove the apples from the casserole. Skim the fat from the pan juices. Return the pheasant to the casserole; surround with the apple slices, bacon bits, onion and garlic, and allow to simmer, covered, for 10 minutes. Stir in the cream, add salt and pepper, to taste; cover the casserole and cook in a slow oven (140°C/275°F/gas 1) until the pheasant is tender.

When ready to serve, remove the pheasant and bacon bits to a clean casserole and keep warm; purée the sauce and the apples. Correct the seasoning; reheat the sauce; pour over the pheasant and serve immediately.

## Pheasant à la Souvaroff
Serves 4 to 6

2 young pheasants, cleaned
100 g/¼ pound *pâté de foie gras*,
    diced
1 truffle, thinly sliced
1 tablespoon cognac
salt and freshly ground
    pepper
butter
dry white wine

2–3 thin slices fat salt pork or
    green bacon
3 or 4 small truffles
4 tablespoons Madeira
2 tablespoons cognac
3 tablespoons truffle juice
3 tablespoons demi-glace
    (if available)
flour and water paste

Stuff your pheasants (partridge and quail are also excellent cooked in this way, and I have often made this delicious casserole with a fine fat capon) with a mixture of the *pâté de foie gras*, truffle, cognac, and salt and pepper, to taste.

Truss the wings and legs of the birds; sew up openings and place in a buttered roasting pan with a little extra butter and some dry white wine. To prevent the birds from drying out in cooking, cover the breasts with slices of fresh fat pork or green bacon and cook for about 40 minutes in a hot oven (200°C/400°F/gas 6). Remove the pork or bacon strips from the breasts, cut the strings and place the birds in an oval casserole just large enough to hold them comfortably. Cover the casserole. Set the pan juices aside to cool; you will use them later. All the above can be done before your guests arrive.

About 25 minutes before you wish to serve the birds, toss the truffles in a little hot butter to bring out their flavour. Then skim the solidified fat from the roasting pan and add the Madeira, cognac, truffle juice, and, if available, *demi-glace* sauce, to the pan juices. Stir this mixture over a low heat until it nearly reaches boiling point, then strain the sauce over the pheasants in the casserole.

Cover the casserole and seal the edges with a band of stiff dough made of flour and water. Bake in a hot oven for 20 minutes. Bring the sealed casserole to the table and break the seal just before serving.

## Quail with White Grapes
Serves 4

4 quail, cleaned
salt and white pepper
2 tablespoons flour
4 tablespoons butter

150 ml/¼ pint dry white wine
2 tablespoons lemon juice
75 g/3 ounces seedless grapes
2 tablespoons blanched almonds

Rub the quail with a mixture of salt, pepper and flour. Melt the butter in a thick-bottomed casserole and sauté the birds in it until golden on all sides. Add the wine and lemon juice; cover and cook over a low heat for 15 to 20 minutes. Add the grapes and the almonds (sliced if you like) and cook for 5 to 10 minutes more, or until the birds are tender.

## Partridge with Juniper Berries
Serves 4

2 partridges, cleaned
4 tablespoons melted butter
salt and freshly ground pepper
4 tablespoons shredded white
bread
2 tablespoons finely chopped
ham
4–6 juniper berries, crushed

grated zest of ½ lemon
dried marjoram
1 beaten egg
2 thin pieces fat salt pork
6 tablespoons dry white wine
150 ml/¼ pint rich chicken stock
1 carrot, finely chopped
1 small onion, finely chopped

Brush the cavities of the partridges with half the melted butter and season liberally with salt and pepper. Combine the remaining melted butter, bread, ham, juniper berries and lemon zest; season to taste with salt, pepper and marjoram; mix in the beaten egg and stuff the birds with this mixture.

Truss the birds; wrap a thin piece of fat salt pork around each and tie it on securely. In a small saucepan combine the dry white wine, chicken stock and chopped vegetables and simmer for 5 minutes or until the vegetables are crisptender. Roast the birds in a moderate oven (190°C/375°F/gas 5) for about 1 hour, or until tender, basting from time to time with the dry white wine, chicken stock and finely chopped carrot and onion.

## Veal and Partridge Pie
Serves 4 to 6

225 g/½ pound lean veal
225 g/½ pound lean pork
100 g/¼ pound fat salt pork
salt and freshly ground pepper
finely chopped parsley,
marjoram and thyme

1 plump partridge, cleaned
100 g/¼ pound bacon, diced
150 ml/¼ pint beef stock
shortcrust pastry, to cover
1 egg yolk

Pass the veal, lean pork and fat salt pork twice through the finest blade of your mincer; season generously with salt, pepper and parsley, marjoram and thyme. Cut the partridge into serving pieces. Line a deep pie dish with the minced meat mixture; on this place a layer of pieces of bird, then a few cubes of bacon and more minced meats. Continue to add layers of these until the dish is well filled. Moisten with the beef stock; cover with a shortcrust pastry lid; decorate and brush with yolk of egg. Bake in a moderate oven (190°C/375°F/gas 5) for 1 to 1½ hours. Serve hot or cold.

# Partridge with Lentils
Serves 2 to 4

2 partridges, cleaned
salt and freshly ground pepper
2 tablespoons butter
2 tablespoons olive oil
100 g/¼ pound fat salt pork,
   diced
1 Spanish onion, sliced
2 carrots, sliced
150 ml/¼ pint white wine

150 ml/¼ pint chicken stock

*Lentils:*
350 g/12 ounces lentils
1 onion, stuck with 2 cloves
2 cloves garlic
1 sprig thyme
2 sprigs flat-leaf parsley
salt and freshly ground pepper

Sprinkle the cavities of the partridges with a little salt and pepper. Sauté the birds in a flameproof casserole in the butter and oil with the diced fat salt pork, onion and carrots. When the birds are golden on all sides, add the white wine and cook until reduced by half. Add the chicken stock and season to taste with salt and pepper; cover the casserole and cook over a low heat until partridges are tender, about 45 minutes.

**To prepare the lentils:**  Soak the lentils overnight. Drain and cover with water, adding the onion, garlic, thyme, parsley, and salt and pepper, to taste. Bring to the boil, reduce the heat and allow to simmer until tender but not too soft. Each lentil should be separate, not mushy. When cooked, drain and remove the onion, garlic and herbs.

**To serve:**  Place the partridges on a hot serving dish and surround with cooked lentils. Skim fat from the pan juices; strain and pour over the birds.

# Salmis of Grouse
Serves 6

3 young grouse, cleaned
100 g/¼ pound butter
1 Spanish onion, finely chopped
2 small carrots, finely chopped
2 cloves garlic, finely chopped
150 ml/¼ pint good red wine
1 rounded tablespoon flour
425 ml/¾ pint well-flavoured
   stock

2 sprigs thyme
1 bay leaf
salt and freshly ground pepper
225 g/½ pound button mushrooms, sliced
juice of ½ lemon
12 small bread triangles
finely chopped flat-leaf parsley

Truss the birds; spread with a little softened butter and roast in the oven until partially cooked. Cut into serving pieces (over a dish to retain juices) and reserve.
   Sauté the onion, carrots and garlic in 4 tablespoons butter until golden. Pour in the wine and simmer, stirring continuously, until it reduces a little. Add the flour

and stir vigorously until the sauce thickens; then add the stock, trimmings and juices from the birds, thyme, bay leaf, and salt and pepper, to taste. Cover the pan and simmer gently for 1 hour.

Sauté the mushrooms in 2 tablespoons butter and the lemon juice until tender. Strain the sauce; add the drained mushrooms and the grouse to the sauce and simmer for 5 minutes, or until they are heated through and the flavour of the sauce has permeated the birds.

Fry the bread triangles in the remaining butter and place 6 on a heated serving dish; cover with the *salmis*; sprinkle with parsley and garnish with the remaining *croûtons*.

# Chapter 12
# Vegetables

## Red Cabbage Normandy

Many men are known to be ardent, if furtive, members of the anti-vegetable school. And who can blame us if we are apt to recoil surreptitiously from the tasteless, soggy blobs of greenery that all too often masquerade on dinner plates throughout the country under the misleading names of 'peas', 'spring beans', 'cauliflower' and 'cabbage'?

Of all vegetables, cabbage particularly seems to suffer from this lack of imagination. Yet the culinary potential of this year-round vegetable is as rich as its history. The ancient Greeks served cabbage with savoury stuffings of meat and rice, flavoured with pine nuts, currants, grated lemon zest and herbs. It was known and used in China as far back as the first century. Indeed, sour cabbage, known throughout the world today as sauerkraut, was, in fact, an early Chinese invention.

The Mediterraneans have used cabbage as the main ingredient for stews and soups for centuries; the Poles call it 'little pigeons' – braised cabbage leaves deliciously stuffed with finely chopped meat, onion, tomatoes and herbs. The Russians immortalise it in a superb peasant soup called *stchi*, made of cabbage, onions, tomatoes and beets simmered in stock; the Germans poach it until tender and stuff it with buttered noodles flavoured with caraway seed; and the Austrians even use this versatile vegetable in a sweet cabbage *strudel*.

There are three main varieties of cabbage. The common or green cabbage, sold everywhere, is bright green in the summer months, whiter, firmer and larger in the winter. The Savoy cabbage – a bright, deep green in colour with a curly leaf – is much more delicate in flavour. I like to use its tender leaves for stuffed cabbage recipes.

White cabbage is used commercially for the preparation of sauerkraut and is also used extensively for salads and coleslaw.

Red cabbage is delicious either raw or cooked. Always add lemon juice or vinegar to water when cooking this attractive vegetable or it will turn purple in cooking. Red cabbage must be firm and the outer leaves must be bright in colour. Cut the head in quarters and remove the heavy veins, then shred the rest of the leaves on a coarse shredder. Often served as an *hors-d'œuvre* salad in France, red cabbage is delicious when shredded in this way, drained to the last drop of the water in which it was cooked and then simmered gently in butter or lard with diced apples and spices, a wonderful accompaniment to all port dishes, goose and many forms of veal and hare.

Perhaps the most noble version of this dish is red cabbage cooked in the fashion of the Norman French.

# Red Cabbage with Apples
Serves 4 to 6

1 red cabbage (about 1 kg/
  2 pounds)
4 tablespoons butter
450 g/1 pound cooking
  apples
225 g/½ pound onions
2 cloves garlic, finely
  chopped

¼ teaspoon each of powdered
  nutmeg, allspice, cinnamon,
  thyme and caraway seed
salt and freshly ground pepper
1 tablespoon grated orange zest
2 tablespoons brown sugar
30 ml/½ pint red wine
2 tablespoons wine vinegar

Wash and shred the cabbage, removing the central core, ribs and outer leaves. Cook in the butter, in a covered saucepan, for 5 minutes. Peel and core the apples and cut into quarters; slice the onions. Place these ingredients in a deep ovenproof casserole in layers, beginning with a layer of cabbage, then onions, then apples, and continue until the casserole is full. Season each layer with finely chopped garlic, spices and salt and pepper, to taste, and grated orange zest. Sprinkle brown sugar over the top and add the wine, wine vinegar and a little hot water.

Cover and simmer very slowly in a moderate oven (180°C/350°F/gas 4) until tender, adding a little more wine if necessary.

# My Colcannon
Serves 4 to 6

1 cabbage
4–6 potatoes
4–6 young carrots
4–6 young turnips
4 tablespoons butter
salt and freshly ground pepper

150 ml/½ pint double cream
2 egg yolks
butter
freshly grated breadcrumbs
freshly grated cheese (optional)

Cook the cabbage and potatoes in water until tender.

Peel and slice the carrots and turnips in thin strips and blanch in sufficient water to cover. Pour off the water; add the butter and 4 tablespoons water to the pan; cover and simmer until vegetables are tender. Season with salt and pepper.

Chop the cabbage finely and mash with the potatoes until smooth. Combine with the cream, egg yolks, additional butter and pepper and salt, to taste.

Spread half of the cabbage-potato mixture in the bottom of a well-buttered ovenproof gratin dish. Arrange a layer of alternating strips of carrots and turnip down the centre and cover with the remaining cabbage-potato mixture. Sprinkle with freshly grated breadcrumbs; top with a little freshly grated cheese (optional) and dot with butter. Cook in a moderate oven (190°C/375°F/gas 5) for 30 minutes or until golden.

## Buttered Cabbage – I
Serves 4 to 6

Remove and discard the discoloured outer leaves from 1 head of green cabbage. Wash, core and cut it into shreds or wedges. Soak the cabbage in cold salted water for ½ hour. Drain and cook, covered, in a small amount of boiling salted water or well-flavoured stock, until just tender. Drain well. Season with salt and freshly ground pepper, and serve with finely chopped flat-leaf parsley and melted butter.

## Buttered Cabbage – II
Serves 4 to 6

Prepare the cabbage as above; soak in cold salted water for ½ hour; drain. Melt 4 tablespoons butter in a large saucepan; add the cabbage; season to taste with salt, freshly ground pepper and the juice of ½ lemon and simmer, covered, until the cabbage is just tender, but not browned. Stir in a little finely chopped flat-leaf parsley and serve.

## Scalloped Cabbage
Serves 4 to 6

**1 head cabbage**
**salt**
**4 tablespoons butter**
**300 ml/½ pint cream sauce**
**  (page 35)**

**freshly ground pepper**
**4 tablespoons freshly grated**
**  Parmesan**

Shred the cabbage and soak in salted cold water for ½ hour. Drain well. Melt the butter; add the shredded cabbage and simmer, covered, until the cabbage is just tender, but not browned.

Line a large casserole with half the simmered cabbage. Add half of the cream sauce; sprinkle with pepper and half the grated Parmesan. Add the remaining cabbage; pour the remaining sauce over the top and add more pepper and the remainder of the Parmesan. Place in a slow oven (170°C/325°/gas 3) and cook until the casserole bubbles and the top is golden brown – about ½ hour.

## Saffron Cabbage
Serves 4

**1 small head cabbage**
**salt**
**600 ml/1 pint rich beef stock**
**1 generous pinch powdered**
**  saffron**

**4–6 tablespoons finely chopped**
**  ham**
**½ Spanish onion, thinly sliced**
**freshly ground pepper**
**1 generous pinch cayenne**

Shred the cabbage and soak in salted cold water for ½ hour. Drain well. Combine in a saucepan with the beef stock and simmer for 15 minutes, or until half cooked.

Mix the saffron with a little boiling water and add to the cabbage together with the ham, onion, salt, pepper and cayenne.

Stir well and simmer until the cabbage is tender, adding a little more stock or water if necessary.

## Cauliflower à la Polonaise

The cabbage family is a large and powerful clan which ranges from the earthy tones of cabbage and sprouts to the more sophisticated flavour of cauliflower, the undoubted aristocrat of the family. I like cauliflower steamed or simmered in salted water with a little lemon juice until it is just tender, not mushy, and then served with melted butter or a delicious sauce such as hollandaise. Or try one of the variations here or, maybe best of all, *à la polonaise,* overleaf.

When buying cauliflower, choose heads that are very white and very firm, with small compact flowers squeezed tightly together. A yellow cauliflower has a very strong flavour and if the flowers are loosely separated from each other this is usually a sign of excess maturity.

## How to Cook Cauliflower

**Whole:** Cut off the stem and remove the green leaves from a medium-sized cauliflower. Soak the head for ½ hour in cold water to which you have added ½ teaspoon salt and the juice of ½ lemon to free it from insects. Fill a deep saucepan with enough water to cover the cauliflower; add ½ teaspoon salt and bring to the boil. Put the cauliflower into the boiling water; cover the saucepan and simmer gently, about 20 minutes, or until the cauliflower is just tender when pierced at the stem end with a fork. Do not overcook.

Drain well; arrange on a heated serving dish or bowl and top with butter. Season to taste with salt and freshly ground pepper.

**Florets:** Break or cut the cauliflower into florets. Prepare as above, but cook for 10 to 15 minutes only, so that the florets are tender but not mushy. Drain and serve as above, or with any of the sauces below.

## Cauliflower variations

Prepare the cauliflower as above, either whole or cut into florets.

**Cauliflower amandine:** Sauté 4 tablespoons blanched slivered almonds in butter; pour the sauce over the hot cauliflower and season to taste with salt and freshly ground pepper.

**Cheesed cauliflower:** Melt 4 tablespoons butter; add 4 tablespoons toasted breadcrumbs, ½ teaspoon grated onion, 4 tablespoons finely grated Gruyère, and salt and freshly ground pepper to taste. Cook over a low heat, stirring continuously until the cheese is melted, and pour over the cooked hot cauliflower.

# Cauliflower à la Polonaise
Serves 4

1 cauliflower
salt

*Polonaise Sauce:*
4 tablespoons butter
4 tablespoons freshly grated
  breadcrumbs

juice of ½ lemon
2 tablespoons each finely
  chopped ham and hard-boiled
  egg
2 tablespoons finely chopped
  flat-leaf parsley
salt and freshly ground pepper

Remove the outer green leaves from the cauliflower; wash and leave in cold salted water for ½ hour. Measure enough water in a deep saucepan to cover the cauliflower; add salt to taste, and bring to the boil. Put the cauliflower into the boiling water; bring to the boil again; lower the heat; cover the saucepan and simmer gently for about 20 minutes, or until the cauliflower is just tender when pierced at the stem end with a fork. Do not overcook.

Drain well, arrange on a heated serving dish and top with Polonaise sauce.

**To make the Polonaise sauce:**   Melt the butter in a frying pan. Add the breadcrumbs and cook until light brown. Stir in the lemon juice, ham, hard-boiled egg and parsley. Season with salt and pepper, to taste.

# Cauliflower au Gratin
Serves 4

1 cauliflower
salt
4 tablespoons butter
4 tablespoons flour
600 ml/1 pint hot milk
100 g/¼ pound freshly grated
  Gruyère
1 teaspoon mustard

juice of ½ lemon
salt and freshly ground pepper
1 egg yolk beaten with 2
  tablespoons crème fraîche
2 tablespoons fresh
  breadcrumbs
butter

Remove the outer green leaves from the cauliflower; wash and leave in cold salted water for ½ hour. Cut the cauliflower into florets and poach in salted water for 10 to 15 minutes, or until tender. Drain.

To make the sauce, melt the butter in the top of a double saucepan; blend in the flour and cook over water, stirring constantly, until smooth. Add the hot milk gradually and cook, stirring constantly, until the sauce comes to the boil. Add the cheese and cook, stirring, until the cheese melts. Season to taste with mustard, lemon juice and salt and pepper. Just before serving, whisk the egg yolk and crème fraîche into the sauce; place the cooked cauliflower in a buttered baking dish; pour the hot sauce over; sprinkle with breadcrumbs and dot with butter. Bake in a moderate oven (190°C/375°F/gas 5) for about 20 minutes, or until the top is golden.

## French Fried Cauliflower

Serves 4

oil for deep-frying
1 egg
150 ml/¼ pint milk
100 g/¼ pound flour

1 teaspoon salt
1 cauliflower
tomato sauce (page 38)

Heat the oil to 190°C/375°F. To make the batter; beat the egg in a bowl; add the milk and beat. Add the flour and salt and beat until smooth.

Clean and prepare the cauliflower as above. Separate into small florets and poach in boiling water, or steam, for 5 minutes. Drain. When ready to cook, dip the drained florets into batter. Deep-fry until golden. Drain and serve immediately with tomato sauce.

## Cauliflower à la Niçoise

Serves 4

1 cauliflower
1 Spanish onion, finely
chopped
2 cloves garlic, finely chopped
3 tablespoons olive oil
2 tablespoons butter

6 tomatoes, peeled and diced, or
1 can chopped tomatoes
2 tablespoons finely chopped
flat-leaf parsley
salt and freshly ground pepper
1 tablespoon breadcrumbs

Prepare and poach the cauliflower florets as above, for about 5 minutes. Sauté the onion and garlic in olive oil and butter until transparent. Add the tomatoes and parsley. Season with salt and pepper. Add the cooked cauliflower and breadcrumbs and simmer for a further 10 minutes, or until tender.

# Gratin Dauphinois

'Let the sky rain potatoes,' cried Sir John Falstaff deliriously as Mistress Ford appeared in the last scene of *The Merry Wives of Windsor*. For the sudden arrival of the potato from America had caused uproar throughout Europe. Denounced as an aphrodisiac from the pulpits of England, prohibited by the Parliament of Besançon as a cause of leprosy, the potato was stolidly ignored by the poor to whom it would have been so useful. But the rich seized on it as a new fad. Elizabeth Tudor feasted on potatoes from Raleigh's Irish estate. Louis XVI brought their flower into high fashion by accepting a bouquet of them from Parmentier – collectors know how widespread was the use of the potato flower as a decorative design for plates. Francis Bacon lauded them with stately phrases in the *History of Life and Death*.

The first excitement soon waned and as they became more common, potatoes slowly sank to the bottom of the menu, following all other vegetables. The problem? We eat them too much; they have become a necessity, not a pleasure. In this country we tend to look at them without imagination, without desire. But give a French chef a potato and he will create a hundred succulent dishes. So do not take the potato for granted. Give it a little credit. Treat it – as the French do – with *panache*!

Select potatoes best suited to your purpose:

**Baking potatoes:**  Large with a fine, mealy texture when cooked. Use floury potatoes for baking and for soups and purées.

**New potatoes:**  Range in size from tiny ones no bigger than a walnut to those the size of a regular potato. The smallest are delicious cooked whole with their skins left on and served with butter, or butter and lemon juice. When *salad potatoes* are hard to come by, larger new potatoes are good for potato salads and cooked dishes such as *gratin dauphinois* for which you want potato slices to keep their shape. Never bake new potatoes.

Whenever possible, cook potatoes with their skins on. Most of the food value of a potato lies just under the skin and is lost if peeled away. After cooking, the skins will slip off easily enough if you prefer serving them without their jackets.

If you peel potatoes when raw, put them immediately into a bowl of cold water to keep them from changing colour.

The major mistake in potato cookery – as with most vegetables – is overcooking. When you boil potatoes, test them with a fork. They are done when you can pierce them easily. Do not allow them to become watery and mushy.

On special occasions that call for a little more than the usual baked, sautéed or puréed potato, apply the Gallic touch and dress your potatoes for company. Cut them in slices or cubes; shape them with a knife to resemble olives. Parboil them for 5 minutes in salted water; drain, then sauté in clarified butter until they are soft and golden. Serve with finely chopped sautéed onions and parsley, crumbled cooked bacon, or a combination of finely chopped parsley, chervil and chives. To clarify butter: place as much butter as desired in a container over hot water until butter has melted. Pour off the butter carefully and discard the remaining white sediment.

Follow on in the French tradition by serving thinly sliced potatoes paired off with the flavours of butter, cream, freshly grated Gruyère or Parmesan and finely chopped onions. *Gratin dauphinois* (recipe below) combines layers of thinly sliced potatoes with cream and freshly grated cheese, dots the whole with knobs of butter and bakes it in a gratin dish in the oven until bubbling and golden-crusted. Serve this delicious dish as a hot first course (as the Italians do *gnocchi* or *pasta*) or with a roast. Potatoes Lyonnaise sautées thin slices of boiled new potatoes in butter and serves them with gently fried chopped onions. *Pommes de terre Anna* sets overlapping layers of sliced raw potatoes in a small buttered baking dish or round mould, each layer dotted with butter and the whole then baked in a hot oven until cooked through. The potatoes are turned out of the mould like a crisp, golden cake just before serving.

# Gratin Dauphinois
Serves 4

**450 g/1 pound new potatoes**
**150 ml/¼ pint double cream**
**8 tablespoons freshly grated**
  **Gruyère**

**4 tablespoons freshly grated**
  **Parmesan**
**butter**
**salt and freshly ground pepper**

Butter a shallow heatproof casserole or deep gratin dish. Peel and slice the potatoes thinly and soak in cold water for a few minutes. Drain and dry thoroughly with a clean tea towel.

Place a layer of sliced potatoes on the bottom of the dish in overlapping rows; pour over a quarter of the cream, sprinkle with 2 tablespoons grated cheese (mixed Gruyère and Parmesan), dot with butter and season with salt and pepper, to taste. Continue this process until the dish is full, finishing with a layer of grated cheese. Dot with butter and cook in a slow oven (170°C/325°F/gas 3) for about 1 hour, or until the potatoes are cooked through. If the top becomes too brown, cover with aluminium foil. Serve very hot.

# Gratin Savoyard
Serves 4

**450 g/1 pound new potatoes**
**150 ml/¼ pint well-flavoured**
  **beef stock**
**6 tablespoons freshly grated**
  **Gruyère**

**2 tablespoons freshly grated**
  **Parmesan**
**salt and freshly ground pepper**
**butter**

Butter a heatproof shallow casserole or gratin dish. Peel and slice the potatoes thinly and soak in cold water for a few minutes. Drain and dry thoroughly with a clean tea towel.

Place a layer of sliced potatoes on the bottom of the dish in overlapping rows; pour over a quarter of the stock; sprinkle with 2 tablespoons grated cheese (mixed Gruyère and Parmesan); dot with butter and season to taste with salt and pepper (not too much salt). Continue this process until the dish is full, finishing with a layer of grated cheese. Dot with butter and cook in a slow oven (170°C/325°F/gas 3) for about 1 hour, or until the potatoes are cooked through. If the top becomes too brown, cover with aluminium foil. Serve very hot.

# Potatoes Lyonnaise
Serves 4

450 g/1 pound boiled new
   potatoes, sliced
4 tablespoons butter
1 small onion, thinly sliced

salt and freshly ground pepper
2 tablespoons finely chopped
   flat-leaf parsley

Sauté the potatoes in the butter over a medium heat until golden on both sides. Remove the potatoes and sauté the onion in the remaining fat until golden. Return the potatoes to the pan; season to taste with salt and pepper and continue cooking until heated through. Sprinkle with parsley.

# Pommes de Terre Anna
Serves 4

450 g/1 pound new potatoes
50–75 g/2–3 ounces softened
   butter

salt and freshly ground
   pepper

Peel and slice the potatoes thinly and soak in cold water for a few minutes. Drain and dry thoroughly with a clean tea towel.

Butter a shallow heatproof casserole or gratin dish and place in it an overlapping layer of sliced potatoes, to come up around the sides of the dish. Spread with 1 tablespoon softened butter and season to taste with salt and pepper. Repeat the layers as above with minimal spreading of butter on top. Bake in a 220°C/425°F/gas 7 oven for 45 minutes to 1 hour, or until the potatoes are cooked through. To serve, invert the golden-brown potato 'cake' on a heated serving dish and serve immediately.

# Latkes
## Jewish Potato Pancakes
Serves 4 to 6

4 large raw potatoes, peeled and
   grated
1 Spanish onion, peeled and
   grated
2 eggs, beaten

2 tablespoons flour
½ teaspoon baking powder
salt and freshly ground pepper
butter and olive oil, for frying

Combine the grated potatoes and onion in a mixing bowl; stir in the beaten eggs, flour and baking powder and add salt and pepper, to taste.

Heat a little butter and olive oil in frying pan. Drop the potato mixture in spoonfuls and fry the *latkes* until browned on both sides. Drain well.

# Hash-browned Potatoes
Serves 6

6 large potatoes, baked in their jackets
1 Spanish onion, coarsely grated

salt and freshly ground pepper
3 tablespoons butter
3 tablespoons lard

Chill the potatoes; peel and shred coarsely. Add the onion and salt and pepper, to taste. Melt the butter and lard in a frying pan.

Put the potatoes into the pan, leaving 1-cm/½-inch space around the edge. Brown for 10 to 12 minutes. When crusty and hot, hold a serving dish over the pan and invert.

Serve hash-browned potatoes with minute steaks or chops and garnish with glazed onion rings.

# Italian Potato Balls
Serves 6

700 g/1½ pounds potatoes
2 egg yolks
4 tablespoons freshly grated Parmesan
2 tablespoons finely chopped onion
1 tablespoon butter

2 tablespoons finely chopped flat-leaf parsley
salt and freshly ground pepper
2 eggs
flour
breadcrumbs
fat, for frying

Peel the potatoes and boil in salted water until cooked. Mash and combine with the egg yolks and cheese in a large mixing bowl.

Sauté the onion in the butter until golden, but not brown. Add to the potato mixture with the parsley and generous amounts of salt and pepper. Mix to a smooth paste and form into small balls the size of a large walnut. Makes about 24 balls.

Beat the eggs with a fork until well blended. Roll the potato balls in flour and then in beaten egg. Coat with breadcrumbs and chill until ready to use.

Heat fat (I prefer a mixture of olive oil and lard) to frying temperature. Fry a few potato balls at a time until they are golden in colour and heated through.

# Lemon Dill Potatoes
Serves 4

700 g/1½ pounds new potatoes
salt
1 tablespoon olive oil
1 tablespoon butter
1½ tablespoons flour
300 ml/½ pint milk

1 teaspoon dill seed
2 tablespoons lemon juice
2 tablespoons finely chopped flat-leaf parsley
salt and freshly ground pepper

Peel or scrape the new potatoes. Cook until just tender in boiling water to which you have added salt and olive oil. Drain and keep warm.

Melt the butter in a saucepan; blend in the flour and gradually stir in the milk. Add the dill seed and cook, stirring constantly, until the sauce is smooth and thick. Add the lemon juice, parsley and salt and pepper, to taste, and pour over the hot potatoes.

# Artichokes

The French believe that if you eat old vegetables you yourself become old. Not for them the jumbo carrots or the giant cabbages so beloved of old by English house-wives. It is the infant vegetables they use. In Italy, too, where the artichoke is very popular, tiny raw artichokes no bigger than a baby's fist are eaten raw as an appe-tiser, preserved in olive oil as an integral part of an Italian *antipasto* platter, or dipped in batter and fried, either alone, or with tiny octopus and prawns in an Italian mixed fry called *fritto misto del mare*.

In Rome, tender young artichokes are often cooked in olive oil, lemon and herbs, *alla romana*, and served as a marvellously flavoured hot or cold *hors-d'œuvre*. I like artichoke hearts done in this manner, too, flavoured with a little finely chopped garlic and oregano. In France, artichokes *au vin blanc* top the bill, the artichokes simmered in dry white wine with a little olive oil and seasonings.

There are so many ways to serve this delicate, nutty-flavoured vegetable – rich in iron, mineral salts and iodine – that I cannot understand why so many people consider it an acquired taste. I like them baked, fried, stuffed, puréed with rich cream as an accompanying vegetable, and even in a soup. But my favourite way of dealing with this sophisticated vegetable is to cook it in boiling water with a little salt, olive oil and lemon juice, and serve it cold with a *vinaigrette* sauce as a first course, or hot as a separate vegetable course. Whole, halved or quartered, a hot artichoke served with a *sauce hollandaise* or melted butter and lemon makes an unbeatable dish; each leaf should be pulled off separately, the large succulent end dipped in the sauce and the soft fleshy bit prised gently off with the teeth.

Artichoke hearts, found at the base of each vegetable, make one of the best garnishes for cold dishes imaginable if cooked and then chilled. They can be served on their own with a *vinaigrette* dressing, as a vegetable, stuffed with various ingre-dients, or used as the decorative base for a host of salads and *hors-d'œuvre* dishes.

## Italian Artichokes with Mushroom Sauce
Serves 4

4 small artichokes
salt
juice of ½ lemon
butter

*Mushroom Sauce:*
2 tablespoons butter
4 tablespoons finely chopped
  mushrooms

2 tablespoons finely chopped
  shallots
4–6 tablespoons dry white
  wine
2 tablespoons tomato purée
2 tablespoons finely chopped
  flat-leaf parsley
salt and freshly ground pepper
pinch of crushed dried chillies

Cut the small artichokes into quarters; trim the tough outer leaves and the tips of the tender leaves and remove the chokes. Poach for 5 minutes in boiling water to which you have added a little salt and lemon juice. Drain and arrange in a buttered shallow flameproof casserole. Cook for 2 minutes on a high heat; spoon over the mushroom sauce, cover the casserole and simmer until tender.

**To make the sauce:**  Melt the butter in a frying pan and sauté the mushrooms and shallots until almost golden; moisten with the white wine and simmer for 3 minutes. Add the tomato purée and parsley; season with salt, pepper and crushed dried chillies.

## Artichoke Hearts with Foie Gras
Serves 4

4 artichokes
1 lemon
2 tablespoons olive oil
salt and freshly ground pepper

4 tablespoons butter
4 slices *pâté de foie gras*
4 tablespoons *sauce béarnaise*

Choose tender artichokes. Cut the hearts out carefully. Rub each heart with ½ lemon and place immediately in a bowl of cold water to keep the colour fresh.

Bring water to the boil with the olive oil and the juice of the remaining ½ lemon. Add salt and pepper to taste and poach the artichoke hearts in this liquid until tender, about 15 to 20 minutes, according to their size. Drain.

Melt the butter in a flameproof gratin dish or shallow casserole; place the artichoke hearts in this upside-down and let them simmer in the butter for a few minutes; turn them delicately and when done place a round of *pâté de foie gras* in each heart; cover each with a spoonful of *sauce béarnaise* and place the dish under the grill for a few seconds to brown the sauce. Serve immediately.

## Artichokes au Vin Blanc
Serves 4

4 medium artichokes
2 tablespoons olive oil
150 ml/¼ pint dry white wine
2 cloves garlic, finely chopped
1 small onion, finely chopped

2 tablespoons finely chopped
  flat-leaf parsley
pinch dried savory
salt and freshly ground
  pepper

Cut the top off the artichokes and remove the chokes.

Combine the olive oil, white wine, garlic, onion, parsley, savory and salt and pepper, to taste. Place the trimmed artichokes in a saucepan just large enough to hold them and pour the mixture over them.

Cover tightly and simmer slowly for 45 minutes, adding a little more wine and olive oil if necessary. When tender, remove and serve with the sauce poured over them.

# Artichokes Vinaigrette
Serves 4

**4 artichokes**
**salt**

**juice of ½ lemon**
**French dressing (page 222)**

Remove the tough outer leaves of the artichokes and trim the tops of the inner leaves. Trim the base and stem of each artichoke with a sharp knife. Cook until tender (30 to 40 minutes) in a large quantity of salted boiling water to which you have added the juice of ½ lemon. Artichokes are cooked when a leaf pulls out easily.

Turn the artichokes upside-down to drain. Serve cold with a well-flavoured French dressing. Pull off a leaf at a time; eat the tender base of each leaf. Remove the choke and eat the artichoke heart.

Artichokes are delicious served as a hot *hors-d'œuvre* or separate vegetable course with seasoned melted butter or, for more special occasions, a *sauce hollandaise*.

# Stuffed Peppers
Serves 4

**4 large green peppers**
**olive oil**
**1 Spanish onion, finely chopped**
**450 g/1 lb pork sausage meat**
**2 tablespoons freshly grated**
**   Parmesan**
**2 tablespoons freshly chopped**
**   chives**

**2 tablespoons chopped flat-leaf**
**   parsley**
**salt and freshly ground pepper**
**freshly grated nutmeg**
**butter**
**300 ml/½ pint chicken stock**
**strips of roasted red pepper**
**parsley sprigs**

Trim the stems of the peppers and then take a thin slice from the side of each one. Remove the pith and seeds. Place the peppers in boiling water with 2 tablespoons olive oil and leave for 5 minutes; drain well and dry.

Sauté the onion in 4 tablespoons olive oil until soft. Add the sausage meat and continue to cook, stirring constantly, until the meat begins to brown. Then add the Parmesan cheese, fresh chives and parsley and mix well. Season to taste with salt, pepper and nutmeg. Place a small piece of butter in the bottom of each pepper and season well.

Stuff the peppers with the meat mixture and place them in a flat ovenproof dish. Pour the chicken stock over them and bake in a moderate oven (190°C/375°F/gas 5) for 30 to 40 minutes. Just before serving, garnish each pepper with strips of roasted (or simply blanched, if you prefer) red pepper and sprigs of parsley.

Serve hot as a main course or cold as an appetiser.

# Chiles Rellenos
## Cheese-stuffed Green Peppers
Serves 4

4 large green peppers
225 g/½ pound *mozzarella*, finely
chopped
225 g/½ pound mild Cheddar,
finely chopped
Tabasco or chilli sauce

salt and freshly ground pepper
flour, to coat
4 eggs, separated
2 tablespoons flour
fat for deep-frying

Roast the whole green peppers under the grill, turning them from time to time until the skins are charred. Remove the charred skins under cold water; dry the peppers and make a small cut down the side without opening the pepper full length. With a spoon, scrape out the seeds and all the pith.

Mix the cheeses together and season to taste with salt and pepper and a little Tabasco or chilli sauce; fill the peppers with the cheese mixture. Re-shape the peppers and roll them lightly in flour. Beat the egg whites until they are stiff and fold in the lightly beaten egg yolks with the 2 tablespoons flour to make a batter.

Dip stuffed peppers in the batter and fry them in deep hot fat until golden brown. Serve immediately.

# Peppers alla Romana
Serves 6

6 large peppers
½ Spanish onion, finely chopped
1 clove garlic, finely chopped
2 tablespoons olive oil
2 tablespoons lard

4 tomatoes, peeled and
chopped
2 tablespoons tomato purée
150 ml/¼ pint dry white wine
salt and freshly ground pepper

Wash the peppers; remove the stalks and seeds and slice thinly. Sauté the onion and garlic in the olive oil and lard until golden. Add the tomatoes, tomato purée and white wine and simmer for 5 minutes.

Add the sliced peppers and salt and pepper, to taste; cover the pan and simmer gently for 30 minutes, or until the peppers are tender, adding more liquid if necessary.

# Ratatouille
Serves 4

8 tablespoons olive oil
2 Spanish onions, sliced
2 green peppers, diced
2 aubergines, diced
2 courgettes, cut in 1-cm/½-inch
  slices
4–6 ripe tomatoes, peeled,
  seeded and chopped

salt and freshly ground pepper
2 tablespoons chopped flat-leaf
  parsley
1–2 pinches dried marjoram or
  oregano
4 fresh basil leaves, slivered
2 large cloves garlic, crushed

Heat the olive oil in a large frying pan, add the onion slices and sauté until transparent. Add the green pepper and aubergines and, 5 minutes later, the courgettes
and tomatoes. The vegetables should not be fried but stewed in the oil, so simmer
gently in a covered pan for 30 minutes. Add salt and pepper to taste, parsley,
marjoram, basil and garlic, then cook uncovered for about 10 to 15 minutes, or
until the *ratatouille* is well mixed and has the appearance of a *ragoût* of vegetables
– which it is. Serve hot from the casserole, or cold as a delicious beginning to a
summer meal.

# Provençal Stuffed Vegetables
Serves 4

*Vegetable cases:*
4 small aubergines
4 courgettes
4 medium onions, peeled
4 small tomatoes

*Provençal Stuffing:*
175 g/6 ounces ground veal
25 g/1 ounce fat salt pork,
  diced
1 onion, finely chopped
olive oil

1 clove garlic, crushed
finely chopped fresh tarragon
finely chopped fresh flat-leaf
  parsley
1 egg, beaten
2 tablespoons freshly grated
  Parmesan
4–6 tablespoons boiled rice
courgette and aubergine pulp
salt and freshly ground
  pepper
butter

Poach the aubergines, courgettes and onions whole for 1 minute in boiling salted
water. Cut the tops off the tomatoes, aubergines, courgettes and onions. Scoop out
the interiors of the vegetables and keep the pulp of aubergines and courgettes for
the stuffing.

**To make the stuffing:** Sauté the meats and onion in olive oil. Mix the other
ingredients (except the butter) in a bowl and add them to the meat and onion
mixture with pepper and salt, to taste. Sauté for a few minutes, stirring continuously, and then stuff the scooped-out vegetables with the mixture. Place the stuffed

vegetables in an ovenproof baking dish to which you have added a little olive oil; place a knob of butter on each vegetable and bake in a moderate oven (190°C/ 375°F/gas 5) for ½ hour. Serve one of each vegetable as a main course.

## Stuffed Tomatoes Provençal
Serves 4 to 6

**12 large ripe tomatoes for cases**
**olive oil and butter**

*Provençal stuffing:*
**175 g/6 ounces ground veal**
**25 g/1 ounce fat salt pork, diced**
**1 onion, finely chopped**
**1 clove garlic, crushed**
**finely chopped fresh tarragon**

**finely chopped fresh flat-leaf**
**parsley**
**1 egg, beaten**
**2 tablespoons freshly grated**
**Parmesan**
**6 tablespoons boiled rice**
**tomato pulp**
**salt and freshly ground pepper**
**butter**

Cut the tops off the tomatoes, scoop out the interiors and keep the pulp for the stuffing.

**To make the stuffing:** Sauté the meats and onion in olive oil. Mix the remaining ingredients (except the butter) in a bowl and add them to the meat and onion mixture with salt and pepper, to taste. Sauté for a few minutes, stirring continuously, and then stuff the scooped-out tomatoes with the mixture. Place the stuffed tomatoes in an ovenproof baking dish to which you have added a little olive oil; place a knob of butter on each tomato and bake in a moderate oven (190°C/375°F/gas 5) for 30 minutes. Serve as a main course.

## Aubergine Casserole
Serves 4

**4–6 aubergines**
**salt**
**2 tablespoons olive oil**
**butter**
**freshly ground pepper**

**8 tablespoons freshly grated**
**Parmesan**
**150 ml/¼ pint fresh cream**
**4–6 tomatoes, peeled and sliced**
**4 tablespoons breadcrumbs**

Peel the aubergines; cut in thin slices; sprinkle with salt and let them 'sweat' in a dish for 2 hours. Drain the aubergine slices; wipe them and fry lightly in the olive oil until soft and golden. Drain.

Butter a deep ovenproof casserole; place a layer of aubergine slices in the bottom; season with pepper and sprinkle generously with Parmesan and cream.

Add a layer of tomatoes, then add pepper and a little more cream and cheese, followed by another layer of aubergine slices and so on, until the dish is full.

Finish with cream on the top; cover with breadcrumbs and Parmesan; dot with 1 tablespoon butter and cook in a moderate oven (190°C/375°F/gas 5) for approximately 45 minutes.

# Stuffed Aubergines

Serves 4 to 6

4 medium-sized aubergines
salt
olive oil
2 Spanish onions, sliced
2 cloves garlic, finely chopped
2 tablespoons finely chopped
  flat-leaf parsley

6 ripe tomatoes, seeded and
  chopped
4 whole tomatoes
sugar
salt and freshly ground
  pepper

Trim the aubergines; cut in half lengthwise and scoop out some of the aubergine flesh, leaving a shell about 6 mm/¼ inch thick. Make 4 incisions lengthwise in each half, being careful not to cut through the skin. Salt the aubergine halves, making sure the salt goes into the incisions, and leave for 20 minutes. Wash the aubergines, squeeze dry and sauté in olive oil until soft and pliable. Reserve the oil.

Sauté the onions in fresh olive oil in another frying pan until transparent. Add the garlic, parsley and tomatoes, and sauté for a few minutes more, stirring from time to time. Allow to cool.

Place the sautéed aubergines, cut side up, in a fairly deep baking dish or shallow casserole. Stuff with the onion and tomato mixture, spooning any left over around the aubergines.

Slice 4 whole tomatoes and place 3 slices on top of each stuffed aubergine; sprinkle with a little sugar and salt and pepper, to taste.

Pour over the reserved oil; add a little water and cook in a slow oven (170°C/325°F/gas 3) for 1 hour, or until tender. Serve cold as appetiser.

# Bouillabaisse d'Épinards

Serves 4 to 6

6 tablespoons olive oil
1 Spanish onion, finely chopped
2 cloves garlic, finely chopped
350 g/¾ pound potatoes, thinly
  sliced
salt and freshly ground pepper
425 ml/¾ pint boiling water
¼ teaspoon powdered saffron

700 g/1½ pounds cooked spinach
1 bouquet garni (flat-leaf
  parsley, thyme, fennel and
  bay leaf)
1 piece lemon peel
1 egg per person
1 fried toast triangle per person

Heat the olive oil in a frying pan and sauté the onion and garlic in it until transparent but not golden. Add the potatoes and let them sauté a minute on both sides without taking colour. Transfer to an earthenware casserole; add salt and pepper and pour over the boiling water, in which you have dissolved the saffron. Drain the cooked spinach, press it between your hands to get rid of all the moisture, chop finely and stir it into the casserole, being careful not to break the potato slices. Add the *bouquet garni* and lemon peel; cover and allow to simmer in a slow oven

(170°C/325°F/gas 3) for at least 1 hour, or until the potatoes are cooked. When ready to serve, break into the pan 1 egg for each person and cook gently until the egg whites set. One toast triangle fried in butter for each guest accompanies this country dish which is so popular in Provence.

## Spinach au Gratin
Serves 4 to 6

1 kg/2 pounds spinach
salt
4–6 tablespoons whipped cream
1–2 tablespoons freshly grated
  breadcrumbs
butter

*Sauce:*
4 tablespoons butter

4 tablespoons flour
600 ml/1 pint hot milk
100 g/¼ pound freshly grated
  Gruyère
1 teaspoon mustard
juice ½ lemon
salt and freshly ground
  pepper

Wash the spinach several times in cold water. Poach in a little salted water for 15 to 20 minutes, or until tender. Drain; squeeze dry and chop finely.

**To make the sauce:** Melt the butter in the top of a double saucepan; blend in the flour and cook over water, stirring constantly, until smooth. Gradually add the hot milk and cook, stirring constantly, until the sauce comes to the boil. Add the cheese and cook, stirring, until it melts. Flavour to taste with mustard, lemon juice, salt and pepper.

**To finish the 'gratin':** Place the chopped, cooked spinach in a buttered baking dish; pour the sauce over; spread with whipped cream; sprinkle with fresh breadcrumbs and dot with butter.

Bake in a moderate oven (190°C/375°F/gas 5) for about 20 minutes or until the top is golden.

## Spinaci con Salsiccia
Serves 4 to 6

1 kg/2 pounds spinach
4 tablespoons olive oil
2 tablespoons butter
1 small clove garlic, kept
  whole

225 g/½ pound dry Italian
  sausage, diced
salt and freshly ground
  pepper
lemon wedges

Bring about 150 ml/¼ pint of water to a vigorous boil in the bottom of a large saucepan; add the carefully washed spinach leaves; cover and boil rapidly for about 3 minutes, adding a little more water if necessary. When the spinach is tender, but not too soft, drain thoroughly.

Heat the olive oil and butter in a large frying pan and sauté the garlic in this mixture until golden. Remove the garlic; add the sausage and sauté until thoroughly cooked. Stir in the cooked spinach, which you have squeezed dry, and heat through. Add salt and pepper, to taste. Serve with lemon wedges.

## Sautéed Spinach
Serves 4 to 6

1 Spanish onion, finely chopped
1 clove garlic, finely chopped
6 tablespoons butter
2 tablespoons olive oil
1.3 kg/3 pounds spinach, cooked and drained
6 tablespoons double cream

4 tablespoons dry breadcrumbs
4 tablespoons freshly grated Parmesan
salt and freshly ground pepper
grated nutmeg
2 slices white bread

Sauté the onion and garlic until transparent in 2 tablespoons of the butter and all of the oil. Chop the cooked spinach finely and add to the pan. Cook over a low heat, stirring constantly, until the fats are absorbed.

Stir in the cream, breadcrumbs and cheese; season to taste with salt, pepper and nutmeg. Heat thoroughly, but do not allow to boil.

Trim the crusts from the bread; cut into cubes and sauté in the remaining butter until golden. Just before serving, stir into the spinach.

## Baked Spinach Mornay
Serves 4 to 6

1 packet young spinach leaves
6 tablespoons butter
salt and freshly ground pepper
4 tablespoons double cream
3 slices white bread

*Mornay Sauce:*
2 tablespoons butter
2 tablespoons flour
300 ml/½ pint milk
½ teaspoon dry mustard
6 tablespoons freshly grated Parmesan
pinch cayenne pepper

Trim the stalks from the spinach then place the leaves in a saucepan with 4 tablespoons of the butter; add salt and pepper, to taste. Cook slowly for 3 to 6 minutes, stirring from time to time. Stir in the cream. Trim the crusts from the bread; dice and fry in the remaining butter until golden. Fold the *croûtons* into the spinach and spoon the mixture into a buttered, shallow, oven-proof dish.

**To make the sauce:**  Melt the butter in the top of a double saucepan; add the flour and cook, stirring continuously, until the mixture is smooth. Pour in the milk and stir over hot water until the mixture begins to thicken. Add the mustard,

5 tablespoons of the cheese and a little cayenne pepper, and simmer slowly for 5 minutes. Pour over the spinach and sprinkle the top with the remaining cheese. Dot with butter and brown quickly under the grill.

## Mushrooms à la Grecque
Serves 4 to 6

2 carrots, coarsely chopped
1 Spanish onion, coarsely
  chopped
2 tablespoons olive oil
2 tablespoons corn oil
150 ml/¼ pint dry white wine
salt and freshly ground pepper
1 *bouquet garni* (2 sprigs flat-
  leaf parsley, 2 sprigs thyme,
  2 bay leaves, 1 branch celery)

1 fat clove garlic
450 g/1 pound button
  mushrooms
225 g/½ pound tomatoes, peeled,
  seeded and chopped
2 tablespoons olive oil
2 tablespoons chopped flat-leaf
  parsley

Sauté the carrots and onion in the oil (half olive oil and half corn) until soft and golden. Moisten with the white wine; add salt and pepper, to taste, a generous *bouquet garni* and a clove of garlic.

Trim the stems of the mushrooms well; add to the vegetables with the tomatoes and a little more wine if necessary. There should not be too much liquid at this stage as the mushrooms will add liquid in cooking.

Cook, uncovered, for about 15 to 20 minutes. Remove from the heat; allow to cool; remove the herbs and add the olive oil. Sprinkle with parsley and serve cold as an *hors-d'œuvre*.

## Baked Stuffed Mushrooms
Serves 4

12 large mushrooms
4 tablespoons olive oil
50 g/2 ounces bacon, finely
  chopped
2 shallots, finely chopped
salt and freshly ground pepper

1 egg
2 tablespoons double cream
1 tablespoon cognac
2 tablespoons breadcrumbs
2 tablespoons butter

Remove and chop the stems of the mushrooms. Brush the caps with olive oil and bake in a hot oven for 5 minutes, or until half cooked. Heat the remaining olive oil in a frying pan and gently sauté the bacon, mushroom stems and shallots for 10 minutes. Add salt and pepper, to taste. Beat the egg with the double cream and cognac, stir in and allow to cool.

Place the mushroom caps on a buttered baking sheet and fill them with the stuffing, piling it up in the centre. Sprinkle with breadcrumbs, place a dab of butter on each mound and brown under the grill.

# Crab-stuffed Mushrooms
Serves 4

100 g/¼ pound crabmeat
4 tablespoons dried breadcrumbs
2 eggs, beaten
2 tablespoons cream
2 tablespoons finely chopped
  flat-leaf parsley

2–3 tablespoons finely chopped
  onion
butter
salt and freshly ground pepper
lemon juice
16 large mushroom caps

Combine the crabmeat, breadcrumbs, eggs, cream and parsley in a mixing bowl. Sauté the onion in 1 tablespoon butter until soft. Stir into the crab mixture and season to taste with salt, pepper and lemon juice. Fill the mushroom caps with this mixture. Dot with butter; arrange the mushroom caps in a buttered baking dish and place in a moderate oven (190°C/375°F/gas 5) for 15 to 20 minutes, or until tender. Serve with mornay sauce (see page 202; or, for an alternative version, page 35: make half).

# Leeks au Gratin
Serves 4 to 6

12 small leeks
4 tablespoons butter
4 tablespoons flour
425 ml/¾ pint hot milk
100 g/¼ pound freshly grated
  Gruyère

1 teaspoon mustard
juice of ½ lemon
salt and freshly ground pepper
2 tablespoons fresh breadcrumbs
butter

Wash the leeks; cut off the roots and green tops to within 2.5 cm/1 inch of the white. Split the leeks from the top almost to the root end and wash thoroughly under running water. Simmer in boiling salted water for 20 minutes, or until tender. Drain thoroughly.

Melt the butter in top of a double saucepan; blend in the flour and cook over water, stirring constantly, until smooth. Add the hot milk gradually and cook, stirring constantly, until the sauce comes to the boil. Add the cheese and cook, stirring, until it melts. Flavour to taste with mustard, lemon juice and salt and pepper.

Place the leeks in a buttered baking dish; pour the sauce over them. Sprinkle with fresh breadcrumbs and dot with butter; bake in a moderate oven (190°C/375°F/gas 5) for about 20 minutes, or until the top is golden.

# Garlic-Stuffed Onions
Serves 6

6 Spanish onions
12 fat cloves garlic
olive oil
salt and freshly ground pepper

6 tablespoons finely chopped
  flat-leaf parsley
freshly grated breadcrumbs
butter

Simmer the onions and garlic in boiling salted water until tender. Scoop out the centres of the onions. Combine the scooped-out onion flesh with the cooked garlic, chop very finely and then pound together until smooth with olive oil, salt, pepper, parsley and 6 tablespoons fresh breadcrumbs. Stuff the onions with this mixture; place on a greased baking dish and sprinkle with breadcrumbs; dot with butter and cook in a moderate oven (190°C/375°F/gas 5) until cooked through.

## Glazed White Onions
Serves 4

| | |
|---|---|
| **450 g/1 pound small white onions** | **4 tablespoons chicken stock** |
| **4 teaspoons butter** | **1 tablespoon sugar** |
| | **salt and freshly ground pepper** |

Peel the onions and place in a small saucepan; cover with cold water and cook over a high heat until the water boils. Remove from the heat and drain.

Replace the blanched onions in the saucepan; add the butter and chicken stock; season with sugar, and salt and pepper, to taste, and simmer over a low flame until the onions have absorbed the liquid without burning and have taken on colour.

## Glazed Carrots
Serves 4

| | |
|---|---|
| **450 g/1 pound small carrots** | **1 tablespoon sugar** |
| **4 tablespoons butter** | **salt** |
| **4 tablepoons chicken stock** | |

Scrape the carrots; slice thickly and place in a small saucepan; cover with cold water and blanch. Drain. Simmer the blanched carrots with the butter, chicken stock, sugar and salt, to taste, until the carrots have absorbed the liquid without burning and have taken on colour.

## Sliced Carrots and Mushrooms
Serves 4 to 6

| | |
|---|---|
| **1 bunch young carrots** | **salt and freshly ground pepper** |
| **2 tablespoons butter** | **1 sprig fresh rosemary, leaves only, chopped** |
| **1 tablespoon olive oil** | |
| **1 small onion, finely chopped** | **seeds from 1 cardamom pod** |
| **½ clove garlic, finely chopped** | **2–4 tablespoons cream** |
| **6 fresh mushrooms, sliced** | |

Scrape the carrots and slice diagonally. Combine the butter, olive oil, onion and garlic in a saucepan and sauté for 1 minute. Add the carrots, mushrooms and seasonings; cover the saucepan and cook over a low heat for 10 to 15 minutes, or until the vegetables are just tender. Stir in the cream and season to taste.

# French-Style Peas
Serves 4

450 g/1 pound frozen peas
4 tablespoons butter
4 tablespoons chicken stock

1 tablespoon sugar
salt

Place the peas in a small saucepan; cover with cold water and blanch. Drain.

Simmer the blanched peas with the butter, chicken stock, sugar and salt, to taste, until the peas have absorbed the liquid and are tender.

# Petits Pois au Lard
Serves 4 to 6

100 g/¼ pound salt pork or
  bacon, diced
4 tablespoons butter
1 kg/2 pounds freshly shelled
  peas

12 tiny white onions, peeled
2 lettuce leaves, shredded
4 tablespoons water
salt and freshly ground pepper
1 tablespoon sugar

Parboil the diced salt pork for 5 minutes in water to cover. Drain. Melt the butter gently in a saucepan; sauté the bacon until golden. Add the peas, onions, lettuce, water, and salt and pepper, to taste. Cover the saucepan and simmer gently for about 30 minutes. Add sugar after the peas have cooked for 20 minutes. Serve hot.

# Braised Celery
Serves 4

2 heads celery
¼ Spanish onion, thinly sliced
2 small carrots, thinly sliced
150 ml/¼ pint chicken stock

salt and freshly ground pepper
2 teaspoons butter
2 teaspoons flour
finely chopped flat-leaf parsley

Cut each celery head in half lengthwise and trim off the tops. Blanch in boiling water for 10 minutes. Drain carefully and put in a heatproof dish with the onion, carrots and chicken stock.

Season with salt and pepper, to taste, then cover the pan and cook slowly until tender (30 to 40 minutes). About 5 minutes before you remove the vegetables from the heat, stir in the butter and flour which you have mixed to a smooth paste (a *beurre manié*). Just before serving, sprinkle with parsley.

# Chapter 13

# Pasta and Rice

## Pasta

Inexpensive, easy to prepare, wonderfully filling and practically imperishable in storage, *pasta* – as typically Italian as Grand Opera and Chianti – has much to recommend it as one of the great dishes of the world.

Though all *pasta* is made of the same basic wheat flour dough, the different shapes and sizes it comes in are as varied as the different towns and regions of Italy. Some varieties – *pasta asciutta* – are eaten with sauce and freshly grated Parmesan; others are stuffed with finely chopped meats, spinach, *ricotta* cheese and other ingredients. Still others – *pasta in brodo* – are meant to be served in soups.

Most of us are familiar with a dozen or so varieties of *pasta*. Italians have more than a hundred different shapes and sizes to choose from – ranging from tiny golden specks called *pastina*, used mainly in light soups and invalid broths, to huge ribbed *rigatoni*, so large and hearty that they are individually stuffed with meat, cheese and tomatoes.

The delightful names the Italians give to the shapes are proof of their great affection for *pasta*. *Spaghetti* (which means little strings) and *macaroni* are, of course, best known to us, but they are just two of the immense *pasta* family; *amorini*, little cupids; *farfalletti*, little bows or butterflies; *conchiglie*, little shells; *cappelletti*, little hats; *tirabaci*, kiss-bringers . . . are a few of the other delicious forms that *pasta* takes. And strange as it seems, the cut and shape of *pasta*, in one or another of these many forms, alters the taste of the finished dish, for it affects the cooking and the amount of sauce included with each mouthful.

Even more important than the size and shape of the *pasta* is the kind of sauce that accompanies it. Not all Italian *pasta* sauces are tomato-based. One of my favourite recipes serves well-drained *spaghetti* with only butter and freshly grated Parmesan cheese; another adds one or two raw egg yolks and a little cream to this basic recipe for a really superb sauce. An 'emergency shelf' sauce that I find useful for *pasta* features a few tablespoons of finely chopped onions sautéed in olive oil, moistened with bottled fish soup and simmered for ten minutes. Coarsely chopped canned clams and fresh cream are added just before serving. I like, too, a sauce made of pounded anchovies, butter and finely chopped onion, garlic and coriander; or, when lots of garden-fresh basil is available, the famous *pesto* or 'green sauce' of Genoa, made by pounding fresh basil with garlic, grated Parmesan and olive oil.

One pint (600 ml) of sauce is enough for a pound (450–500 g) of *pasta*, as there should be just enough to flavour, moisten and coat each strand or piece of *pasta* but not enough to leave a pool of sauce in the bottom of the serving dish.

# How to Cook Pasta Perfectly

One pound (450–500 g) of *pasta* serves 4 people for a main course, 6 people for a first course. Cook *pasta* in boiling, well-salted water (3.4–4.5 litres/6–8 pints of water per pound of *pasta*).

Let the water boil briskly for a minute before adding the *pasta*. For long *spaghetti* or *macaroni*, hold a handful at one end and dip the other into the boiling water. As the *pasta* softens, curl it round in the pan until the whole length goes in. Do not cover; use a kitchen fork or a long wooden spoon to stir at the start of the cooking to prevent *spaghetti* from sticking to the pan. Stir frequently during cooking.

Cook *pasta* until tender, but still firm – '*al dente*', as the Italians say, which means just firm enough to bite comfortably but not so soft that it is mushy. And remember, cooking time varies with the shape, thickness and freshness of *pasta*. Dried *pasta* – the commercial variety available in this country – should be cooked for 10 to 12 minutes: check the packet instructions. *Pasta fatta in casa* – the home-made kind – takes only about 5 minutes to cook. Lift out one strand with a fork and bite it to test whether it is ready.

Be careful not to overcook *pasta*. When done, drain at once in a big colander, shaking it to remove as much water as possible. For best results, serve *pasta* immediately.

**To keep pasta hot:**  If it is impractical to serve *pasta* as soon as it is cooked, set the colander of drained *pasta* over a saucepan containing a small amount of boiling water. Cover with a damp towel until ready to serve.

# Home-made Egg Pasta

**450 g/1 pound sifted flour**       **3 well-beaten eggs**
**1 teaspoon salt**                 **4–5 tablespoons water**

Mix the flour, salt, eggs and a little of the water with a fork until the *pasta* dough is just soft enough to form into a ball, adding a little more water if the mixture seems too dry.

Sprinkle a large pastry board with flour and knead the dough until smooth and elastic (about 15 minutes) on this board with the flat of your hand, sifting a little flour on hands and board from time to time.

Divide the dough into 6 equal parts and, using a rolling pin, roll out a piece at a time into paper-thin sheets. To do this, roll out in one direction, stretching the *pasta* dough as you go, and then roll out in the opposite direction. Sprinkle with flour, fold over and repeat. The dough should be just dry enough not to stick to the rolling pin. Repeat this process of rolling, stretching and folding the dough another 2 or 3 times. Repeat with other pieces of *pasta* dough.

**To make tagliatelle:**  Prepare egg *pasta* as above. Dust liberally with flour. Fold loosely and cut into 6-mm/¼-inch strips. Spread on a clean cloth to dry for at least 1 hour before cooking in the usual way.

**To make lasagne:** Prepare egg *pasta* as above. Dust with flour. Fold loosely and cut into 5-cm/2-inch strips. Spread on a clean cloth to dry for at least 1 hour before cooking in the usual way.

**To make cannelloni:** Prepare egg *pasta* as above. Cut into rectangles of 7.5 × 10 cm/3 × 4 inches. Dry for 1 hour. Drop into boiling salted water, 6 to 8 at a time, and boil for 5 minutes. Remove and drop immediately into cold water. Drain and spread on a clean cloth to dry. Fill as desired and bake until the stuffing is cooked through. Serve with tomato sauce and freshly grated Parmesan.

## Spaghetti Soufflé
Serves 4

2 tablespoons butter
2 tablespoons flour
300 ml/½ pint hot milk
100 g/¼ pound freshly grated
  Parmesan

1 teaspoon mustard
cayenne pepper and salt
100 g/¼ pound *spaghetti*
5 eggs
tomato sauce (page 38)

Melt the butter in the top of a double saucepan. Add the flour and blend well. Add the milk and stir until the sauce begins to thicken; then add the Parmesan and stir until the sauce is smooth and thick. Season to taste with mustard, cayenne pepper and salt.

Cook the *spaghetti* in boiling water until tender. Drain well. Separate the eggs and stir the yolks, one by one, into the slightly cooled cheese mixture. Stir the *spaghetti* into the cheese mixture. Beat the egg whites until they are stiff, but not dry. Fold gently into the *spaghetti* and cheese mixture and pour into a well-buttered soufflé dish. Cook in a preheated oven (180°C/350°F/gas 4) for about 25 minutes, or until done. Serve immediately with well-flavoured tomato sauce.

## Spaghetti alla Matriciana
Serves 4

100 g/¼ pound fat salt pork,
  diced
1 Spanish onion, finely chopped
2 cloves garlic, finely chopped
2 tablespoons olive oil
1 large can Italian peeled
  tomatoes

2 tablespoons tomato purée
½ large red pepper, diced
salt and freshly ground pepper
450 g/1 pound *spaghetti*
freshly grated Parmesan
butter

Sauté the fat salt pork, onion and garlic in the olive oil until golden. Add the tomatoes, tomato purée and red pepper; season to taste with salt and pepper and simmer for 1 hour.

Cook the *spaghetti* in boiling salted water until *al dente*. Drain. Serve with the sauce and freshly grated Parmesan. Dot with butter.

## Spaghetti alla Bersagliera
Serves 4

1 onion, finely chopped
4 tablespoons olive oil
100 g/¼ pound *salame*, cut in
  strips
4 tablespoons dry white wine
1 kg/2 pounds tomatoes, peeled
  and seeded

salt and freshly ground pepper
450 g/1 pound *spaghetti*
100 g/¼ pound *provolone* cheese,
  cut in strips
freshly grated Parmesan
butter

Sauté the onion in the olive oil until golden. Cut the *salame* in thin strips and add to the onion mixture. Allow the *salame* to take on colour; moisten with white wine and cook, stirring, until the wine evaporates. Stir in the tomatoes; season to taste with salt and pepper, and simmer gently for at least 45 minutes. Keep warm.

Cook the *spaghetti* in salted water until *al dente*. Cut the *provolone* cheese into thin strips and when the *pasta* is almost cooked, add the cheese to the tomato and *salame* sauce and mix well. Drain the *pasta*; cover with sauce and sprinkle with Parmesan. Serve with butter and additional Parmesan.

## Tagliatelle Verde
Serves 4

450 g/1 pound green noodles
  (*tagliatelle verde*)
6 tablespoons butter
1 can Italian white truffles
4 egg yolks

150 ml/¼ pint cream
1–2 pinches nutmeg
butter
freshly grated Parmesan

Boil the green noodles in salted water until cooked to *al dente* tenderness. Drain. Melt half the butter in a large saucepan. Slice the truffles thinly and sauté for a minute. Add the noodles and pour over the egg yolks beaten with the cream and a grating of nutmeg. Stir for a minute; remove from the heat and add the remaining butter.

The sauce should be creamy and the egg yolks should blend in perfectly. Serve with additional quantities of butter and with Parmesan.

## Spaghetti with Mushroom Sauce
Serves 4

4 tablespoons olive oil
4 tablespoons butter
2 onions, coarsely chopped
450 g/1 pound mushrooms, sliced
  thinly
2 cloves garlic, crushed

1 teaspoon salt
freshly ground pepper
550–600 g/1¼ pounds peeled
  tomatoes, roughly chopped
chopped oregano, basil or
  marjoram, to taste

**450 g/1 pound** *spaghetti*

butter
freshly grated Parmesan

Combine the olive oil and butter in a heavy-bottomed iron *cocotte* or casserole and sauté the onions until golden but not brown. Add the mushrooms, garlic, salt and pepper to taste and simmer, stirring frequently, for 10 minutes. Add the tomatoes and herbs and simmer for 30 minutes.

While the sauce is simmering, cook the *spaghetti* in rapidly boiling salted water until just tender. Drain and place on a hot serving dish. Pour the sauce over and serve with a generous knob of butter and with Parmesan.

## Spaghetti alla Marinara
Serves 4

**1 Spanish onion, finely
  chopped**
**2 cloves garlic, finely chopped**
**4 tablespoons olive oil**
**450 g/1 pound ripe tomatoes,
  peeled, seeded and coarsely
  chopped**
**salt and freshly ground
  pepper**
**1–2 teaspoons brown sugar**

**chopped oregano, basil or
  marjoram, to taste**
**450 g/1 pound shelled tiger
  prawns, chopped**
**150 ml/¼ pint dry white wine**
**4 tablespoons finely chopped
  flat-leaf parsley**
**450 g/1 pound** *spaghetti*
**butter**

Sauté the onion and garlic in the olive oil until transparent. Add the tomatoes, salt and pepper, to taste, brown sugar and herbs and simmer gently for 15 to 20 minutes.

Combine the prawns and white wine in another saucepan and simmer gently for 5 minutes. Add the prawns to the tomato sauce with the parsley and simmer for 10 minutes longer. Correct the seasoning.

While the sauce is simmering, cook the *spaghetti* in rapidly boiling salted water until just tender. Drain and place on a hot serving dish. Pour the sauce over and serve with generous knob of butter.

## Spaghetti al Tonno
Serves 4

**1 clove garlic, kept whole**
**4 tablespoons olive oil**
**6–8 tablespoons tomato purée**
**300 ml/½ pint water**
**100 g/¼ pound fresh tuna fish**
**4 anchovy fillets**

**salt and freshly ground pepper**
**450 g/1 pound** *spaghetti*
**finely chopped flat-leaf
  parsley**
**butter**

Sauté the garlic in the olive oil until golden. Discard the garlic. Mix the tomato purée with the water and add to the oil. Simmer for 30 minutes.

Chop the tuna fish coarsely; chop the anchovies finely; add to the tomato mixture. Season to taste with salt and pepper and simmer for 15 minutes, stirring occasionally.

Cook the *spaghetti* in boiling salted water until *al dente*. Drain and mix with the sauce; sprinkle with parsley; dot with butter, and serve.

## Fettuccine with Pesto Sauce
Serves 4

2–3 cloves garlic, finely
chopped
4–6 tablespoons finely chopped
basil
4–6 tablespoons finely chopped
flat-leaf parsley
2–3 tablespoons pine nuts

6–8 tablespoons freshly grated
cheese (Romano, pecorino or
Parmesan), plus extra to serve
olive oil
freshly ground pepper
450 g/1 pound *fettuccine*
butter

Pound the garlic, basil, parsley, pine nuts and cheese in a mortar until smooth. Gradually add olive oil and whisk until the sauce is thick and smooth. Season to taste with pepper.

Cook the *fettuccine* in rapidly boiling salted water until just tender. Drain and place on a hot serving dish. Spoon the *pesto* sauce over and serve with a generous knob of butter and grated cheese.

## Spaghetti with Oil and Garlic Sauce
Serves 4

450 g/1 pound *spaghetti*
4 cloves garlic, finely chopped
4 tablespoons finely chopped
flat-leaf parsley
4 tablespoons butter

4 tablespoons olive oil
salt and freshly ground pepper
freshly grated Parmesan
butter

Cook the *spaghetti* in boiling salted water until just tender. Drain and keep warm.

Simmer the garlic and parsley in the butter and olive oil until hot, but do not allow the garlic to take on colour.

Add the drained *spaghetti* to the oil and garlic mixture and stir until thoroughly moistened, adding a little more warm oil if necessary. Season to taste with salt and pepper.

Turn the *spaghetti* into a heated serving dish, sprinkle with Parmesan, dot with butter and serve immediately.

# Tagliatelle con Tartufi

Serves 4

450 g/1 pound *tagliatelle*
4 tablespoons butter
2 raw egg yolks
6 tablespoons freshly grated
  Parmesan, plus extra to serve

6 tablespoons double cream
salt and freshly ground pepper
canned white truffles, finely
  sliced
butter

Boil the *tagliatelle* in salted water until cooked to *al dente* tenderness. Drain and place in a hot serving bowl or chafing dish, with the butter, egg yolks, grated cheese and cream. Toss the noodles in this mixture until the heat of the noodles 'cooks' the egg and cream sauce. Season to taste with salt and pepper; sprinkle with white truffles and serve immediately with additional butter and freshly grated Parmesan.

# Cannelloni Ripieni

Serves 4 to 6

450 g/1 pound *cannelloni* (follow
  the recipe on page 208 or buy
  ready-made)

2 tablespoons freshly grated
  Parmesan
salt and freshly ground pepper

*Filling:*
450 g/1 pound button
  mushrooms, chopped
225 g/½ pound cooked ham or
  veal, diced
½ Spanish onion, chopped
2 tablespoons butter
2 tablespoons olive oil

*Cheese Sauce:*
2 tablespoons butter
2 tablespoons flour
600 ml/1 pint hot milk
4 tablespoons freshly grated
  Parmesan, plus extra for
  topping
salt and freshly ground pepper

**To make the filling:** Sauté the mushrooms, ham or veal and onion in the butter and olive oil until cooked. Cool. Add the Parmesan, and salt and pepper, to taste. Place 2 tablespoons mushroom filling on each square and roll the *pasta* carefully around the filling. (Or spoon into ready-made *cannelloni*.)

**To make the sauce:** Melt the butter in the top of a double saucepan; stir in the flour to make a smooth *roux*. Add the hot milk gradually, stirring continuously over simmering water; season to taste with the cheese, salt and pepper and cook, stirring from time to time, until smooth and thick.

**To complete the dish:** Arrange the filled *cannelloni* in a buttered shallow baking dish; cover with the sauce; sprinkle generously with Parmesan and bake in a moderate oven (180°C/350°F/gas 4) for about 30 minutes, or until golden brown.

# Creole Jambalaya

For me, one of the most romantic places in the United States, and perhaps the world, is the shadowy, unreal swampland of Louisiana where the grey streamers of Spanish moss trail heavily from the branches of oak trees, removing all sense of distance and turning the *bayoux* into a series of dreamy backdrops from some gigantic ballet.

The trees, growing straight out of the water, seem to float in space, balanced precariously over their own writhing reflections. Strange creatures of these wastes – alligators, racoons and swimming snakes – contest possession of the dark waterways with men in canoes, Cajun Indians, who have lived in this area for centuries and yet (almost the strangest fact of all about this lost land) speak among themselves perfect seventeenth-century French.

It was from this magic country and its capital, New Orleans, where Indian, Spanish, Negro and French cultures have combined to produce the Creole, that I first discovered how foreign and exotic American regional food could be. It was here that I first tasted baked *pompano* with spicy Creole sauce, red snapper *court-bouillon*, fluffy oyster cutlets, feathery-light beaten biscuits and the heady delights of Creole *gumbos* (high-flavoured soups of chicken, oysters, shrimps and crabs, seasoned with okra and powdered sassafras) and Creole *jambalaya*, my favourite of them all.

This great Creole speciality seems to sum up the troubled history of Louisiana, combining the subtlety of the French, the exoticism of the *Conquistadores* and the earthy magic of the Negro plantation cooks. Ham and shrimps or prawns are a necessity for this dish; hot Spanish sausage (*chorizo*) and cubed poached chicken are often added for festive occasions; and even chickpeas can go into the pot with the spices, herbs, rice and tomatoes that give such character and flavour to this great dish.

Creole *jambalaya* takes time to prepare and more time to cook but the results make the operation more than worth the extra effort involved. I particularly like this dish for its easy stretchability. The recipe below feeds six lavishly, will stretch comfortably to eight, and can be doubled for twelve. Easily manageable with a fork, it is an admirable standby for buffet party suppers.

## Creole Jambalaya

Serves 6

350 g/¾ pound cooked ham
350 g/¾ pound jumbo prawns, shelled
225 g/½ pound *chorizo* sausage
4 tablespoons olive oil
2 tablespoons butter
2 tablespoons lard
1 Spanish onion, finely chopped

350 g/¾ pound *risotto* rice
1 stalk celery, chopped
1 green pepper, finely chopped
6 tomatoes, peeled, seeded and chopped
1 small can tomato purée
1.2 litres/2 pints well-flavoured chicken stock
1 small glass dry white wine

| | |
|---|---|
| **4 tablespoons finely chopped flat-leaf parsley or a handful black olives (optional)** | **½ teaspoon dried oregano** |
| | **⅛ teaspoon dried thyme** |
| | **⅛ teaspoon ground cloves** |
| | **2 cloves garlic** |
| ***Seasonings:*** | **salt, freshly ground pepper and** |
| **1 bay leaf, crumbled** | **cayenne** |

Cut the ham into 2.5-cm/1-inch squares; cut the prawns into smaller pieces if they seem a little large; slice the *chorizo* sausage (if not available, substitute pork or garlic sausage).

Heat the olive oil in a thick-bottomed frying pan and sauté the ham, prawns and sausage until golden brown. Reserve.

Melt the butter and lard in the bottom of a large flameproof casserole and sauté the onion until transparent. Stir in the rice and cook over a low heat, stirring gently until the rice is golden. Add the ham, prawn and sausage mixture to the rice; and stir in the celery, green pepper, tomatoes, tomato purée and all the seasonings.

Bring the chicken stock to the boil and pour over the *jambalaya* mixture. Cover the casserole and simmer over a low heat for 25 to 30 minutes – or until the rice is tender, but still separate – adding a little more liquid from time to time if necessary. Just before serving, stir in the white wine, correct the seasoning and keep warm in the lowest of ovens – or on a candle warmer – until ready to serve. A little parsley or a handful of black olives may be added if desired.

# Spanish Paella

One of the prime pleasures of travelling is the chance we have to sample foods that differ from our own. Spain is famous for its *empanados*, deep-fried 'little pies' of finely chopped seafood or meat, served in tiny pastry cases for *hors-d'œuvres,* slightly larger for luncheon or supper; its savoury *tortillas,* thick flat omelettes rich with vegetables and meats; and *gazpacho*, a cold tomato and garlic-based soup with finely chopped trimmings – spring onions, radishes, pimento, cucumber, green pepper, hard-boiled egg and olives, served in individual bowls on the side so that *aficionados* may flavour it as they see fit.

Hearty soups – *cocida*, a knife-and-fork soup that blends the flavours of chicken, beef, smoked ham, chickpeas and other vegetables – and fragrant combinations of beans, beans and pork, chicken and rice, or lobster and rice, are intrinsic parts of this exotic fare, as rich in tradition as the country itself. But perhaps the most famous and most exciting of all is the famous *paella valenciana* – one of the great dishes of the world – which combines many of these ingredients in one delicious dish.

*Paella* gets its name from the flat, round frying pan with two handles in which this dish is traditionally cooked and served. In Spain these pans range from 15 cm/ 6 inches in diameter for one portion to about 1.2 metres/4 feet for large parties.

I always think of *paella* as the perfect party dish – glamorous and attractive and as easy to make as it is easy to serve. It combines its four essential ingredients

– saffron, pimentos, Spanish onion and rice – with a selection of the following: fried chicken, rabbit, ham, veal or pork, *chorizo* sausage, mussels or cockles, prawns or shrimps, and (for gala occasions) a lobster.

## Spanish Paella

Serves 4 to 6

12 mussels, with shells
6 tablespoons dry white wine
2 tablespoons finely chopped
  onion
4 tablespoons finely chopped
  flat-leaf parsley
1 frying chicken, cut in pieces
225 g/½ pound lean pork, diced
100 g/¼ pound *chorizo* or pork
  sausage, sliced
150 ml/¼ pint olive oil
1 small lobster, cut in pieces
8 large whole prawns
1 Spanish onion, finely chopped

4 small cloves garlic, finely
  chopped
4 large tomatoes, peeled and
  chopped
2 canned pimentos, cut in strips
  (or strips of fresh red
  pepper)
salt and freshly ground pepper
¼ teaspoon cayenne pepper
½ teaspoon powdered saffron
425 ml/¾ pint chicken stock or
  water, boiling
450 g/1 pound uncooked risotto
  rice

Steam the mussels in the white wine with the onion and half of the parsley until the shells open. Reserve the mussels. Strain the liquor and reserve.

Sauté the chicken, pork and sausage in the olive oil in a *paella* or large frying pan until golden on all sides. Remove the meats and reserve. Sauté the lobster and prawns in the same pan. Remove and reserve. Add the Spanish onion and half the garlic to the pan and sauté until transparent. Then add the tomatoes and pimentos and simmer the mixture for about 5 minutes, stirring constantly.

Return the sautéed chicken, pork, sausage and half the lobster, prawns and mussels to the pan; add the mussel liquor; season to taste with salt, pepper and cayenne pepper, and heat through.

Mix the remaining garlic and parsley with the powdered saffron in a cupful of the boiling stock or water; add to the remaining stock or water and pour over the meat and seafood mixture; stir well and slowly bring to the boil again. Add the rice and cook, uncovered, for 15 minutes without stirring. Stir well with a wooden spoon; garnish with the remaining lobster, prawns and mussels and cook for 10 to 15 minutes more, or until the rice is tender.

# Italian Rice

Italians love rice and are wonderfully creative in their methods of cooking it. Not for them the pallid plain-boiled variety so often served here as a sop for undistinguished gravies of curry and casserole. Instead they combine rice with butter, finely chopped onion and rich chicken stock, and simmer it gently until it is magically tender – neither mushy soft nor unpleasantly hard, but *al dente* just like their *spaghetti*. And then they flavour it with saffron, wild mushrooms or, for more special occasions, chicken, shrimps, prawns or thinly sliced white truffles.

Italian cooks respect rice: rarely do they wash it under the tap. Instead they clean it by placing it in cold water for a few minutes, carefully picking out any possible bits of grit, and then they rub it dry, after draining it, between the folds of a clean tea towel.

For the best results rice should be cooked in only as much liquid as it can absorb, and special care is required in handling it once it is cooked. The grains mash very easily and so, once cooked, they should never be stirred with a spoon, but tossed lightly with a fork. Serve your rice as soon as possible after cooking.

## The Risotto

One of the easiest and most delicious methods of cooking rice I know is the *risotto*. Wash Italian *risotto* rice in cold water. Drain and dry thoroughly. Add 3 to 4 tablespoons butter; season to taste with salt and pepper and then add enough chicken stock and dry white wine, beef stock, or a combination of the three, to cover the rice. Bring to the boil, stirring; reduce the heat, cover tightly and simmer gently for 15 to 18 minutes, adding a little more liquid if necessary. Uncover, toss lightly with a fork, add a little extra butter and some grated Parmesan cheese and serve. The rice should have absorbed all the liquid and all the grains will be separate and moist.

If a rich chicken stock is used in cooking the rice, and you have sautéed the rice with a little finely chopped beef marrow and onion before adding the liquid, it will take on extra strength and flavour. Try adding to it 225 g/½ pound diced cooked chicken or lamb that has been heated in a little stock, with ½ Spanish onion, finely chopped and cooked until golden in 2 tablespoons butter. Or, substitute cooked prawns, shrimps, lobster or diced white fish. Then, to ring the changes, add to any of these a teaspoon or two or curry powder, or ½ teaspoon of powdered saffron. Chopped nuts, diced raw apples or plumped-up raisins will also do much to change the taste and texture of your *risotto*. This with a salad, followed by a sweet or cheese and fruit, will make a delicious and satisfying meal.

## Risotto alla Milanese

Serves 4 to 6

½ **Spanish onion, finely chopped**
4 **tablespoons butter**
4 **tablespoons diced raw beef**
 **marrow**
350 **g/¾ pound *risotto* rice**
900–1200 **ml/1½–2 pints hot beef**
 **stock**

½ **teaspoon powdered saffron**
**salt and freshly ground**
 **pepper**
**pinch of crushed dried chillies**
**butter**
**freshly grated Parmesan**

Place the onion in a deep saucepan with the butter and beef marrow. Cook slowly for 2 to 4 minutes, taking care that the onion does not become brown. Add the rice and cook over medium heat, stirring constantly with a wooden spoon. After a minute or so stir in a cupful of the hot beef stock in which you have dissolved the powdered saffron.

Continue cooking, adding stock as needed and stirring from time to time, until the rice is cooked (15 to 18 minutes). Season generously with salt and pepper and a pinch of crushed dried chillies. By this time all the stock in the pan should have been absorbed by the rice, leaving the rice tender but still moist. Serve immediately with extra butter and freshly grated Parmesan.

## Easy Saffron Rice
### Serves 4

½ teaspoon powdered saffron
6 tablespoons dry white wine
900 ml/1½ pints hot chicken
   stock

350 g/¾ pound Italian rice
salt and freshly ground
   pepper

Dissolve the saffron in the white wine; add it to the hot chicken stock and combine in a large saucepan with the rice and salt and pepper, to taste. Cover the pan and simmer until all the liquid is absorbed and the rice is tender (about 30 minutes).

## Saffron Rice Salad
### Serves 4

6–8 tablespoons olive oil
2 tablespoons wine vinegar
4 tablespoons finely chopped
   flat-leaf parsley
1–2 cloves garlic, finely
   chopped
dry mustard

350 g/¾ pound rice, cooked as
   above
350 g/¾ pound flaked cooked
   haddock
salt and freshly ground pepper
4 tomatoes, sliced
ripe olives

Make a highly flavoured dressing with the olive oil, wine vinegar, parsley, garlic and dry mustard, to taste. Toss the cooked saffron rice and flaked cooked fish in a bowl with the dressing and season generously with salt and pepper, adding more oil and vinegar if necessary. Garnish with tomatoes and olives.

## Risi e Bisi
### Serves 4

1 Spanish onion, chopped
2 slices bacon, chopped
4 tablespoons butter
225 g/½ pound shelled fresh
   peas
2 tablespoons chopped flat-leaf
   parsley

900–1200 ml/1½–2 pints beef or
   chicken stock
350 g/¾ pound Italian rice
salt and freshly ground
   pepper
freshly grated Parmesan
butter

Sauté the onion and bacon in the butter until the onion is soft and lightly golden. Stir in the peas and parsley; pour half the stock over; cover and simmer for 15 to 20 minutes (5 minutes only if frozen peas are used). Add the rice; cover and cook for 15 to 18 minutes, stirring occasionally. Add stock from time to time when needed. Season with salt and pepper, to taste. When the rice is done, all the stock in the pan should have been absorbed by the rice, which should be quite moist. Serve sprinkled with cheese and dotted with butter.

## Italian Green Rice
Serves 4

350 g/¾ pound Italian rice
salt
1 clove garlic, kept whole
½ teaspoon powdered sage
50 g/2 oz butter
2 tablespoons olive oil

2 tablespoons cooked strained
  spinach or watercress
crushed dried chillies
50 g/2 ounces freshly grated
  Parmesan

Cook the rice in boiling salted water for 15 to 18 minutes. A few minutes before the rice is done, gently sauté the garlic and sage in the butter and oil, being careful not to let the butter become brown. Discard the garlic as soon as it becomes lightly golden. Drain the rice and place it in a serving dish. Stir in the spinach or watercress, and pour the hot pan juices over it. Season with salt and a pinch of crushed dried chillies. Mix well. Sprinkle with the cheese and serve.

## Risotto Provençal
Serves 4

4 tablespoons olive oil
1 Spanish onion, finely
  chopped
225 g/½ pound *risotto* rice
hot water
salt and freshly ground pepper

*Risotto Sauce:*
2 tablespoons finely chopped
  onion
4 tablespoons olive oil

150 ml/¼ pint dry white wine
4–6 tomatoes, peeled, seeded
  and coarsely chopped
salt and freshly ground
  pepper
2 cloves garlic
4 tablespoons finely chopped
  flat-leaf parsley
¼ teaspoon powdered saffron
½ green pepper, finely chopped

Heat the oil in a thick-bottomed saucepan and sauté the onion until golden. Stir in the rice and cook, stirring continuously, until the rice is golden. Moisten with 300 ml/½ pint hot water and simmer gently, stirring from time to time and adding more hot water as the liquid is absorbed by the rice. Continue cooking in this way until the rice is cooked through, but not mushy. Season generously with salt and pepper. Serve with the risotto sauce (see over).

**To make the sauce:** Sauté the onion in the olive oil until transparent. Stir in the white wine and tomatoes. Season to taste with salt and pepper; add 2 whole cloves garlic, finely chopped parsley and the saffron. Simmer gently for 20 minutes. Add chopped green pepper and simmer for a further 10 minutes.

## Chinese Fried Rice
Serves 4

2 eggs
1 tablespoon butter
4 tablespoons corn oil
½ Spanish onion, finely chopped
2 Chinese bowls cold cooked rice
4 tablespoons diced cooked pork

4 tablespoons diced cooked chicken
4 tablespoons diced Italian sausage
4 mushrooms, diced
2 teaspoons soy sauce
salt and freshly ground pepper

Make a thin omelette with the eggs and butter; cut it in strips and set aside. Heat the corn oil in a large frying pan, and when it is very hot add the onion and sauté until golden. Add the next five ingredients and sauté gently for 3 to 5 minutes. Just before serving, add the egg strips, soy sauce and salt and pepper, to taste. Serve immediately.

## Risotto al Tonno
Serves 4

4 tablespoons olive oil
2 tablespoons butter
½ Spanish onion, finely chopped
2 tablespoons tomato purée
6 tablespoons dry white wine
175 g/6 ounces fresh tuna fish, pounded
½ Spanish onion, finely chopped

4 tablespoons butter
350 g/¾ pound *risotto* rice
6 tablespoons dry white wine
900–1200 ml/1½–2 pints hot chicken stock
salt and freshly ground pepper
freshly grated Parmesan
butter

For the sauce, combine the olive oil and butter in a deep saucepan and sauté the onion until golden. Combine the tomato purée and white wine and stir into the onion mixture with the tuna fish. Heat through, stirring constantly, and keep warm.

For the risotto, sauté the onion in the butter until transparent. Add the rice and cook, stirring continuously, until golden. Add the white wine and hot chicken stock and simmer, covered, until the rice is tender.

Five minutes before serving, stir in the tuna sauce. Season and serve with Parmesan cheese and additional butter.

# Rice Pilaff
Serves 4

4 tablespoons butter
½ Spanish onion, finely chopped
350 g/¾ pound basmati rice
600–900 ml/1–1½ pints boiling
chicken stock

salt and freshly ground pepper
2 tablespoons butter
100 g/¼ pound sliced
mushrooms, sautéed in butter

Melt the butter in a casserole and brown the onion in it. Add the rice and stir for a minute or two, until the grains of rice are coated with butter. Add 600 ml/1 pint of the boiling chicken stock and salt and pepper, to taste, and cover the casserole tightly. Bake the rice in a moderate oven (190°C/375°F/gas 5) for about 30 minutes, or until the grains are tender, stirring occasionally and adding a little more chicken stock if necessary. Or cook the rice in a tightly covered pan over direct heat for about 25 minutes. Remove the rice to a serving dish, add the 2 tablespoons butter and the sautéed mushrooms and toss with a fork.

# Risotto alla Paesano
Serves 6

100 g/¼ pound dried red kidney
beans, soaked overnight
4 tablespoons butter
2 tablespoons olive oil
3 slices bacon, diced
1 small onion, finely chopped
50 g/2 ounces carrots, diced

2 courgettes, diced
50 g/2 ounces celery, diced
300 ml/½ pint hot beef stock
350 g/¾ pound *risotto* rice
salt and freshly ground pepper
freshly grated Parmesan

Place the beans in a saucepan with lightly salted water to cover. Bring to the boil; boil rapidly for 10 minutes then cover and cook over a lower heat for 1 hour, or until tender. Reserve.

Combine the butter and oil in a large frying pan and sauté the bacon and onion until the onion is transparent. Add the carrots, courgettes and celery and continue to cook, uncovered, for 3 or 4 minutes, stirring occasionally. Pour the hot beef stock over and simmer uncovered until almost all the liquid has evaporated. Add the rice to this mixture and cook for 2 minutes, stirring occasionally, over a low heat.

Drain the beans, reserving the stock. Add the beans to the rice, together with 3 cupfuls of the bean stock; cook over medium heat for 15 to 18 minutes, stirring occasionally, and continue adding bean stock as needed until the rice is done. When the rice is tender, season with salt and pepper, to taste. Add cheese and serve.

# Chapter 14
# **Salads**

## **Tossed Green Salad**

What is simpler or more summery than a freshly tossed salad of green and bitter leaves? The very sound of the word salad evokes visions of crisp green lettuce leaves, carefully washed and dried leaf by leaf, liberally bathed with fruity olive oil and flavoured with a touch of lime juice or red wine vinegar, a hint of garlic and a dusting of salt and freshly ground pepper.

There are two secrets to perfect salad making: the preparation of the salad itself and the preparation of the dressing. Salad greens must be thoroughly washed and dried and preferably chilled before being mixed with the dressing. No water should be allowed to drip from the greens into the dressing. If you do not own a salad basket, an easy way to dry well-washed salad greens is to pile them loosely in the centre of a clean tea towel and pat the leaves dry. Then gather up the edges and corners of the towel; shake out any remaining moisture over the sink and chill in the refrigerator in the tea towel until crisp.

There seems to be a mystery about a simple so-called French dressing; so many people put sugar, water, paprika or mustard into it; some use Worcestershire sauce or Tabasco. Others depend on bottled preparations rather than use their own initiative and skill to achieve what should be one of the most individual dishes of the meal.

I usually prefer to mix my salad dressing directly in the salad bowl, blending the extra virgin olive oil and lime juice or vinegar with pepper, sea salt, finely chopped garlic and herbs, before I add the lettuce and salad greens. Then all one has to do at table is to give a final toss to the ingredients to ensure that every leaf is glistening with the dressing. A final check for flavour, and the salad is ready to serve.

### **Salad dressings**

Here are my recipes for salad dressings to make a tossed salad for four.

**French dressing:** To 2 tablespoons of wine vinegar add coarse sea salt and freshly ground pepper to taste; stir the mixture well; add 6 to 8 tablespoons extra virgin olive oil and beat with a fork until the mixture thickens. For a creamier dressing, put an ice cube in the mixing bowl and stir the dressing for a minute or two longer. Remove the cube and serve.

**Tarragon dressing:** Add 1 teaspoon chopped fresh tarragon leaves to the French dressing.

**Curry dressing:** Add ½ teaspoon curry powder and 1 teaspoon finely chopped shallots to the French dressing.

**Anchovy and caper dressing:**  To the French dressing add 1 teaspoon chopped capers, ½ clove garlic, crushed, and anchovy paste to taste. Blend well.

**Roquefort dressing:**  Add 2 to 4 tablespoons crumbled Roquefort cheese to the French dressing and blend well. Chill thoroughly before using.

## To Make Salad

Break into the bowl some tender lettuce leaves, well washed and dried. Leaves should be left whole, or torn, never cut. Wash them well in a large quantity of water. Drain well and dry thoroughly in a cloth or a salad basket so that there is no water on them to dilute the dressing.

For variety's sake, I like to add other salad greens in season to the lettuce leaves – baby Cos, rocket, endive, chicory, spinach leaves if they are very young and tender, watercress and French *mâche*. Fresh green herbs – chervil, basil and tarragon – are often used to add flavour and freshness to green salads. I also like *eau-de-Cologne* mint, which lends a certain purple spiciness to a summer salad, or even a chopped nasturtium leaf or two from the garden.

Shallots, so finely chopped they are almost minced, are excellent in a tossed green salad, as are chives, especially when combined with diced or finely sliced avocado pear as a garnish.

Sometimes a little 'crunch appeal' seems warranted in a summer salad; in these cases I use a little chopped celery, green pepper, or *finocchio*, the green-white root of fennel with its delicate aniseed flavour.

## Chilled Watercress Salad

Serves 4 to 6

4 bunches watercress
2 oranges
6–8 tablespoons olive oil
2 tablespoons wine vinegar
1 tablespoon lemon juice

1 tablespoon curry powder
salt and freshly ground pepper
1 tablespoon finely chopped
  shallots

Prepare the watercress and chill in a damp towel.

Peel the oranges, cut into thin slices and chill.

Prepare a curry dressing: combine the olive oil, wine vinegar, lemon juice and curry powder. Season with salt and pepper, to taste, and chill. Just before serving, place the watercress in a salad bowl; arrange the orange slices on top; add the shallots to the curry dressing and pour over the salad.

Toss at table so that each leaf is glistening.

# Salade Niçoise

I like basking by the lazy blue of the Mediterranean, with a glass of chilled *vin rosé* in my hand, or better yet, an iced glass of smoke-filled Pernod. Who could ask for anything more?

Lunch in the sun, perhaps, under the striped awning of a *quai*-side restaurant, on a hillside terrace, or in the cool depths of a summer garden. It would be a refreshing Provençal salad – a combination of both cooked and raw vegetables, with hard-boiled eggs, tuna fish and anchovies in the Mediterranean manner. I like *Salade Niçoise*, quartered tomatoes and eggs, sliced sweet onions, celery and green peppers, black olives, tuna fish and anchovies, bathed in a rich dressing of Provençal olive oil and wine vinegar made from the robust red wines of the Var.

## Salade Niçoise

| | |
|---|---|
| 4 tomatoes, seeded and quartered | 8 black olives |
| ½ Spanish onion, sliced | *Salad Dressing:* |
| 1 sweet green pepper, sliced | 2 tablespoons wine vinegar or lemon juice |
| 8 radishes | |
| 2 hearts of lettuce | 6 tablespoons pure olive oil |
| 4 stalks celery, sliced | salt and freshly ground pepper |
| 1 can tuna fish | 12 leaves of fresh basil, coarsely chopped |
| 8 fillets of anchovy | |
| 2 hard-boiled eggs, quartered | |

Combine the prepared vegetables in a salad bowl, placing neatly on top the tuna fish, anchovies and quartered eggs. Dot with black olives. Mix the salad dressing of wine vinegar, olive oil, seasoning and herbs, and sprinkle over the salad.

## Tossed Green Salad with Avocado

Serves 4 to 6

| | |
|---|---|
| 2 heads lettuce | wine vinegar |
| 1 bunch watercress | coarse salt and freshly ground pepper |
| 1 clove garlic, halved | |
| 2 tablespoons finely chopped chives | 1 avocado pear, peeled and sliced, marinated in lemon juice |
| olive oil | |

Wash and prepare the lettuce and watercress. Shake dry in a salad basket, or dry each leaf carefully in a clean tea towel. Wrap in the tea towel and allow to crisp in the refrigerator until ready to use.

Rub a wooden salad bowl with the cut clove of garlic. Arrange the lettuce and watercress in the bowl. Chop the garlic finely; sprinkle with the chives over the salad and dress with an olive oil and wine vinegar dressing (3 to 4 parts oil to 1 part vinegar), and season with coarse salt and pepper, to taste. Just before serving, toss the salad until each leaf is glistening. Garnish with avocado.

## Tossed Green Salad with Herbs
Serves 4 to 6

2 heads lettuce
choice of salad greens: endive,
  young spinach, watercress,
  chicory, dandelion, *mâche*,
  etc
1 clove garlic, finely chopped

1 teaspoon each finely chopped
  basil, marjoram, chervil and
  chives
olive oil
wine vinegar
salt and freshly ground pepper

Wash and prepare the lettuce and salad greens of your choice. Shake dry in a salad basket, or dry each leaf carefully in a clean tea towel. Wrap in the tea towel and allow to crisp in refrigerator until ready to use.

Make the salad as in the recipe above, adding finely chopped garlic and fresh herbs to the dressing.

## Salade Paysanne
Serves 4 to 6

2 heads lettuce
100 g/¼ pound fat salt pork,
  finely diced
2 tablespoons olive oil
2 hard-boiled eggs, chopped

salt and freshly ground pepper
1–2 tablespoon(s) finely chopped
  chervil, tarragon or basil
wine vinegar

Wash and dry the lettuce leaves thoroughly and chill. Sauté the fat salt pork in the olive oil until golden brown.

Place the lettuce in a salad bowl; sprinkle with the pork and hot fat. Add the eggs, salt, pepper, herbs and vinegar, to taste. Mix well and serve immediately.

## Chef's Salad
Serves 4 to 6

1 head lettuce
100 g/¼ pound cooked chicken
100 g/¼ pound smoked ox
  tongue
100 g/¼ pound cooked ham

100 g/¼ pound Swiss cheese
2 hard-boiled eggs
4 tomatoes
1 bunch watercress
150 ml/¼ pint French dressing

Wash and dry the lettuce carefully; chop coarsely and arrange in the bottom of a large salad bowl. Cut the chicken, tongue, ham and cheese into thin strips and arrange according to colour on a bed of the lettuce with the hard-boiled eggs, cut in quarters, and the tomatoes, cut in wedges. Place a cluster of prepared watercress in the centre and serve with well-flavoured French dressing.

# Russian Salad
Serves 4 to 6

450 g/1 pound cooked new
  potatoes, diced
225 g/½ pound cooked string
  beans, sliced
4–6 cooked carrots, sliced
100 g/¼ pound dried beans,
  soaked and boiled
150 g/5 oz cooked peas
2 tablespoons wine vinegar

2 tablespoons olive oil
salt and freshly ground pepper
1 tablespoon each capers and
  chopped baby gherkins
2 tablespoons finely chopped
  flat-leaf parsley
2–3 hard-boiled eggs
300–425 ml/½–¾ pint well-
  flavoured mayonnaise

Combine the potatoes with the string beans, carrots, beans and peas, reserving a few of each vegetable for garnish. Moisten with the wine vinegar and olive oil and season to taste with salt and pepper. Toss and chill.

Add the capers, pickles and parsley, chopped egg whites and enough mayonnaise to bind the mixture loosely. Toss the ingredients and mound them in a salad bowl. Decorate the top and sides with the remaining mayonnaise and assorted vegetables. Sprinkle sieved egg yolks over the top.

# Salade Caroline Cochonne
Serves 4 to 6

350 g/¾ pound Gruyère cheese,
  diced
350 g/¾ pound ham, diced
6–8 tablespoons olive oil

2–3 tablespoons wine vinegar
salt and freshly ground pepper
1 head lettuce
finely chopped flat-leaf parsley

Combine the Gruyère cheese and ham in a large bowl. Prepare the salad dressing (see page 222); pour over the cheese and ham; toss well. Allow to marinate in the refrigerator for 1 hour.

Just before serving, place the washed and dried lettuce leaves in the bottom of a salad bowl. Pile the cheese and ham in the centre. Sprinkle with parsley and serve with additional salad dressing.

# Italian Vegetable Salad

Serves 4 to 6

4 tomatoes
olive oil
wine vinegar
salt and freshly ground pepper
1 small cucumber
2 small green peppers
100 g/¼ pound button mushrooms
2 tablespoons finely chopped
   flat-leaf parsley

lettuce
2 hard-boiled eggs

*Italian Dressing:*
150 ml/¼ pint olive oil
4 anchovy fillets, finely
   chopped
juice of 1 large lemon
salt and freshly ground pepper
1–3 teaspoons capers

Quarter the tomatoes and toss lightly in a small bowl with a little olive oil, wine vinegar, salt and pepper. Peel the cucumber and slice thinly; place in a small bowl with a little wine vinegar, olive oil, salt and pepper. Remove the seeds and pith from the green peppers; slice in thin strips and place in a small bowl with the same dressing as above. Wash and thinly slice the mushrooms. Dress with a little wine vinegar and olive oil and add the parsley.

Just before serving, assemble the salads on a bed of lettuce in a large wooden bowl. Garnish with quartered hard-boiled eggs and sprinkle liberally with Italian dressing.

**Italian dressing:**   Warm the olive oil slightly and add the anchovy fillets, mashing them with a fork until well blended with the oil. Add the lemon juice and salt, pepper and capers, to taste.

# Bean and Raw Spinach Salad

Serves 4 to 6

350 g/¾ pound broad beans
6–8 tablespoons olive oil
3 tablespoons wine vinegar or
   lemon juice
1 teaspoon chopped marjoram
1–2 tablespoons chopped
   basil

1–3 tablespoons chopped
   flat-leaf parsley
1 clove garlic, finely chopped
salt and freshly ground pepper
450 g/1 pound raw spinach
   leaves
1 small onion, thinly sliced

Cook the broad beans until tender; cool and drain. Mix with a dressing made of the olive oil, wine vinegar or lemon juice, herbs and garlic, and season to taste with salt and pepper. Serve on tender young spinach leaves and garnish with onion rings.

# Roasted or Grilled Peppers for Salads

Perfectionists prefer to peel the sweet pepper. The easiest way I know of preparing peppers for use in appetiser salads and other dishes is to grill or roast the peppers as close to the heat as possible, turning them until the skin is charred on all sides. The skins can then be easily rubbed off under running cold water. The peppers are then cored, seeded, sliced into thick strips and marinated in a well-flavoured French dressing. Peppers prepared in this way will keep a long time under refrigeration if packed in oil in tight sterilised jars. Serve as a salad on a bed of lettuce with a lattice of anchovy fillets for garnish.

## Provençal Pepper Salad
Serves 4 to 6

2 large green peppers
2 large red peppers
6 firm ripe tomatoes
6 hard-boiled eggs
24 anchovy fillets
24 black olives

*Herb Dressing:*
2 cloves garlic, finely chopped
1 tablespoon each finely
   chopped flat-leaf parsley,
   tarragon, chervil and chives
6–8 tablespoons olive oil
3 tablespoons wine vinegar
salt and freshly ground pepper

Prepare the herb dressing by combining the garlic and fresh herbs with the oil, vinegar, and salt and pepper, to taste.

Prepare the peppers as follows: wash and dry whole; place under the grill, as close to the heat as possible. Cook, turning the peppers continually, until the skin on all sides has charred. Remove the charred skin under cold water. Cut the peppers in lengths – 4 to 6 to each pepper – and wash off the seeds and excess fibre; drain on absorbent paper. Slice the tomatoes thickly and cover the bottom of a large flat serving dish with them. Sprinkle with a quarter of the salad dressing; add a layer of green pepper slices; sprinkle with salad dressing; add a layer of red pepper slices and sprinkle with dressing. Shell the eggs and slice into rings; cover the red pepper with a layer of sliced eggs and pour over the rest of the dressing. Arrange the anchovy fillets in a lattice on top and place an olive in the centre of each lattice square. Chill in refrigerator for at least 30 minutes before serving.

## German Potato Salad
Serves 4 to 6

1 kg/2 pounds new potatoes
1 tablespoon sugar
2 tablespoons wine vinegar
150 ml/¼ pint sour cream
1 teaspoon mustard

½ Spanish onion, finely chopped
1 teaspoon celery seed
lemon juice
salt and freshly ground pepper
lettuce

| | |
|---|---|
| **2 tablespoons finely chopped** | **tomato wedges** |
| **flat-leaf parsley** | **2 hard-boiled eggs, sliced** |

Scrub the new potatoes; cook in boiling salted water until just tender, 15 to 20 minutes; drain, peel and slice. Place the warm potatoes in a bowl and sprinkle with the sugar and wine vinegar. Add the sour cream blended with the mustard, onion, celery seed, and lemon juice, salt and pepper, to taste. Toss well and serve in a lettuce-lined bowl. Garnish with the parsley, tomato wedges and hard-boiled eggs.

## Watercress and Radish Salad
Serves 4 to 6

| | |
|---|---|
| **1 head lettuce** | *French Dressing:* |
| **1 bunch watercress** | **2 tablespoons wine vinegar** |
| **1 bunch radishes** | **6–8 tablespoons olive oil** |
| | **dry mustard** |
| | **salt and freshly ground pepper** |
| | **1 clove garlic, finely chopped** |

Wash and trim the lettuce and watercress. Dry thoroughly. Trim the radishes and slice paper-thin. Chill.

To assemble the salad, arrange the lettuce leaves in a salad bowl and spread the watercress on top. Scatter the radishes over this. Make the French dressing and add it just before serving; toss until every ingredient glistens.

## Waldorf Salad
Serves 4 to 6

| | |
|---|---|
| **6 red-skinned eating apples** | **50 g/2 ounces halved walnuts** |
| **juice of 2 lemons** | **mayonnaise or French dressing** |
| **6 stalks celery** | **1 head lettuce** |

Core and dice the apples and sprinkle with the lemon juice. Add the celery and walnut halves. Toss together in mayonnaise or French dressing according to taste, and pile into a salad bowl lined with lettuce leaves.

## Chicken Waldorf
Serves 4 to 6

Make the salad as above; but add 350 g/¾ pound diced cooked chicken.

## Apple Herring Salad
Serves 4 to 6

2 filleted salt herrings
olive oil
vinegar
4 boiled potatoes, sliced
4 tart apples, diced
2 hard-boiled eggs, chopped

1 dill pickle, chopped
4 tablespoons sliced stuffed
  olives
1 small onion, freshly chopped
salt and freshly ground pepper

Cut the filleted herrings in small pieces and marinate in olive oil and vinegar. Combine the potatoes, apples, eggs, pickle, olives and onion in a bowl. Add the herrings. Make a dressing of 3 parts olive oil to 1 part vinegar; add salt and pepper and toss the salad just before serving.

## Spanish Seafood Salad
Serves 4 to 6

1 head lettuce, washed and
  chilled
1 head Cos lettuce, washed and
  chilled
225 g/½ pound cooked prawns
225 g/½ pound cooked lobster
  meat
225 g/½ pound cooked white fish
225 g/½ pound cooked crabmeat
4 ripe tomatoes

8 large black olives

*Saffron Dressing:*
150 ml/¼ pint mayonnaise
4 tablespoons lemon juice
2 tablespoons grated onion
1 teaspoon prepared mustard
salt and white pepper
1 generous pinch powdered
  saffron

Line a salad bowl with the lettuce and Cos leaves. Arrange the prawns, lobster, white fish and crabmeat, cut in cubes, on the bed of salad leaves. Garnish with wedges of ripe tomato, and ripe olives. Serve with saffron dressing.

**To make the dressing:** Combine the mayonnaise with the lemon juice, onion and mustard, and season to taste with salt and white pepper. Dissolve the saffron in a little hot water and stir into the dressing. Chill.

## Cauliflower Salad
Serves 4 to 6

1 cauliflower
6 anchovy fillets, finely chopped
12 black olives, pitted and
  chopped
3 tablespoons finely chopped
  flat-leaf parsley

1 clove garlic, finely chopped
1 tablespoon finely chopped
  capers
6 tablespoons olive oil
2 tablespoons wine vinegar
salt and freshly ground pepper

Remove the green leaves from the cauliflower, trim the stem and cut off any bruised spots. Break or cut into florets and poach in lightly salted water for about 5 minutes. Drain and place in a bowl of cold salted water until ready to use. Drain well. Mix the anchovies, olives, parsley, garlic and capers with the oil and vinegar; add the cauliflower and season to taste.

## Raw Mushroom Salad
Serves 6

**450 g/1 pound button**
  **mushrooms**
**juice of 1 lemon**
**8 tablespoons olive oil**
**salt and freshly ground pepper**

**1 tablespoon finely chopped**
  **chives**
**1 tablespoon finely chopped**
  **flat-leaf parsley**

Remove the stems from the mushrooms; wash and dry the caps but do not peel. Slice the caps thinly, arrange them in a salad bowl and pour a well-flavoured lemon and olive oil dressing over them. Toss carefully and chill in the refrigerator for 2 hours before serving. Sprinkle with chives and parsley.

## Coleslaw
Serves 4 to 6

**1 head cabbage (about 1 kg/**
  **2 pounds)**
**4 tablespoons tarragon vinegar**
**2 tablespoons sugar**
**salt and freshly ground pepper**
**paprika**
**1 small green pepper, chopped**

**2 tablespoons finely sliced**
  **spring onion**
**¼ teaspoon celery seeds**
**¼ teaspoon caraway seeds**
**6 tablespoons mayonnaise**
**150 ml/¼ pint sour cream**

Shred the cabbage and then crisp in cold water for ½ hour. Drain and dry thoroughly.

Combine the vinegar, sugar, salt, pepper and a sprinkling of paprika in a salad bowl. Add the shredded cabbage, toss well and marinate for 1 hour. Add the green pepper, spring onion, celery and caraway seeds and toss lightly.

Combine the mayonnaise and sour cream and pour over the cabbage mixture. Toss lightly, correct the seasoning and serve.

# Red Cabbage Salad

Serves 4

1 red cabbage (about 1 kg/
  2 pounds)
tarragon vinegar
salt and freshly ground pepper
4 hard-boiled egg yolks
300 ml/½ pint cream

juice of 1 large lemon
1 tablespoon each finely
  chopped chervil, chives and
  fennel
½ cucumber, thinly sliced
radishes, thinly sliced

Wash the cabbage leaves and shred them. Blanch the strips in boiling salted water. Drain; place in cold water; then drain again. Allow to marinate for at least 1 hour in tarragon vinegar with salt and pepper, turning from time to time. Remove and drain.

Pass the hard-boiled egg yolks through a fine sieve; combine with the cream and lemon juice and add salt and pepper to taste. Add the herbs to this dressing and mix well with the red cabbage. Serve decorated with thin rounds of cucumber and radish.

# Red Bean Salad

Serves 4

350 g/¾ pound kidney beans
salted water
1 Spanish onion, finely
  chopped
finely chopped flat-leaf parsley

6 tablespoons olive oil
4 tablespoons wine vinegar
salt and freshly ground pepper
generous pinch dry mustard
lettuce

Soak the kidney beans overnight in salted water. Bring the beans to the boil in their liquid and simmer for about 2 hours or until tender.

Drain the beans. Add the onion and some parsley; moisten with the olive oil and wine vinegar and season to taste with salt, pepper and a pinch of dry mustard. Mix the salad lightly and chill it. Serve the bean salad on lettuce leaves and sprinkle generously with the remaining parsley.

# Moroccan Orange Salad

Serves 6 to 8

6 ripe oranges
6–8 dates, chopped
6–8 blanched almonds, slivered

orange flower water (or lemon
  juice and powdered sugar)
powdered cinnamon

Peel the oranges, removing all the pith, and slice crosswise. Place in a salad bowl with the dates and almonds and flavour to taste with orange flower water or lemon juice and sugar.

Chill. Just before serving, sprinkle lightly with cinnamon.

# Pears Vinaigrette
Serves 4

4 ripe dessert pears

*Mint Vinaigrette:*
6 tablespoons olive oil
3 tablespoons wine vinegar
2 tablespoons finely chopped
   mint

2 tablespoons finely chopped
   flat-leaf parsley
salt, freshly ground pepper and
   mustard
lettuce, to garnish

Peel, core and slice the pears.

**To make the sauce:**  Combine the olive oil, vinegar, mint and parsley in a mixing bowl. Season to taste with salt, pepper and a little dry mustard. Mix well.
    Toss the pears in the *vinaigrette* and serve on lettuce leaves.

# Orange Vinaigrette
Serves 6

6 ripe oranges

*Olive and Herb Vinaigrette:*
6 tablespoons olive oil
2 tablespoons wine vinegar
12–18 black olives, pitted and
   finely chopped
½ Spanish onion, finely chopped

1 tablespoon finely chopped
   mint
1 tablespoon finely chopped flat-
   leaf parsley
2 tablespoons finely chopped
   basil
salt, freshly ground pepper and
   cayenne

Peel the oranges, removing all the pith, and slice crosswise.

**To make the sauce:**  Combine the olive oil, vinegar, olives, onion and herbs in a mixing bowl. Season to taste with salt, pepper and cayenne. Mix well.
    Toss the orange slices in the *vinaigrette*.

# Chapter 15

# Desserts

## Rum Baba

King Stanislas of Poland, father-in-law of Louis XV of France, Duke of Lorraine and Bar, was an ardent cook. Among the many creations credited to this noble *cuisinier* is the *baba-au-rhum*, one of the world's most delicious sweets. History tells us that Stanislas dunked his favourite *kugelhupf* in a rum-flavoured syrup and declared the result a triumph! Later generations of cooks added a scattering of raisins to the dough, and the baba as we know it was born. Based on a *savarin* recipe (see below), the rum baba is a featherlight concoction of flour, sugar and eggs, made airy with powdered or granulated yeast and moistened with syrup and rum.

The *savarin* cake mixture, which is the basis of rum baba as well as of many other famous sweets, is quite easy to make if you follow these rules:

Dissolve the yeast (regular, not the easy-blend type) in liquid (water, milk, or a mixture of the two) just a little warmer than body temperature. The liquid should feel warm, not hot.

Warm a mixing bowl with boiling water. Dry it thoroughly. Sift the flour, sugar and salt into the warm bowl; gradually add the yeast mixture and beaten eggs and blend the batter ingredients by hand. (The warmth of your hand is important to the handling of the yeast.)

Beat by hand until the batter is smooth and well blended, then cover it with a towel and leave to rise in a warm place protected from draughts.

Do not allow the batter to stand too long: at most 45 minutes to an hour, or until it doubles its bulk.

Punch the batter down and beat it again, using the bread hook of your food processor, if you have one, to facilitate this task, until the dough leaves the sides of bowl (about 5 minutes with a bread hook).

Butter the moulds; fill them one-third to one-half full with yeast batter; cover with a towel and leave for the final rising (about 45 minutes). When the batter rises to top of the moulds, the cakes are ready for baking and should be put into the oven immediately.

Bake small shapes in a moderately hot oven (200°C/400°F/gas 6). Larger shapes are baked in a very hot oven (230°C/450°F/gas 8) for 10 minutes, then the temperature is reduced to moderate (190°C/375°F/gas 5) and the cake is baked for 30 to 40 minutes longer until it acquires a rich brown colour.

To turn out; invert each mould on a wire cake rack for 5 or 10 minutes; then loosen with a knife and turn out of the mould. Saturate with hot syrup while the cake is still warm, spooning the syrup over the cake until most of it is absorbed.

# Basic Savarin Recipe
Makes 1 baba

7 g/¼ ounce powdered or
  granulated yeast
4 tablespoons warm water
4 tablespoons warm milk
225 g/½ pound flour

50 g/2 ounces sugar
1 pinch salt
2 eggs, beaten
½ teaspoon vanilla essence
50 g/2 ounces softened butter

**Step 1:**  Mix the yeast with the warm water and milk and leave for 5 minutes. Sift the flour, sugar and salt into a warm mixing bowl. Beat the eggs with the vanilla essence. Make a well in the centre, add the yeast mixture, then the beaten eggs, little by little, mixing the soft, sticky dough very lightly with your hand.

**Step 2:**  When the dough is well blended, distribute the softened butter in small quantities over it; cover lightly with a towel and leave for 1 hour, or until it has doubled its bulk. Punch the batter down and beat it again, using the bread hook of your food processor if you have one, until the dough leaves the sides of the bowl, about 5 minutes.

**Step 3:**  Butter a deep cake tin or *savarin* mould and half-fill it with dough; put in a warm place until the dough rises to the top of the tin (about 45 minutes). Tie a band of buttered paper around the top (and 5 cm/2 inches above) and bake in a moderately hot oven (200°C/400°F/gas 6) for 10 minutes, then lower the heat to 180°C/350°F/gas 4 for 25 to 30 minutes, or until the cake is a rich brown. Leave to cool and then turn out.

# Baba-au-Rhum

1 basic *savarin* recipe (above)
2 tablespoons currants
1 tablespoon sultanas

*Syrup for Baba:*
syrup (225 g/½ pound sugar and
  300 ml/½ pint water)
6 tablespoons rum

**Steps 1 and 2:**  Follow the basic recipe.

**Step 3:**  Add the currants and sultanas to the dough and mix well. Then put the dough into a large, well-buttered ring mould, or into small individual moulds, filling the moulds only up to one-third of their height. Put in a warm place, covered with a towel, until the dough rises to the top of the tin. Bake a large mould in a hot oven (230°C/450°F/gas 8) for 10 minutes, then reduce the temperature to 190°C/375°F/gas 5; small moulds are baked at 200°C/400°F/gas 6 until the cakes are golden. Leave to cool and then turn out. Pour syrup over the cake and sprinkle with more rum just before serving.

**To make the syrup:**  Combine the sugar and water in a saucepan. Simmer gently until it thickens. Stir in the rum. Prick the cake all over with a fork and spoon syrup over it. If desired, pour a little more rum over the baba just before serving.

# Gâteau à l'Ananas

**1 basic *savarin* recipe (page 235)**

*Garnish:*
**1 large can pineapple slices**

**3 tablespoons sugar**
**6 tablespoons Kirsch**
**glacé cherries (optional)**

**To make the savarin:**   Follow the basic *savarin* recipe, baking the mixture in a buttered cake tin.

**To make the syrup for the garnish:**   Pour the pineapple juice into a saucepan. Add the sugar and simmer gently until it thickens. Stir in the Kirsch. Prick the cake all over with a fork and spoon half of the syrup over it. Cook the remainder until it is reduced by half. Cut the pineapple slices into segments; arrange in concentric rings on the cake; garnish with glacé cherries and, just before serving, cover with the thickened caramel sauce.

# Savarin aux Pommes

**1 basic *savarin* recipe (page 235)**

*Crème Pâtissière:*
**4 egg yolks**
**50 g/2 ounces sugar**
**2 teaspoons flour**
**300 ml/½ pint warm milk**
**¼ teaspoon vanilla essence**

*Poached Apple Halves:*
**3–4 ripe eating apples**
**juice of 1 lemon**

**4 tablespoons sugar**
**vanilla essence**

*To Finish the Cake:*
**300 ml/½ pint apple sauce**
   **with 2–4 tablespoons Jamaica**
   **rum stirred in**
**4–6 tablespoons apricot jam,**
   **warmed**
**300 ml/½ pint double cream,**
   **whipped**

**To make the savarin ring:**   Follow the basic *savarin* recipe, making the mixture in a buttered ring mould.

**To make the crème pâtissière:**   Beat the yolks and sugar together until lemon-coloured. Mix in the flour, then add the milk and vanilla and mix thoroughly. Place in a saucepan over a low flame and cook, stirring constantly, until it reaches boiling point. Cook until thick; remove from the heat; put through a sieve and allow to cool.

**To poach the apples:**   Peel and core the eating apples; slice in half and poach gently in water with the lemon juice, sugar and vanilla essence, until slightly softened. Drain.

**To assemble the cake:** Fill the centre of the *savarin* ring with equal quantities of *crème pâtissière* and rum-flavoured apple sauce. Place a ring of well-drained, poached apple halves on the *savarin* ring. Brush the apples with warmed apricot jam and serve with the whipped cream.

## Genoese Sponge
Makes 1 cake

4 eggs
100 g/¼ pound caster sugar
½ teaspoon vanilla essence or
  grated zest of ½ lemon

75 g/3 ounces flour
25 g/1 ounce cornflour
8 tablespoons unsalted butter

Combine the eggs, sugar and vanilla essence or lemon zest, and whisk the mixture in the top of a double boiler until very light and thick and lukewarm. Transfer the mixture to an electric mixer and beat at high speed for 3 to 5 minutes, or until it holds shape.

Sift the flour and cornflour and fold carefully into the mixture a little at a time until thoroughly blended. Melt the butter in the top of a double boiler, taking care that it does not bubble or separate; add it immediately to the batter and pour the batter into a buttered and floured sandwich tin. Bake in a slow oven (180°C/350°F/gas 4) for 45 minutes, or until golden brown. (If desired, the mixture may be put in two shallow tins and baked for 15 minutes.) Invert the cake on a wire rack to cool. Slice into two layers; sandwich and ice to choice. Excellent for all layer cakes, iced cakes and *petits fours*.

## Chocolate Date Nut Torte
Makes 6 to 8 portions

175 g/6 ounces sugar
2 tablespoons flour
1 teaspoon baking powder
2 eggs
100 g/¼ pound coarsely chopped
  walnuts

225 g/½ pound coarsely chopped
  dates
50 g/2 ounces finely grated
  bitter chocolate
¼ teaspoon cinnamon
whipped cream

Sift 150 g/5 ounces sugar together with the flour and baking powder. Beat the eggs until light and fluffy. Add the dry ingredients and mix well. Fold the coarsely chopped nuts, dates and finely grated chocolate into the mixture. Pour into a well-greased and floured 22.5-cm/9-inch cake tin. Sprinkle with a mixture of the remaining sugar and the cinnamon. Bake in a very slow oven (150°C/350°F/gas 2) for 30 to 40 minutes, until golden brown. Serve warm with whipped cream.

# Summer Lemon Cake
Makes 8 to 12 portions

*Cake Mixture:*
**6 eggs, separated**
**175 g/6 ounces sugar**
**2 tablespoons water**
**grated zest of 1 lemon**
**1 generous pinch salt**
**75 g/3 ounces flour**
**25 g/1 ounce cornflour**

*Lemon Topping:*
**1 egg**
**150 g/5 ounces sugar**
**grated zest and juice of 1 lemon**
**made up to 150 ml/¼ pint with**
**water**
**25 g/1 ounce flour**
**300 ml/½ pint double cream,**
**whipped**
**100 g/¼ pound chopped toasted**
**almonds**

**The cake:** Beat the egg yolks, sugar, water, lemon zest and salt until light and fluffy (5 minutes in a mixer at high speed). Sift the flour and cornflour and gradually blend into the egg yolk mixture. Whisk the egg whites until stiff but not dry and fold gently into the yolk mixture. Place equal quantities of batter into three round 20-cm/8-inch cake tins which have been buttered and lightly dusted with flour. Bake in a moderately slow oven (180°C/350°F/gas 4) for 45 minutes, or until golden brown. Invert the layers on wire racks. When cool, loosen the edges and remove the pans.

**The topping:** Beat the egg, sugar and lemon zest together until foamy; add the sifted flour and the lemon juice and water and cook in the top of a double boiler, stirring all the time, until smooth and thick. Cool. Fold in the whipped cream. Spread 2 cake layers with some of the lemon topping and put together. Cover the top and sides of the cake and then pat chopped almonds firmly around the sides.

# Lemon Devil's Food
Makes 8 portions

**3 tablespoons cocoa**
**3 tablespoons sugar**
**3 tablespoons water**
**150 ml/¼ pint milk**
**1 teaspoon vanilla essence**
**100 g/¼ pound butter**
**225 g/½ pound brown sugar**
**3 egg yolks**
**75 g/3 ounces plain flour**
**25 g/1 ounce cornflour**
**1 teaspoon baking powder**

**pinch salt**
**3 egg whites, beaten until stiff**

*Lemon Icing:*
**300 g/10 ounces icing sugar**
**225 g/½ pound softened butter**
**grated rind and juice of 2**
**lemons**
**2 tablespoons Grand Marnier**
**(optional)**

**The cake:** Combine the cocoa, sugar and water in the top of a double saucepan and cook over simmering water, stirring, until smooth and thick. Stir in the milk and vanilla essence; blend well and set aside to cool.

Cream the butter and brown sugar. Beat in the egg yolks one at a time; then beat in the chocolate mixture. Sift the flour and cornflour 3 times with the baking powder and salt and beat into the cake mixture. Fold in the egg whites. Pour into 2 cake tins and bake for 30 to 35 minutes in a slow oven (180°C/350°F/gas 4).

**To make the icing:** Cream the sugar and softened butter. Add the lemon zest and juice and Grand Marnier. Beat until smooth and creamy. Spread between the layers and over the cake.

## Gâteau Basque
Makes 6 portions

*Crème Pâtissière:*
**4 egg yolks**
**50 g/2 ounces sugar**
**2 teaspoons flour**
**300 ml/½ pint warm milk**
**¼–½ teaspoon vanilla essence**

*Cake Mixture:*
**225 g/½ pound flour**
**100 g/¼ pound butter**
**2 eggs**
**150 g/5 ounces sugar**
*crème pâtissière*
**egg or milk, to glaze**

**The crème pâtissière:** Beat the egg yolks and sugar together until lemon-coloured. Mix in the flour, then add the milk and vanilla essence and mix thoroughly. Place the mixture in the top of a double saucepan and cook over water, stirring constantly, until smooth and thick; remove from the heat, put through a sieve and allow to cool.

**The cake:** Mix the flour, butter, eggs and sugar. Knead lightly to a smooth dough. Form into two equal-sized, round layers. Cover the first layer with *crème pâtissière*. Top with the second layer of dough. Brush with egg or milk and bake in a moderate oven (190°C/375°F/gas 5) for about 40 minutes or until golden brown. Serve cold.

## American Strawberry Shortcake
Serves 4

*Shortcake Mixture:*
**225 g/½ pound flour**
**1 tablespoon baking powder**
**½ teaspoon salt**
**2 tablespoons sugar**
**4–6 tablespoons softened butter**
**150 ml/¼ pint milk**
**2 egg yolks, lightly beaten**

*Berry Mixture:*
**softened butter**
**fresh strawberries**
**sugar**
**juice of ½ lemon**
**300 ml/½ pint cream**

Sift the flour with the baking powder, salt and sugar. Work in the butter with a fork. Add the milk and eggs little by little, stirring continuously, until the mixture holds together but is still soft.

Turn out on to a floured board. Roll out or pat into 4 rounds; place on a greased baking sheet and bake for 10 to 15 minutes in a fairly hot oven (220°C/425°F/gas 7).

To serve: split carefully with a fork; spread with softened butter and spoon halved strawberries (to which you have added sugar and lemon juice) between the layers and on top. Serve warm with cream.

# The Bombe

Legend has it that ice cream first reached these shores eight centuries ago in the form of a recipe for orange ice, brought back from the Crusades by Richard Cœur de Lion. It was given to him by Saladin, the great warrior Sultan of Egypt and Syria. Ever since, ices have been firm favourites of the English; the ice-houses buried in hillsides on great estates all over the country bear solid witness to that. Unprotected by our blanket of smog, winters were colder in the past, summers hotter, and only by burying could the thick blocks of ice sawn from rivers and ponds after Christmas be preserved throughout the summer to provide the delights of iced sweets.

'Take two Pewter Basons, one larger than the other,' wrote Mrs Glasse in 1747. 'The inward one must have a close Cover, into which you are to put your Cream, and mix it with Raspberries or whatever you like best, to give it a Flavour and a Colour. Sweeten it to the Palate; then cover it close, and set it into the larger Bason. Fill it with Ice, and a Handful of Salt; then let it stand in this Ice three Quarters of an Hour, then uncover it, and stir the Cream well together; cover it close again, and let it stand Half an Hour longer, after that turn it into your Plate.'

The method was cumbersome but the principle was sound. Fresh fruit and fresh cream are the only possible foundation for ice cream, even if you do only have to pop it into the refrigerator to freeze. The juice of peaches, of white grapes, of plums and strawberries and currants, of apples and pears even, will provide the climax to any summer meal.

But to get this perfection, you will have to make the ice cream yourself. Gunter's used to make fresh fruit ice cream in London before the war; many shops in Paris still do. But it is in the tiny village of St Tropez that I discovered the best ices in the world. In a side turning at the end of the port, Mme Lamponi produced ice cream of such perfection that her customers begged her to open in Paris. They promised her backing, they found her a shop, they guaranteed her a clientele, but nothing would budge her. As the last yacht left the harbour every year, she put up her shutters and firmly remained closed until the following spring brought the first boats nosing once more into the little port. Then she would open again and all summer long a procession of people would be seen leaving her shop, bearing the round cylinders in which the best ice cream in the world was packed. Mme Lamponi was wise. By opening during the summer months only, she used nothing but fresh fruit purées in her confections . . . and fresh is the operative word, for no finer tastes have been devised than the blends of fresh fruits, butterscotch and praline that she used to make in her little shop.

Take a leaf from Mme Lamponi's book. Experiment with different flavours. Quince and tangerine, fresh lime or banana will amaze you with their flavour in this new setting. Almost anything will work, as I found myself from Mme Lamponi. I had heard of a legendary ice served by Gunter's at garden parties before the war – a grape ice cream. When I asked Mme Lamponi to make some for me, she told me indignantly that it could not be done – the flavour was too subtle to be captured. Disappointed, I gave up; but she did not. Behind her closed shutters that winter she worked away, experimenting until she had perfected the new flavour. And when I visited St Tropez the next year, Grape Ice Cream was her top seller!

Home-made fresh fruit ices, iced soufflés and glamorous iced *bombes* can add enormously to the excitements of summer entertaining. A *bombe*, so named because it is usually made in a round or conical-shaped mould, is always a combination of two or more creams or ices frozen together. In most cases an ice or ice cream is used to line the mould and a creamy *bombe* mousse is used to fill the centre.

*Bombes* make a wonderfully elegant ending to a meal. And as they can be prepared the day, or even days, before the event, they provide a perfect iced pudding for a small dinner party. Well-flavoured fruit ices or ice creams can be bought in most areas for the outside casing and all that is required is a home-made centre to give a personal touch to your *bombe* recipe.

A delicious basic *bombe* mixture for the filling can be made of egg yolks, sugar and water. It will keep in a well-sealed jar in the refrigerator for a week and is added to whipped cream with the desired flavourings and garnishes when ready to use. Fruits, nuts, crushed macaroons, cake crumbs, raisins or coarsely grated chocolate are wonderful additions to *bombe* mixtures.

## Basic Bombe Mixture

Bring 150 g/5 ounces granulated sugar and 150 ml/¼ water to the boil, stirring continuously, and cook over a medium heat until the thermometer reads 103°C/217°F. Set aside to cool.

Beat 5 egg yolks until light and creamy. Place the beaten yolks over boiling water in the top of a double saucepan and add the cooled sugar syrup gradually, beating constantly, until well mixed. Cook the mixture, still beating, until it is thick and doubled in volume, about 15 minutes.

Remove from the heat; set in a pan of iced water and whisk again until the mixture is smooth and cold. Use immediately or store in a sealed container in the refrigerator for up to 7 days.

Add 300 ml/½ pint whipped cream flavoured with vanilla essence, rum, cognac or the liqueur of your choice. Stir in any one of the following garnishes and pour into the centre of a well-chilled mould lined with ice or ice cream of a contrasting colour. Chill until ready to serve (2 to 4 hours).

**Bombe garnishes:**   *Coarsely grated chocolate, crumbled macaroons, finely chopped glacé cherries, chopped toasted almonds, halved strawberries, crushed raspberries, chopped peaches, bananas or pears and chopped nuts.*

## Raspberry Bombe

Serves 4–6

½ recipe basic *bombe* mixture
  (page 241)
1.2 litres/2 pints raspberry ice
300 ml/½ pint cream, whipped
  until stiff

1 tablespoon grated orange zest
1–2 tablespoons Grand Marnier
1 egg white, beaten stiff
1–2 tablespoons coarsely
  chopped nuts

Line a chilled mould with raspberry ice and smooth into a coating about 2 cm/
¾ inch thick. Chill the lined mould.

In the meantime, whip the cream and flavour to taste with orange zest and
Grand Marnier. Whisk into the basic *bombe* mixture. Fold in the stiffly beaten egg
white and chopped nuts and pour into the lined mould. Freeze until ready to serve.

## Bombe au Chocolat

Serves 4–6

½ recipe basic *bombe* mixture
  (page 241)
1.2 litres/2 pints chocolate ice
  cream
1–1½ teaspoons instant coffee

2 tablespoons Kirsch
300 ml/½ pint cream, whipped
  stiff
1 egg white, beaten stiff

Line a chilled mould with chocolate ice cream and smooth into a coating about
2 cm/¾ inch thick. Chill the lined mould.

In the meantime, dissolve the instant coffee in the Kirsch and whisk into the
basic *bombe* mixture. Fold the mixture gently into the whipped cream. Fold in
the stiffly beaten egg white and pour into the lined mould. Freeze until ready
to serve.

## Iced Soufflés

Serves 6 to 8

4 tablespoons diced sponge cake
4 tablespoons Grand Marnier
4 eggs
100 g/¼ pound sugar

2 tablespoons orange juice
grated zest of 1 orange
300 ml/½ pint cream
powdered chocolate

Soak the sponge cake in 2 tablespoons Grand Marnier. Separate the eggs and beat
the yolks with the sugar until the mixture is lemon-coloured and thick. Stir in the
remaining Grand Marnier, orange juice and orange zest.

Whisk the cream and egg whites separately and fold into the mixture. Half-fill
6 or 8 individual soufflé dishes or custard cups; divide the diced sponge cake among
the cups; add the remaining soufflé mixture and freeze for 4 hours. Dust with
powdered chocolate or cocoa.

# Chocolate Ice Cream
Serves 4 to 6

4 egg yolks
100 g/¼ pound sugar
1 pinch salt
425 ml/¾ pint single cream

50 g/2 ounces melted chocolate
1 teaspoon vanilla essence
300 ml/½ pint double cream,
 whipped

Beat the egg yolks, sugar and salt until light and lemon-coloured. Scald the single cream and add to the egg and sugar mixture, whisking until well blended.

Pour the mixture into the top of a double saucepan and cook over simmering water, stirring continuously, until the custard coats the spoon.

Strain through a fine sieve; stir in the melted chocolate and vanilla and set aside to cool.

Mix the whipped cream with the chocolate custard mixture and freeze for at least 3 hours.

# Orange Ice
Serves 4 to 6

350 g/¾ pound sugar
900 ml/1½ pints water
425 ml/¾ pint orange juice

150 ml/¼ pint lemon juice
finely grated zest of 1 orange
 and 1 lemon

Bring the sugar and water to the boil; boil for 5 minutes. Cool slightly and add the orange juice, lemon juice and orange and lemon zest. Cool; strain through a fine sieve and freeze.

# Iced Coffee Soufflés
Serves 4

4 eggs
100 g/¼ pound sugar
2 tablespoons powdered coffee
50 g/2 ounces chocolate

2 tablespoons water
2 tablespoons rum
300 ml/½ pint double cream
grated chocolate

Separate the eggs and beat the yolks with the sugar and powdered coffee until the mixture is thick and creamy. Melt the chocolate and water in a small saucepan; add the rum and stir into the egg and coffee mixture.

Whip the cream and fold it into the soufflé mixture. Whisk the egg whites and fold into the mixture. Pour into 4 or 6 individual soufflé dishes or custard cups and freeze for 4 hours. Decorate with grated chocolate.

## Frozen Banana Cream
Serves 6 to 8

3–4 bananas, mashed
50 g/2 ounces sugar
pinch salt
6–8 tablespoons pineapple juice
2 tablespoons lemon juice

2 tablespoons rum
300 ml/½ pint double cream,
  whipped
2 tablespoons chopped toasted
  almonds

Combine the bananas, sugar, salt, pineapple and lemon juices and rum. Fold in the cream. Turn into a freezer container and freeze until firm. Turn into a bowl and whisk until frothy. Fold in the almonds; return to the tray and freeze until set.

## Coupe Créole
Serves 4

150 ml/¼ pint milk
300 ml/½ pint double cream
4 egg yolks
100 g/¼ pound caster sugar
½ teaspoon vanilla essence

4 tablespoons *crème de marrons*
300 ml/½ pint cream, whipped
hot melted chocolate
4 *marrons glacés*
toasted slivered almonds

To make the vanilla ice cream, combine the milk and cream in a saucepan and bring to the boil. Place the egg yolks in a bowl and whisk, adding the sugar slowly, until light-coloured and creamy. Pour the hot cream mixture over the egg and sugar mixture, stirring well. Cook over a very low heat until thickened sufficiently to coat the back of a wooden spoon. Do not let it come to the boil or it will curdle.

Strain through a fine sieve into a freezer container and allow to cool. Stir in the vanilla and freeze, stirring from time to time.

Just before serving, place a tablespoon of *crème de marrons* at the bottom of 4 individual *coupes* or champagne glasses, together with a little whipped cream. Place a large ball of ice cream on top and cover with hot melted chocolate. Top with a *marron glacé* and garnish with whipped cream and toasted slivered almonds.

## Tulipe Glacée
Serves 8

150 g/5 ounces flour
150 g/5 ounces icing sugar
2 egg yolks
3 egg whites
1 large orange, greased, to form
  pastry shapes

1 fresh pineapple, peeled, cored
  and diced
Kirsch
vanilla ice cream
double cream, whipped

Sift the flour and icing sugar into a mixing bowl; add the egg yolks and whites and mix well.

Grease a cold baking sheet and mark 4 circles on it with a saucer. Spread 1 dessertspoon of mixture over each circle, using the back of a teaspoon. Bake in a slow oven (170°C/325°F/gas 3) for 5 to 6 minutes, or until just turning brown at the edges.

Remove each round from the baking sheet; turn over and, working quickly, place each circle over the top of the greased orange. Place a tea towel over the pastry to prevent burning your hands and mould the pastry to fit the orange. Remove and continue as above, baking 2 to 4 circles each time and shaping them over the orange as you go. The cases will keep for days in a biscuit tin. This recipe makes 12 to 16 *tulipes*.

To serve, fill 8 cases with diced fresh pineapple which you have marinated in Kirsch; add a scoop of vanilla ice cream and decorate with whipped cream.

## Ananas Glacé 'Laurent'
Serves 4

| | |
|---|---|
| **4 slices fresh pineapple** | **150 ml/¼ pint double cream,** |
| **orange quarters, peeled** | **whipped** |
| **4 scoops vanilla ice cream** | **chocolate vermicelli** |
| | **toasted slivered almonds** |

Remove the hard central core from the slices of pineapple. Arrange on a plate; add orange quarters in a flower shape; keep cool. Just before serving, place a scoop of vanilla ice cream in the hollow of each pineapple slice; top with whipped cream and sprinkle with chocolate vermicelli and toasted slivered almonds.

## Orange Apricot Chantilly
Serves 6

| | |
|---|---|
| **450 g/1 pound dried apricots** | **2–4 tablespoons Cointreau** |
| **1 orange (rind and pulp), finely** | **150 ml/¼ pint cream, whipped** |
| **shredded** | **2 tablespoons blanched slivered** |
| **100 g/¼ pound granulated sugar** | **almonds** |

Rinse the apricots well and put them in a saucepan with the shredded orange pulp, rind and just enough water to cover. Simmer gently, uncovered, for 15 minutes. Stir in the sugar and continue to cook over a very low heat until most of the liquid is absorbed and the apricots are cooked through, adding more water if necessary.

Allow the apricot mixture to cool and purée it in a blender or rub through a fine sieve. Add Cointreau to taste, stir in the whipped cream and almonds, and chill in 6 individual soufflé dishes or *pots de crème*.

# Baked Apple Compote
Serves 4

900 g/2 pounds cooking apples,
  peeled and cored
zest and juice of 1 lemon

175 g/6 ounces brown sugar
50 g/2 ounces butter
double cream

Slice the apples into a buttered baking dish. Sprinkle with lemon juice, grated lemon zest and brown sugar and dot with butter. Bake, uncovered, in a moderate oven (190°C/375°F/gas 5) for 30 minutes, or until tender. Serve with double cream.

# Poires à la Bourguignonne
Serves 4 to 6

900 g/2 pounds small pears
225 g/½ pound sugar
150 ml/¼ pint water

cinnamon
150 ml/¼ pint red Burgundy
whipped cream

Peel the pears but do not core them. Put them in a saucepan with the sugar, water and cinnamon. Simmer, covered, for about 15 minutes. Add the Burgundy and continue to cook over a low heat, uncovered, for 15 minutes.

Put the pears in a deep serving dish. Reduce the liquid to the consistency of a light syrup; pour over the pears and chill. Serve very cold with whipped cream.

# Marquise à l'Ananas
Serves 4

2 small fresh pineapples
sugar
300 ml/½ pint pineapple juice
150 ml/¼ pint water

225 g/½ pound sugar
zest and juice of 1 lemon
300 ml/½ pint cream, whipped
3 tablespoons Kirsch

Cut the pineapples in half lengthwise, leaving on the green tops. With a fork, scrape the flesh and juice into a bowl, discarding the hard core and being careful not to break through the shell. Sprinkle the insides of the shells with a little sugar and chill in the refrigerator until ready to use.

Mash the flesh of the two pineapples with a fork. Add the pineapple juice, water, sugar and the grated lemon zest. Bring to the boil and boil for 5 minutes. Strain; add the lemon juice and freeze in the usual way.

Whisk with a fork, fold in the whipped cream and Kirsch and return to the freezer. Just before serving, spoon the mixture into the chilled pineapple shells and serve immediately.

# Fresh Fruit Compote

Serves 4 to 6

| | |
|---|---|
| **1 medium-sized pineapple** | **icing sugar** |
| **4 pears** | **2 tablespoons brandy** |
| **4 Cox's orange pippins** | **2 tablespoons lemon juice** |
| **4 plums** | **¼ bottle champagne** |
| **1 bunch grapes** | |

Peel, core and slice the pineapple into rings. Reserve the top. Slice each ring in half and combine in a mixing bowl with the peeled, cored and sliced pears and apples, sliced plums and halved, seeded grapes. Dust with icing sugar to taste; moisten with brandy and lemon juice; toss well and chill.

Just before serving, transfer to a serving bowl; pour over the champagne and decorate with the pineapple top.

# Baked Pears in White Wine

Serves 6

| | |
|---|---|
| **6 pears** | **sugar** |
| **dry white wine** | **whipped cream** |

Peel the pears and place in an ovenproof baking dish with white wine to cover and sugar, to taste. Cover and bake in a moderate oven (190°C/375°F/gas 5) for about 45 minutes. Serve cool or chilled with whipped cream.

# Rum Charlotte

Serves 4 to 6

| | |
|---|---|
| **150 ml/¼ pint water** | **2 tablespoons brown sugar** |
| **100 g/¼ pound caster sugar** | **50 g/2 ounces butter** |
| **6 tablespoons rum** | **4 eggs, separated** |
| **100 g/¼ pound good quality dark** | **sponge fingers** |
| **chocolate** | **unsweetened whipped cream** |
| **150 ml/¼ pint coffee** | |

Make a rum syrup by boiling the water, sugar and rum together for 3 to 5 minutes. Make a chocolate sauce by melting the chocolate in a small saucepan. Add the coffee and cook for 5 minutes. Remove the saucepan from the heat; add the brown sugar, butter and egg yolks, and mix well. Stiffly beat the egg whites and fold in. Line small moulds with sponge fingers which have been sprinkled with some of the rum syrup and pour in the chocolate mixture.

Arrange more sponge fingers over the top of the moulds to cover the filling completely. Chill for 12 hours. Unmould, sprinkle with the remaining syrup and serve with whipped cream.

# English Trifle
Serves 8

175 g/6 ounces dried apricots,
  soaked overnight
1 sponge cake
150 ml/¼ pint sweet Marsala
2 tablespoons cornflour
2 tablespoons sugar
300 ml/½ pint hot milk

3 eggs
8–10 macaroons, crumbled
600 ml/1 pint double cream
½ teaspoon vanilla essence
sugar
fresh or crystallised fruits, to
  decorate

Drain the apricots, keeping the soaking liquid. Purée them in a food processor or blender with enough of the soaking liquid to make a smooth mixture. Cut the sponge cake into 2 layers and spread half the apricot purée between the layers. Assemble the cake again and cut into small strips.

Arrange the cake strips in the bottom of a large glass serving bowl. Pour Marsala over the cake and spread the remaining apricot purée on top.

To prepare the custard, mix the cornflour and sugar to a smooth paste with a little milk; combine with the remaining hot milk in the top of a double saucepan and bring to the boil. Cook over simmering water, stirring continuously, until the mixture thickens. Remove from the heat and beat in the eggs, one by one. When well blended, simmer gently over water, stirring continuously, for 10 minutes. Stir in the crumbled macaroons and leave to soak until soft. Beat well to dissolve the macaroons. Cool the custard and then pour over the apricot purée. Chill for 2 hours.

Just before serving, whisk the double cream with the vanilla essence and sugar until thick. Cover the custard with whipped cream and decorate with fruits.

# Crème Renversée au Grand Marnier
Serves 4 to 6

425 ml/¾ pint single cream
3 tablespoons Grand Marnier or
  other liqueur

4 eggs
4 egg yolks
100 g/¼ pound sugar

Scald the cream with the Grand Marnier and let it cool slightly. Beat the whole eggs and egg yolks with the sugar until light and lemon-coloured. Add the cream, stirring constantly until well blended. Strain through a fine sieve into a buttered baking dish. Set the dish in a pan of hot water; cover and bake in a moderate oven (180°C/350°F/gas 4) for 35 to 45 minutes, or until the custard is set and a knife inserted near the centre comes out clean.

To serve: cool the custard, loosen it from the sides of the dish with a knife and invert the mould on to a serving platter.

# French Rice Pudding

Serves 4 to 6

50–75 g/2–3 ounces pudding rice
600 ml/1 pint milk
water
100 g/¼ pound sugar

½ teaspoon salt
2 egg yolks
2 egg whites, stiffly beaten
½ teaspoon vanilla essence

Cook the rice in the milk and a little water with the sugar and salt until tender but not mushy. Beat the egg yolks in a bowl and add the hot rice mixture slowly. Cook in the top of a double saucepan until thick. Cool slightly and fold in the beaten egg whites. Flavour with vanilla essence and, if necessary, more sugar. Bake in a fairly hot oven (220°C/425°F/gas 7) for 5 to 10 minutes or until golden brown.

# Zabaglione Pudding

Serves 4

6 egg yolks
50 g/2 ounces granulated
sugar
6–8 tablespoons Marsala or
sherry
7 g/¼ ounce gelatine
2 tablespoons cold water
3 tablespoons brandy

225 ml/⅜ pint double cream

*Zabaglione Sauce:*
3 egg yolks
25 g/1 ounce granulated sugar
3–4 tablespoons Marsala or
sherry
1½ tablespoons brandy

To make the pudding, combine the egg yolks with the sugar and Marsala or sherry in the top of a double boiler, and whip the mixture over hot, but not boiling, water until it thickens. Stir in the gelatine, softened in the cold water and dissolved over hot water. Put the pan in a bowl of ice and stir the *zabaglione* well until it is thick and free of bubbles. When it is almost cold, fold in the brandy and whipped cream and pour into 4 individual moulds. Chill the *zabaglione*, unmould it, and serve with *zabaglione* sauce.

**To make the sauce:** Repeat the process as above, stirring the egg yolks and sugar over hot water until the sauce is of the desired consistency. Stir in the Marsala (or sherry) and brandy, and serve immediately.

# Figs in Wine and Honey

Serves 4

450 g/1 pound fresh figs
dry white wine

125 ml/4 fluid ounces honey
fresh cream

Place the figs in a saucepan with enough white wine to cover. Bring to the boil; add the honey and simmer until the figs are tender. Chill. Serve with fresh cream.

## Elizabeth Moxon's Lemon Posset
Serves 4 to 6

grated zest and juice of 3 to 4
  lemons
600 ml/1 pint double cream

150 ml/¼ pint dry white wine
sugar
whites of 3 eggs

Add the lemon zest to the cream and whisk until stiff. Stir in the white wine and enough lemon juice to make a lemony mixture. Add sugar to taste. Whisk the egg whites until they form peaks and fold into the whipped cream mixture. Serve in a glass serving dish or in individual glasses.

## Bread and Butter Pudding
Serves 6

2–3 tablespoons dried currants
4 slices white bread, brioche or
  panettone
butter
4 egg yolks

100 g/¼ pound sugar
freshly grated nutmeg
600 ml/1 pint warm milk
¼–½ teaspoon vanilla essence
3 egg whites, beaten until stiff

Wash and pick over the dried currants and scatter a few in the bottom of a well-buttered baking dish. Trim the crusts from the bread if necessary; cut each slice in half; butter generously and place in layers in the baking dish, scattering a few currants between each layer.

Twenty minutes before you are ready to bake the pudding, beat the egg yolks with the sugar and a little nutmeg. Stir in the warm milk and vanilla essence. Fold in the beaten egg whites and pour over the bread and currants. Bake in a moderate oven (190°C/375°F/gas 5) for about ¾ hour, or until the pudding is set and lightly browned.

# Crêpes Suzette

Pancakes, in one form or another, have been a universal delight since man first discovered that if he mixed crushed grain with water and baked it, he would have a new kind of food.

Under more elaborate conditions – and a host of different names and fillings – they have been enjoyed around the world for centuries. In Mexico, it is the peasant *tortilla*; in China, the crisp egg roll; while America prefers hers for breakfast, swimming in melted butter and maple syrup; and the Russians like theirs as *blini*, a delicious appetiser topped with caviare and sour cream.

But of all the pancake recipes in the world, the greatest – *Crêpes Suzette* – originated in France. The legends of the origin of this famous dish are as varied as the recipes for making it. The one I like best is the version recounted by Morrison Wood in his excellent cookery book, *With a Jug of Wine*. According to Mr Wood, a well-known French chef, Henri Carpentier, was preparing *crêpes* in liqueur for Edward VII when the dish accidentally burst into flames. Chef Henri, not at all abashed at this misadventure, carried the flaming pan in which the *crêpes* were immersed to the table, and when the fire had died out, he served the little pancakes to the king and his party.

Edward pronounced them delicious and asked what they were called. 'They have just been invented, sir,' Henri replied, 'and they shall be called *Crêpes Princesse.*' The king smiled, but shook his head. 'Where is your gallantry, Henri?' he asked. Then, indicating the young daughter of his host, he announced: 'They shall be called *Crêpes Suzette*, in Mademoiselle's honour.' Whatever you call them, these paper-thin pancakes are wonderfully easy to make. They can be prepared hours or even the day before you plan to serve them, as their flaming sauce calls more for showmanship than for skill.

You will need a good *crêpes* pan made of cast iron or lined copper, for the delicate pancakes may scorch in lighter materials. It should be the size of the ultimate pancake (about 12.5 cm/5 inches across), for the batter should be so creamy and thin that it will run ragged over a larger pan. And your pan should have rounded or sloping sides so that you will be able to turn the pancakes over with your spatula without tearing them.

If your *crêpes* pan is new, season it before using: fill it with vegetable oil; bring the oil slowly to a simmer; remove from heat and let the oil-filled pan stand until the oil is cold. Then pour out the oil and wipe the pan clean with cloth or kitchen paper. To keep your pan in prime condition: wipe it out with oil, never with water, after every use, and your *crêpes* will never stick.

## Basic Crêpes Mixture

Makes 20 to 24 golden *crêpes*

225 g/½ pound flour
1 tablespoon sugar
pinch of salt
3 eggs
425 ml/¾ pint milk

2 tablespoons melted butter or
  oil
2 tablespoons cognac or rum
butter

Sift together the flour, sugar and salt. Beat the eggs and add them to the dry ingredients. Mix in the milk, melted butter and cognac gradually to avoid lumps. Strain through a fine sieve and leave the batter to stand for at least 2 hours before cooking the *crêpes*. The batter should be as thin as cream. (Add a little water if it is too thick.)

For each *crêpe*, melt 1 teaspoon butter in a small thick-bottomed *crêpes* pan; spoon in about 2 tablespoons batter, swirling the pan to allow the batter to cover the entire surface thinly; brush a piece of butter around the edge of the hot pan with the point of a knife and cook over a medium heat until just golden, but not brown (about 1 minute each side). Repeat until all the *crêpes* are cooked, stacking them on a plate as they are ready. If they are to be filled, cover with waxed paper or aluminium foil to prevent drying while you prepare the filling.

# Lemon Crêpes Mixture

Makes 20 to 24 thin lemon pancakes

| | |
|---|---|
| 100 g/¼ pound flour | 225 ml/¾ pint milk |
| 1 tablespoon sugar | 2 tablespoons melted butter |
| 1 pinch salt | 1 teaspoon grated lemon zest |
| 2 eggs | 2 tablespoons lemon juice |
| 2 egg yolks | butter |

Sift together the flour, sugar and salt. Beat together the whole eggs and egg yolks and add them to the dry ingredients. Mix in the milk, melted butter, lemon zest and juice smoothly. Strain through a fine sieve and let the batter stand for at least 2 hours before cooking the *crêpes*. The batter should be as thin as cream.

For each *crêpe*, melt 1 teaspoon butter in a small thick-bottomed frying pan (15 to 20 cm/6 to 8 inches in diameter); add about 2 tablespoons batter, swirling the pan to allow the batter to cover the entire surface thinly; brush a piece of butter around the edge of the hot pan with the point of a knife and cook over a medium heat until just golden (about 1 minute each side).

## Variations on the Basic Crêpes Theme

**Apple crêpes:**  Simmer 3 to 4 apples, peeled and sliced, with ½ teaspoon cinnamon, 4 tablespoons brown sugar and 4 tablespoons butter for 15 minutes, or until the apples are soft. Cook *crêpes* as on page 251; place 1 or 2 tablespoons of apple filling on each; roll up and brown in butter. Sprinkle with cinnamon and sugar before serving.

**Fresh berry crêpes:**  Cook *crêpes* as on page 251 and fill with crushed raspberries or strawberries mixed with whipped cream. Garnish with whole berries.

**Apricot crêpes:**  Cook *crêpes* as on page 251 and fill with a combination of chopped pineapple and apricot jam flavoured with Kirsch.

**Marron crêpes:**  Cook *crêpes* as on page 251. Keep warm. When ready to serve, butter them generously with *crème de marrons* (canned puréed chestnuts); roll them up and cover with a sauce made of heated apricot jam. Top with toasted slivered almonds.

## Crêpes Suzette

Serves 4

| | |
|---|---|
| 100 g/¼ pound butter | 6 tablespoons Cointreau |
| 50 g/2 ounces icing sugar | ½ basic *crêpes* mixture |
| 1 tablespoon grated lemon zest | (page 251) |
| grated zest and juice of 1 | 4 tablespoons cognac |
| orange | |

Cream the butter and icing sugar together; add the lemon and orange zest, orange juice and 4 tablespoons of the Cointreau. (You can substitute either curaçao or Grand Marnier for the Cointreau.)

Make the *crêpes* as in the basic recipe on page 251.

When ready to serve: heat the orange-flavoured butter in a hot chafing dish (or electric frying pan) for about 5 minutes or until it bubbles and reduces a little. Dip each cooked *crêpe* into this hot mixture; then fold in quarters, using a fork and spoon, and push to one side of the pan. When all the *crêpes* are in the pan, sprinkle with a little sugar and add the remaining Cointreau with the cognac. Stand well away from the pan and light the liquid with a match. Keep spooning the flaming liquid over the *crêpes* until the flames die down. Serve immediately with the sauce.

## Palatschinken
Serves 4 to 6

½ **basic *crêpes* mixture (page 251)**
**225 g/8 ounces apricot jam**
**2 tablespoons cognac**

**25 g/1 ounce finely chopped almonds**
**icing sugar**

Make about 12 *crêpes*, transferring them to a warm plate as you cook them. Combine the apricot jam, cognac and almonds; spread the *crêpes* with the apricot-nut mixture; roll them up neatly, place on an ovenproof serving dish and keep hot in a very slow oven (130°C/250°F/gas ½) until ready to serve. Just before serving, dust the *palatschinken* with icing sugar.

## Crêpes au Mocha
Make 20–24 thin *crêpes*

**100 g/¼ pound flour**
**1 tablespoon sugar**
**pinch of salt**
**1 tablespoon powdered chocolate**
**1 tablespoon powdered coffee**
**2 eggs**

**2 egg yolks**
**425 ml/¾ pint milk**
**2 tablespoons melted butter**
**butter, to cook *crêpes***
**300 ml/½ pint cream, whipped**
**1 tablespoon rum**
**sugar**

Sift together the flour, sugar, salt, chocolate and coffee. Beat together the whole eggs and egg yolks and add them to the dry ingredients. Mix in the milk and melted butter smoothly. Strain through a fine sieve and let the batter stand for at least 2 hours before cooking the *crêpes*. The batter should be as thin as cream.

Melt a bit of butter for each *crêpe* in a small thick-bottomed frying pan (15 to 20 cm/6 or 8 inches in diameter); add about 2 tablespoons batter, swirling the pan to allow the batter to cover the entire bottom of the pan thinly; brush a piece of butter around the edge of the hot pan with the point of a knife and cook over a medium heat until crisp (about 1 minute each side).

Fill *crêpes au mocha* with whipped cream flavoured to taste with rum and sugar.

## Strawberry Dessert Pancakes

Serves 4

½ lemon *crêpes* recipe (page 252)        Kirsch or Grand Marnier
1 large punnet ripe strawberries        lightly toasted slivered almonds
sugar        whipped cream

Make about 12 *crêpes*. Slice the strawberries; add sugar and a little Kirsch or Grand Marnier to taste and spoon 2 tablespoons sliced and sugared strawberries on to each pancake.

Roll the *crêpes* to enclose the filling and arrange the rolls side by side in a shallow buttered baking dish. Sprinkle the *crêpes* with the almonds and put the dish under the grill for a few minutes. Serve hot with whipped cream, sweetened and flavoured with a little Kirsch or Grand Marnier.

# English Apple Pie

It is quite amazing the subtleties of flavour that our ancestors managed to create when you realise how few ingredients they had to play with.

Sated as we are with the riches of the world (asparagus from Kenya, strawberries from California and courgettes from Morocco as early as January), we can hardly imagine that the cabbage and the carrot were once exotic imported vegetables, that Henry VIII himself brought back from the Field of the Cloth of Gold the first cherries ever to be seen here, and that the pineapple was considered so extraordinary when it first arrived on these shores that the reigning monarch, Charles II, was painted receiving the first specimen as if it were a rare treasure.

But for nearly two thousand years, ever since the Romans first planted apple trees in Somerset and found that the flavour of the fruit surpassed that of any in all their Empire, the apple has been our dominant fruit, and by far and away our favourite.

Along with roast beef, game and salmon, the apple pie is one of the great dishes of this island, and one that has spread right round the world, recognisably British still, perfected over the centuries, impossible to improve.

I find a special satisfaction, in these days of quick and easy cooking, in making this traditional dish just for the sheer pleasure of it. The warm and spicy smell of apple pie baking in the oven – its filling rich with cinnamon and nutmeg and the tart rind of orange or lemon, its crust part butter, part flour and part poetry – is one of the most tantalising and appetising aromas I know. For British cooks have been making superb apple pies ever since 1296 when the first British cooking apple of real importance, the Costard, came on the scene.

Costards are no longer to be had today, for time has marched over them. But from those far-off origins stem their descendants, the Lord Derby, the Grenadier, the Newtown Wonder, and my own personal favourite, Bramley's Seedling.

The Bramley keeps firm and well, and cooks to perfection. Tart, but not too tart; juicy, but not too juicy; its highly flavoured flesh breaks down when cooked to a fluffy mass that is as delicious hot as it is cold. It is the perfect apple for making apple sauce and baked apples and, of course, apple pie.

## Deep Dish Apple Pie

550–600 g/1¼ pounds cooking
  apples
juice of ½ lemon
fingertip pastry for shell and top
  (page 12)
50 g/2 ounces granulated sugar
50 g/2 ounces dark brown
  sugar
1 tablespoon flour

⅛ teaspoon freshly grated
  nutmeg
¼ teaspoon powdered cinnamon
grated zest of 1 orange
grated zest of ½ lemon
50 g/2 ounces chopped raisins
  and sultanas
2 tablespoons orange juice
2 tablespoons butter

Peel and core the apples and slice thickly. Soak them in water to which you have added lemon juice to keep their colour. Line a deep 23-cm/9-inch oval pie dish with pastry.

Combine the sugars, flour, nutmeg and cinnamon and rub a little of this mixture into the pastry lining. Add the zests to the remaining sugar mixture. Cover the bottom of the pastry shell with the sliced apples and sprinkle with a few chopped raisins and sultanas and some of the sugar mixture, to taste. Repeat layers until the pie shell is richly filled.

Sprinkle with the orange juice; dot with the butter and fit the top crust over the apples, pressing the edges together or fluting them. Decorate the pastry; cut slits in the top crust to release steam and bake in a moderately hot oven (200°C/400°F/gas 6) for 35 to 40 minutes, or until tender. Serve warm, with cream or Cheddar cheese.

## English Treacle Tart

fingertip pastry (page 12)
1 cooking apple
225 g/8 oz freshly grated
  breadcrumbs
juice and grated zest of 1
  lemon
¼ teaspoon salt

¼ teaspoon ground ginger
1 tablespoon sugar
2 tablespoons milk
2 tablespoons warmed golden
  syrup
milk
caster sugar

Butter a pie tin and line with the pastry. Peel, core and grate the apple and mix with the breadcrumbs, lemon juice and zest, salt, ginger, sugar, milk and golden syrup. Blend well and spread evenly over the pastry.

Make thin strips of pastry out of the remaining dough; lay in lattice fashion over the treacle filling; brush lightly with a little milk and sprinkle with caster sugar. Bake in a moderate oven (190°C/375°F/gas 5) for 40 minutes.

## Creamy Apple Pie

1 pastry case
1 kg/2 pounds cooking apples
175 g/6 ounces sugar
25 g/1 ounce flour

¼ teaspoon salt
¼ teaspoon cinnamon
300 ml/½ pint double cream

Prepare a 23-cm/9-inch unbaked pastry shell. Bake 'blind'. Peel, core and slice the apples thickly. Combine the sugar, flour, salt and cinnamon and add to the apples. Toss lightly and turn into the pastry shell. Pour double cream over the top and bake in a hot oven (200°C/400°F/gas 6) for 35 to 40 minutes, or until firm. Serve warm.

## Lemon Meringue Pie

4 tablespoons cornflour
½ teaspoon salt
275 g/10 ounces sugar
425 ml/¾ pint water
2 tablespoons butter
6 tablespoons lemon juice

grated zest of ½ lemon
4 egg yolks, slightly beaten
1 baked pastry case
4 egg whites
salt and sugar

Combine the first four ingredients in the top of a double saucepan and cook over direct heat, stirring continuously, until the mixture comes to the boil. Place over simmering water and cook gently for 15 minutes, stirring from time to time.

Remove from the heat, beat in the butter and lemon juice and zest. Stir in the egg yolks and cook over simmering water until thick. Cool. Fill the baked pastry shell.

Make a meringue with the egg whites, beaten until stiff with a pinch of salt and sugar. Spoon the meringue in peaks on to the pie filling and bake until golden brown in a fairly hot oven (220°C/425°F/gas 6).

## Strawberry Flan Chantilly

450 g/1 pound ripe strawberries
6 tablespoons Grand Marnier
sugar

1 egg white
300 ml/½ pint cream, whipped
1 baked pastry case

Wash, hull and slice the strawberries into a bowl. Pour the Grand Marnier over them; add sugar to taste; stir and let marinate in the refrigerator for at least 30 minutes. Beat the egg white until stiff and fold into the whipped cream to make the *chantilly* mixture.

Just before serving, fold the sliced strawberries and the liquid into the *chantilly*; correct the flavouring and pile into the baked pastry case. Serve immediately.

# French Lemon Tarts

*Pastry:*
100 g/4 ounces butter
50 g/2 ounces icing sugar
juice of 1 lemon
175 g/6 ounces flour
½ teaspoon salt

*Filling:*
1 egg
150 g/5 ounces sugar
1 lemon
50 g/2 ounces softened butter

**The pastry:** Cream the butter and sugar; add the lemon juice and the flour sifted with the salt. Mix quickly to a firm paste, using a little water if necessary. Chill for 15 minutes. Roll out and fit into tart cases. Prick the bases lightly and bake 'blind' in a hot oven (230°C/450°F/gas 8) for 10 minutes.

**The filling:** Beat the egg with the sugar until light and creamy; add the juice and grated zest of the lemon and the softened butter, and continue beating until smooth paste. Fill the tart shells with this mixture and bake in a slow oven (170°C/325°F/gas 3) for 10 to 15 minutes, or until the filling is firm. Cool before serving.

# French Raspberry Tart
Serves 6

*Cinnamon Pastry:*
225 g/½ pound plain flour
1½ tablespoons powdered
   cinnamon
pinch of salt
2 tablespoons icing sugar
150 g/5 ounces butter, at room
   temperature, diced
1 egg yolk

2 tablespoons iced water

*Cardinale Sauce:*
225 g/½ pound fresh raspberries
3 tablespoons icing sugar
1–2 tablespoons Grand Marnier
lemon juice

350 g/¾ pound fresh raspberries

**First make the pastry:** Sieve the flour, cinnamon, salt and icing sugar into a mixing bowl. Rub in the butter with your fingertips (or a pastry blender) until the mixture resembles fine breadcrumbs. Do this gently and lightly, or the mixture will become greasy.

Beat the egg yolk; beat in the iced water; sprinkle this mixture over the dough and work in lightly with your fingers. Shape the moist dough lightly into a flattened round; wrap in foil or cling-film and leave in the refrigerator for at least 1 hour to ripen.

If the chilled dough is too firm for handling, allow it to stand at room temperature until it softens slightly. Then turn it on to a floured board and roll out as thinly as required to line a loose-bottomed 23–25-cm/9–10-inch tart tin. Press the dough into the tart tin with your fingers and prick the bottom of the case evenly with a fork. Chill for 20 minutes in the refrigerator.

Prepare the case for baking blind by covering the pastry with a piece of foil; fill with a layer of dried beans (or raw rice) and bake in a fairly hot oven (220°C/425°F/gas 7) for 10 minutes. Lower the heat to 180°C/350°F/gas 4 and bake for 20 minutes more; then remove the foil and beans (or rice) and continue cooking for 5 to 10 minutes, or until the bottom of the case is golden. If the crust becomes too brown at the edges at any time during baking, cover the edges loosely with a little crumpled foil.

Cool the pastry in the tin on a wire cake rack.

**To make the sauce:**   Place the raspberries in a fine sieve and, with the back of a wooden spoon, force them through the sieve into a bowl. Discard the pips from the sieve. Add the sifted icing sugar to the purée, with the Grand Marnier and a little lemon juice to taste, and chill.

**To serve:**   Arrange the raspberries evenly in the baked pastry case. Just before serving, remove the edges of the tin, leaving the tin bottom under the tart case to support it. Then spoon the chilled raspberry sauce over the berries and serve and eat immediately.

# INDEX